University of St. Francis
907.6 F983
Furay, Conal.
The methods and skills of hist

P9-AQS-308

1994

THE METHODS AND SKILLS OF HISTORY

A Practical Guide

1994

Arthur S. Link
GENERAL EDITOR FOR HISTORY

THE METHODS AND SKILLS OF HISTORY

A Practical Guide

by

Conal Furay
Michael J. Salevouris
Webster University

HARLAN DAVIDSON, INC.
ARLINGTON HEIGHTS, ILLINOIS 60004

Copyright © 1988
Harlan Davidson, Inc.
All Rights Reserved

This book, or parts thereof, must not be used or reproduced in any manner without written permission. For information, address the publisher, Harlan Davidson, Inc., 3110 North Arlington Heights Road, Arlington Heights, Illinois 60004-1592.

Library of Congress Cataloging-in-Publication Data
Furay, Conal.
   The methods and skills of history.

   Rev. ed. of: History, a workbook of skill development. 1979.
   Bibliography: p.
   1. History—Examinations, questions, etc.
I. Salevouris, Michael J. II. Furay, Conal. History, a workbook of skill development. III. Title.
D21.F947 1987   907.6   86-16733
ISBN 0-88295-851-8

Manufactured in the United States of America
97 96 95 94 93 7 8 9 10 11   EB

907.6
F983

To Our Parents
Guy and Marguerite
Mike and Gretchen

1-21-94 B&T $16.41

College of St. Francis Library
Joliet, Illinois

149,578

THE AUTHORS

Conal Furay received a B.S.C. and an M.A. at Creighton University and a Ph.D. at St. Louis University. Currently Professor of History at Webster University, his teaching fields are American cultural history, business and management history, and American studies. He is a Commander in the U.S. Coast Guard Reserve (retired) and lists among his avocations the care and feeding of nine children, horse race gambling (a bit incompatible, those two), sea stories, golf, and following the football fortunes of the Nebraska Cornhuskers. His publications include *The Grass-Roots Mind in America* (1977).

Michael J. Salevouris earned a B.A. in history at Colorado College and an M.A. and Ph.D. at the University of Minnesota. He is Professor of History and Chairman of the Department of History-Political Science at Webster University in St. Louis. He teaches courses in historical methodology, British and European history, the history of disease and medicine, and the history of warfare. His interests include running, tennis, the recorder (the instrument, not the machine), stamp collecting, mystery and spy novels, and model ships. In addition to this book he has published articles, reviews, and, in 1982, a monograph entitled *"Riflemen Form": The War Scare of 1859–1860 in England.*

CONTENTS

PREFACE

Two recent trends in American education have been instrumental in moving us to write this book. First, there has been a drift away from traditional forms of history in many high schools and colleges in favor of "relevant" topic courses in the social sciences. Valuable though they may be, such courses often make students aware of many contemporary problems but leave them innocent of the historical background of those problems. Further, these courses do little to encourage students to develop the conceptual tools to think historically. Second, there has been of late an exodus from "liberal arts" curricula to professional and preprofessional programs of study. The assumption, explicit or not, is that courses in the liberal arts—especially those in the humanities—do little to prepare one for a career in the "real world."

Both trends are deeply disturbing, since we are convinced (and there is evidence to support the conviction) that a good liberal arts education often can provide better all-around career preparation than many narrowly focused professional or vocational programs. Further, we firmly believe that, within the context of a liberal arts education, the development of basic historical literacy is essential. Not only can history give one a perspective on the world that no other discipline can provide, but the serious study of history will help the student develop skills that can be applied directly to the world of work.

The purpose of the book is thus twofold:

1. To provide a general introduction to the nature and methods of history that will help students think historically and better appreciate the importance of historical literacy.
2. To help students develop the intellectual and communication skills that are applicable not only to the study of history, but also to many other academic disciplines and to a wide variety of post-college professional pursuits.

To accomplish these goals we combine theory and practice, with slightly more emphasis on the latter. In each chapter we provide a brief introductory overview of a topic followed by one or more exercises. The aim of the essays and exercises is not to teach sophisticated research skills to prospective graduate students, but to make the study of history more meaningful for the countless students who major in history, take history courses, or simply read history on their own. It is our hope that this book will enhance students' appreciation of history on a purely intellectual level and at the same time help them develop skills that can be used in other academic subjects and in the outside world of work.

The exercises in this book range from the relatively simple to the complex. Many of the exercises have two sets of questions—Set A and Set B. Few instructors will want to assign every exercise to every student, but in instances where the instructor feels that the repetition of an exercise might be beneficial to a student, a second set of materials is provided. Although most of the exercises call for written responses, ideally students should have the opportunity to discuss their answers in a classroom setting. History, obviously, is not like arithmetic, where only one answer is "correct." The value of many exercises, therefore, will be greatly enhanced by general debate and discussion. It might be worth noting here that we have deliberately included exercises or sections of exercises for which there are no universally acceptable "right" answers. In using this book in our own classes we find that "offbeat" questions are often more useful educationally than many others. They require careful definition of terms and frequent reorganization of ideas on the students' part.

Another important point: Although we have ordered the chapters in a way we think makes sense, both students and instructors should feel free to use the chapters in whatever order seems most appropriate to their immediate purposes. For example, students beginning to collect information for research papers might want to skip ahead to the section on taking research notes in Chapter 10. Or, students who have had a thorough indoctrination in the use of the library could very well skip Chapter 3, "The Search for Information."

This book can also be used as a programmed text for individual students if circumstances so dictate. The programmed approach may be especially valuable for students with family and work responsibilities who find it difficult to conform to class schedules designed for the resident nonworking student. It is also quite conceivable that a teacher might wish to assign certain exercises to individual students in "content" courses so that they might strengthen their skills in a particular area—e.g., writing book reviews, reading secondary sources, etc.

We might note here that many of the quoted extracts from historical literature reveal a bias toward the more traditional narrative varieties of history. This may seem peculiarly old-fashioned at a time when so many researchers have abandoned the narrative approach to history in favor of analyses with a distinctly sociological flavor. But we have our reasons: 1) First, for a person to think historically, he or she must be able to see events as part of an organic continuum linking past ages and experiences to our own. We believe that narrative, chronological history facilitates the development of this sense of historical continuity better than many purely analytical studies. 2) Furthermore, narrative histories still constitute the bulk of most library collections, and such histories are a logical place for students to begin. Moreover, the critical skills needed to interpret and evaluate narrative histories are equally applicable to analytical histories. 3) Finally, we share the conviction that when history is true to its intellectual heritage it *does* tell a story. A sense of chronological development—one thing happening after another—is one of the basic characteristics that distinguishes history from other academic pursuits.

Notes on the Text: This book is based on *History: A Workbook of Skill Development*, published originally in 1979. In this new version we retained the sections of the first book that proved especially effective and added some promising new elements. In doing so, we hope to avoid a famous criticism once given by Samuel Johnson: "Your manuscript is both good and original; but the part that is good is not original, and the part that is original is not good."

We are deeply indebted to a number of people who assisted us along the way. Of most value was the careful, intelligent editorial criticism offered by our friend and colleague, Margaret Brockmann. Her critique of both style and content saved us from more infelicities, unnecessary jargon, and outright blunders than we would care to admit. We also owe our thanks to Professor Dennis Mihelich of Creighton University for his searching criticism of several chapters; Mary Lauranne Lifka of Mundelein College for many valuable suggestions; Anne Moedritzer of Eden-Webster library for ideas and comments on "The Search for Information" chapter; Jane Coad O'Brien of Creighton Prep in Omaha for assistance with some of the exercises; students Susan Kincaid and Alice L. Furay for their clear and uncompromising reactions to the text and exercises; C. R. (Rob) Brown for his timely research assistance; and Ginny Miller and Sue Meredith of Webster University for typing portions of the manuscript. Finally, who can write a book such as this and fail to thank the many scholars from whose works we have sought counsel? Indeed, we stand on their shoulders. Of course, the standard closing line is appropriate: For all errors of commission and omission, we are fully responsible.

Conal Furay
Michael Salevouris

CHAPTER 1

THE USES AND NATURE OF HISTORY

*"He to whom the present is the only thing that is
present knows nothing of the age in which he lives."*
Oscar Wilde

On May 20, 1927, a foolhardy young mail pilot began a perilous journey across the Atlantic. Charles A. Lindbergh set out to be the first to fly a plane nonstop from New York to Paris. Defying the elements, more than 3,000 miles of ocean, and his own desire to sleep, "Lucky Lindy" made the trip in just over thirty-three hours. Overnight Lindbergh became a hero; and he and his silver monoplane, the *Spirit of St. Louis*, became symbols of the fledgling air age.

It had taken humanity countless generations to conquer the air, but it took only a few short decades to take the next step: the conquest of space. Thirty years after Charles Lindbergh vaulted the Atlantic, the Soviet Union launched the first artificial space satellite. A mere twelve years later, in 1969, American astronauts walked on the surface of the moon. Within less than a single lifetime the air age had given way to the space age. This scientific and technological leap symbolizes a central reality of the modern period: in many areas of life—in science and technology, government, economic organization, and social relations—the pace of change is accelerating. Tomorrow often seems to be here before today has been fully comprehended.

In a society undergoing such frantic, and often revolutionary, changes it is easy to question the relevance of historical studies. How, after all, can the experiences of imperial Rome, Elizabethan England, or colonial America have any relevance for individuals who view the 1970s or 1960s as ancient history? How can history teach anything to a society that is present oriented?

The Uses of History   Such questions are heard frequently these days, but they miss the mark. Significant and rapid changes *have* occurred, but in countless areas of life organic connections with the past have not been broken. The legacies and burdens of the past, the long-term continuities, are with us still. Further, the study of history has hardly become irrelevant. In fact, one could argue that precisely *because* change has been rapid in our time, the need for good history has actually increased. There is much truth in the aphorism "the more things change, the more they stay the same." Without historical perspective we are in danger of falling into the mistaken and perhaps arrogant notion that the problems we face and the solutions we propose are unprecedented and bear no relationship to human problems of the past. Just one of the contributions history can make is to serve as a useful antidote to such narrow present-mindedness.

Even the rapid change we see around us should not hide the basic reality that all we do, all we think, indeed all we are is the cumulative result of past experiences. The future is an abstraction; the "present" is but a fleeting moment; all else is history. The past and judgments about the past are inescapable. Daily we speak and act according to some perception of past events; and though our knowledge of the past may be incomplete or fallacious, we are thinking historically nevertheless. When we choose a school course because we like a teacher; when we vote Democratic or Republican on the basis of our assessment of the party's record; when we decide not to go to a movie with someone who "isn't our type"—we are making judgments based on our analysis of past experience. We are functioning as historians.

Not only is it impossible to escape history, it would be catastrophic to try. Imagine for a moment what life would be like if you totally lost your memory. You would, in a very real sense, have no sense of belonging—no family, no friends, no home, no memories to guide your behavior, no identity. Clearly, your sense of personal identity is not so much a function of what you *are* at the moment, but what you *have been* your entire life. The same can be said of society as a whole. A society's identity is the product of the myriad individuals, forces, and events that constitute its past. History, the study of the past, is society's collective memory. Without that collective memory, society would be as rootless and adrift as an individual with amnesia. Of the many legitimate reasons for studying history, this seems to us to be one of the most compelling. Individually and collectively *what we are* is the product of *what we have been.* In the words of philosopher George Santayana, "A country without a memory is a country of madmen."

There are, of course, many other sound reasons to study history, and you will have the opportunity to think about some of them in the exercise section of this chapter. But now there is a more important item on the agenda: we must define "history" more precisely and delve more deeply into the nature of historical study.

What Is History? There is a curious ambiguity in the English language that makes the answer to the above question less obvious than it might appear. The main difficulty is that "history" has two distinct meanings. First, "history" is the sum total of everything that has actually happened in the past—every thought, every action, every event. In this sense, "history" is surely one of the broadest concepts conceived by the human intellect. "History," broadly defined, encompasses the entire scope of the human experience on this planet. And, this meaning of the word—*things that happened in the past*—is what most people have in mind when they use the term in daily conversation.

There is a second meaning, one actually more central to this book. If "history" *is* the past, it is also an **account** *of the past*—i.e., books, articles, lectures, etc. It should be clear with just a moment's thought that the past (all of those thoughts and events that really happened) is lost forever. Our only contact with the past is through the relatively scant records left by those who lived before us and through the accounts written by historians on the basis of those records. It is this "history"—accounts of the past—that we read, think about, and study in school. And it is this meaning of "history"—history as a creation of human intelligence—that is the subject of this book. As historians James Davidson and Mark Lytle put it, "History is not 'what happened in the past;' rather, it is *the act of selecting, analyzing, and writing about the past.* It is something that is done, that is constructed, rather than an inert body of data that lies scattered through the archives."[1]

The Nature of History

"History," then, is both the past and the study of the past. In order to appreciate better the vast intellectual gulf that separates the past-as-it-actually-happened (history in the first sense) from historians' *accounts* of that past (history in the second sense) we ask you to take a brief journey of the imagination. Try to visualize yourself walking at night amidst a rugged landscape punctuated by dramatic peaks and valleys. As you walk a companion turns on a powerful beam that lights up some of the recesses and promontories that have been veiled in darkness. As the light moves, the previously illuminated objects disappear and new features of the landscape come into view. You want to see the entire landscape spread before your eyes, but the beam of light, narrow and imperfect, lets you see only a tiny fraction of the reality that lays before you. When the light is turned off, you can see nothing at all. The peaks and valleys and forests are still there, and remain there, awaiting other beams, projected from other angles to further illuminate their contours.

In this allegory the peaks and valleys of the landscape represent the "past-as-it-actually-happened"—history in its broadest meaning. The person with the searchlight is the historian who, by using the beam, reveals some of the outlines of the landscape. Essentially, the historian "lights up" some segment of the past that we cannot perceive directly, just as the person carrying the spotlight illuminated a landscape hidden in darkness. The glimpse of the landscape provided by the beam, as transient and incomplete as it is, is analogous to an account of the past written by a historian.

This analogy is imperfect in that the historian cannot even shine a weak beam of light on the real past as if it were a mountain or a valley. The past, unlike any existing geological feature, is gone forever. To the extent we can know anything about the past-as-it-actually-happened, that knowledge must be based on surviving records. Still, the analogy *is* useful. Just as the landscape was real, so, too, was the past that historians study. The actual events of the past are gone forever, but they were just as "real" as all the human activities you see around you every day. Further, as inadequate as the beam of light was in illuminating the total reality of the landscape, the beam *did* provide useful and accurate glimpses of that reality. Similarly, historians' accounts can and do provide "useful and accurate" glimpses of the contours of the past, but those accounts constitute only a pale reflection of that reality.

To reiterate the central point: Even though a relationship exists between the past-as-it-happened and the historian's account of a segment of the past, the historical account can no more show past events as they actually took place than the narrow beam of light could illuminate an entire landscape. The historian can "illuminate" a tiny piece of the past, the historian

---

[1] James Davidson and Mark Lytle, *After the Fact: The Art of Historical Detection* (New York: Knopf, 1982), p. xvii.

can present us with *an individual version* of a segment of the past, but cannot present the past as it actually was.

This leads us to another central point. All historical accounts have an element of subjectivity. Whether written or spoken, every piece of history is an individualized view of a segment of past reality—a particular vision, a personalized version. Writing history is an act of creation, or more accurately, an act of *re-creation*, in which the mind of the historian is the catalyst. Any piece of history that we read or hear ought to be treated as an individual creation, respectable insofar as it calls forth in the reader or hearer a clear image or understanding of some past. In fact, one might even say that any history we read is as much a product of the historian who wrote it as of the people who actually lived the events it attempts to describe!

The Process of History

The subjective, recreative, nature of written history becomes clearer if we look more closely at the process whereby the historian bridges the chasm between the past being studied and the account that is the product of that study. Actually, the historian's intellectual task is as challenging as any on earth. Unlike the scientist who can experiment directly with tangible objects, the historian is many times removed from the events under investigation. The historian, as noted before, cannot study the past directly, but must rely on surviving records.

It should be obvious that surviving records, compared to the real past they reflect, are like a few drops of water in a large bucket. For instance, most past events left no records at all! Think of the number of events in your own life for which there is no record but your own memory. Multiply those unrecorded events in your own life by the billions of human beings who inhabit the earth and you get some idea of the number of events each day that go unrecorded. That is only the beginning of the problem. In the words of historian Louis Gottschalk:

> Only a part of what was observed in the past was remembered by those who observed it; only a part of what was remembered was recorded; only a part of what was recorded has survived; only a part of what has survived has come to the historians' attention; only a part of what has come to their attention is credible; only a part of what is credible has been grasped; and only a part of what has been grasped can be expounded or narrated by the historian. . . . Before the past is set forth by the historian, it is likely to have gone through eight separate steps at each of which some of it has been lost; and there is no guarantee that what remains is the most important, the largest, the most valuable, the most representative, or the most enduring part. In other words the "object" that the historian studies is not only incomplete; it is markedly variable as records are lost or recovered.[2]

If all this were not enough, the historian is also a factor in the equation. Not only is the historian fallible and capable of error, but personal biases, political beliefs, economic status, religious persuasion, and idiosyncrasies can subtly and unconsciously influence the way in which existing sources

[2] Louis Gottschalk, *Understanding History* (New York: Knopf, 1950), pp. 45–46.

are interpreted. For instance, conservative Republicans often read and interpret the political history of the United States in a very different way than do liberal Democrats. Protestants and Catholics frequently disagree when writing about the religious upheavals known as the Reformation, and Northerners and Southerners are notorious in their differences concerning the history of the American Civil War.

These matters will be discussed in greater detail later in this book. For now it is sufficient to note that the historian can never get the full truth about a given past (see Fig. 1). The best that can be provided, even under ideal conditions, is a partial sketch of a vanished past. "Even the best history," said historian Bruce Catton, "is not much better than a mist through which we see shapes dimly moving." Or, in the words of W. S. Holt, "History is a damn dim candle over a damn dark abyss." Small wonder written history is "subjective."

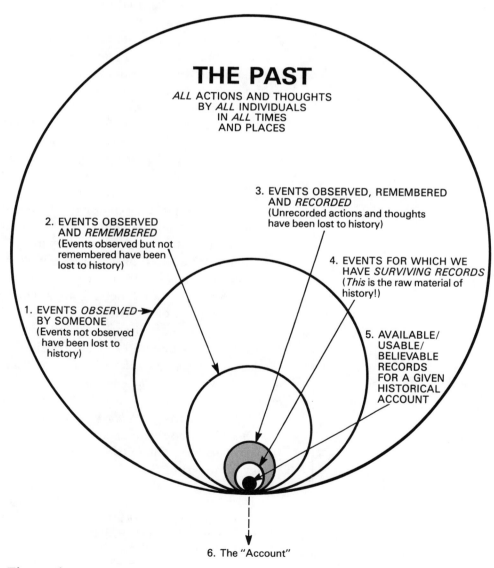

Figure 1

HISTORY AND THE
FORMATION OF PUBLIC POLICY

In this chapter we discussed the "uses" of history. More is said on the subject in the exercises that follow. Skeptics might dismiss these ideas as rationalizations developed by history teachers to keep themselves employed. But we can easily show that talk about the "uses of history" is not empty chatter. History often has been used by high government officials to guide their deliberations on public policy. One good example is the Swine Flu "fiasco" of 1976.

In 1976, during the brief administration of President Gerald Ford, the Federal government launched a massive influenza immunization program. Public health officials feared a reappearance of the deadly "swine flu" which was responsible for a worldwide epidemic in 1918. In fact, more people died of swine flu than died in the four years of World War I (1914–1918). To avoid a similar disaster, millions of dollars were appropriated to inoculate everyone as a safeguard against the outbreak of a second epidemic.

The dreaded killer never arrived. There was no massive outbreak of the swine flu. As for the immunization program, it was increasingly seen by government and public health officials as a mistake. Because of that perception, in 1977 Health, Education and Welfare Secretary Joseph Califano, Jr., decided to review what had happened in order to prevent similar fiascoes in the future. "He sought lessons for the future useful to a man in his position," says a Department of HEW publication on the subject.

Where did Califano turn for his lessons? To history. Two scholars, Richard Neustadt and Harvey Fineberg of Harvard University, were commissioned to write a study of the swine flu affair. Neither Neustadt nor Fineberg are formally historians, but they are respected scholars who decided that a written history of the episode was the most effective way to give Secretary Califano what he wanted. Neustadt and Fineberg wrote in the Foreword of their book: *"[W]e know no better way to draw most lessons than to tell the applicable portions of the story. . . . [U]nderstanding is imparted best by a selective narrative. This calls for a reconstruction of events, which we have undertaken by combining press accounts, hearings, official files, and interviews with participants. . . ."* In other words, history was the most useful vehicle for identifying the "lessons" of a public policy gone wrong.

SOURCE: Richard E. Neustadt and Harvey V. Fineberg, M.D., *The Swine Flu Affair* (Washington, D.C.: Dept. of HEW, 1978), pp. 1–3. In 1983 Vintage republished the report and additional material by the authors under the title *The Epidemic That Never Was*.

The Question of Truth At this point many readers may throw up their hands in despair. Why study history at all if historical accounts are so far removed from the past they attempt to understand? What happens to the search for "truth" if we acknowledge that historical accounts are by nature subjective and incomplete? How can we justify the pursuit of knowledge that appears so shallow and fleeting?

These are good questions, but they imply that there is a total incompatibility between "subjectivity" and "truth." There is no such incompatibility. The "subjectivity" of literature and the arts is perhaps most apparent, since every work of art is to a great degree a highly personal statement. Yet who would deny that Shakespeare's plays or Rembrandt's paintings have much "truth" in them?

Even the disciplines that make a crusade of their quest for "objective knowledge"—i.e., knowledge uninfluenced by personal bias or values—are, in fact, subject to many of the same limitations that plague historians. Daily it becomes more apparent that to some extent all knowledge is conditioned by cultural circumstance and personal temperament—that is, there is an element of subjectivity involved.

For instance, the social sciences—sociology, psychology, political science, economics, anthropology—make the claim that the knowledge they seek is "objective" and value-free. Yet we should view these claims to neutrality and objectivity with a degree of caution.

After all, human beings—unpredictable, illogical, defiantly individualistic human beings—are both the *researchers* and the *objects* of social scientific investigations. This being the case we can hardly be surprised when an element of subjectivity intrudes here and there. This fact does not mean that we should reject the conclusions of the social sciences as hopelessly tainted by personal and cultural bias. Nor does it imply that the social sciences can never discover "truth." It simply means that you should be as alert to the influence of "subjectivity" in social science research as you are when you study history.[3]

The hard sciences—physics, chemistry, biology, etc.—have long been considered the most "objective" of the scholarly disciplines. Scientists claim that their researches have steadily revealed more and more about the workings of the natural world *as it really is.* They further assert that scientific knowledge of the natural world is not conditioned by cultural values and the personal biases of the researchers. There is, of course, a good deal of validity to these claims. But, even the sciences are not totally immune from the intrusion of subjective influences. In his recent critique of Darwinism, Jeremy Rifkin writes: "The traditional view that knowledge and truth about nature are independent of context is now being challenged by a new generation of scholars."[4] Rifkin, for example, shows how Charles Darwin, the

---

[3] Many historians would categorize history as a social science. Others think the discipline of history belongs with the humanities (along with literature, philosophy, etc.). Although we understand the position of the first group, we lean toward the second view—or at least to the school that argues that history—sharing as it does characteristics of the sciences, social sciences, and humanities—should be given a category all its own.

[4] Jeremy Rifkin, *Algeny* (Harmondsworth, Middlesex, England: Penguin, 1984), p. 32.

originator of the modern theory of evolution, was strongly influenced by the social and economic value system of the Victorian era in which he lived and worked. It was no accident, claims Rifkin, that Darwin's theory of natural selection reflected almost exactly the economic doctrines of the early industrial era. Darwin's view that, in nature, "progress" was based on a biological struggle for survival reflected the basic belief of nineteenth-century economists—that competition among individuals would gradually increase the wealth of the entire community. In other words, here is a case in which scientific "truth" was conditioned by the value system of the surrounding culture.

Our excursion into the nature of the various academic disciplines was perhaps somewhat premature at this point. (See the Appendix for more on this topic.) But we would like you to remember this central insight: *History is not unique in its subjectivity. To a greater or lesser degree all disciplines (fields of study) are conditioned by circumstance and personal frames of reference.*

This fact does not prevent us from pursuing the "truth" of the past with vigor and sound historical method. It is worth reminding ourselves that the past *did happen.* Even though the records of those events are inadequate and misleading, they do constitute a link between the present and that real if inaccessible past. Even though researchers are fallible human beings who can never totally escape their personal frames of reference, that does not preclude the writing of credible, coherent, and "true" accounts of segments of the past. Historical "truths" will always be conditional and open to revision, but so, too, are "truths" in all the other academic disciplines.

The critical question then is: How do you go about pursuing such knowledge given the numerous obstacles that lay in your path? That is what this book is about. There are a number of skills, habits of mind, and critical methods that make up the mental processes of the good historian. These skills and attributes are essential to good history and are also useful in a wide range of professional activities.

The methods of history are not especially complicated or confusing. Most of them derive from basic common sense, but that is not to say that "doing" history is easy. (One historian, for instance, compared writing intellectual history to trying to nail jelly to the wall.) It takes time and effort to develop the skills of historical thinking, but the effort is worth it.

EXERCISES

Set A, Exercise 1 In this chapter we briefly discussed the "uses" of history or the reasons for studying history. Central to that discussion was our argument that 1) it is impossible to escape or ignore history since all our judgments are to some extent based on past experience, and 2) history provides us with a sense of personal and social identity. These notions only scratch the surface. Through the ages (the study of history has a long and noble heritage) numerous claims have been made concerning the utility of history. Among the most prominent are:

A. **History provides a source of personal and social identity.** This we have already discussed.

B. **History helps us understand the problems of the present.** The cliché is true that to understand the present one must study the past. History, of course, cannot provide clear answers to today's problems (past and present events never exactly parallel each other), but a knowledge of relevant historical background is essential for a balanced and in-depth understanding of many current world situations.

C. **History—good history—is a corrective for misleading analogies and "lessons" of the past.** Many who believe the proposition that history is relevant to an understanding of the present often go too far in their claims. Nothing is easier to abuse than the historical analogy or parallel. Time and again politicians, journalists, and sloppy historians can be heard declaring that "history proves" this or "history shows" that. The fact is, the historical record is so rich and varied that one can always find examples that seem to support one position or another. (History in this sense is much like the Bible. If one reads selectively, Biblical passages can be found to support almost any notion under the sun.) Good history, on the other hand, can expose the *inapplicability* of many inaccurate, misleading analogies.

D. **History can help one develop tolerance and open-mindedness.** We believe that the study of many different times and places can help us overcome cultural provincialism. As the French philosopher Descartes put it: "It is good to know something of the customs of different peoples in order to judge more sanely our own."

E. **History helps us better understand all human behavior and all aspects of the human condition.**

F. **History provides the basic background for many other disciplines.** Here the assertion is that historical knowledge is extremely valuable for the pursuit of other disciplines—political science, sociology, etc. Further, it is fair to argue, with Jacques Barzun and Henry Graff, that the social sciences "are in fact *daughter* disciplines [to history], for they arose, each of them, out of historical investigation, having long formed part of avowed historical writing."[5]

G. **History can be entertainment.** This may seem trivial, but it certainly must be counted as one of the central "uses" of history. Much written history is also good literature, and the stories historians recount are often far more engaging and entertaining than those we find in works of fiction.

H. **The study of history can teach many critical skills.** That is, studying history helps sharpen the critical "thinking" and communication skills essential to success in school and in most professions.

Below are a number of reasons for the study of history written by different individuals. Using the letters A through H (see list above), indicate which category best describes each quotation. If you think a quotation includes more than one reason for the study of history use more than one letter.

---

[5] *The Modern Researcher*, rev. ed. (New York: Harcourt, Brace and World, 1970), p. 218.

If none of the categories above seem to fit, write "O" for "Other." The first item is completed for you.[6]

    _C_   1. "The chief practical use of history is to deliver us from plausible historical analogies." *James Bryce*

    _____ 2. "History is the shank of the social sciences." *C. Wright Mills*

    _____ 3. "In reality, what more agreeable entertainment to the mind, than to be transported into the remotest ages of the world. . . . What amusement, either of the sense or imagination, can be compared with it." *David Hume*

    _____ 4. "With the historian it is an article of faith that knowledge of the past is a key to understanding the present." *Kenneth Stampp*

    _____ 5. "To be ignorant of what happened before you were born is to be ever a child." *Cicero*

    _____ 6. "The chief lesson to be derived from the study of the past, is that it holds no simple lesson, and . . . the historian's main responsibility is to prevent anyone from claiming that it does." *Martin Duberman*

    _____ 7. "Everything is the sum of its past and nothing is comprehensible except through its history." *Pierre Teilhard de Chardin*

    _____ 8. "The ultimate reason for studying history is to become conscious of the possibilities of human existence." *Rudolf Bultman*

    _____ 9. "History can help us shake off the shackles of ethnocentrism and the debilitating bias of cultural and racial purity. . . . History helps us to illuminate the human condition." *Lester Stephens*

    _____ 10. "History is a means of access to ourselves." *Lynn White, Jr.*

Discussion   You have been reading what others consider to be the important reasons for studying history. Now it is time to discuss what *you* think. First, on the lines below indicate how important or valid the major reasons for the study of history are (use the letters A through H as before).

    1. Very Important/Valid: _____

    2. Moderately Important/Valid: _____

    3. Of Little Importance/Validity: _____

Once you have established a set of priorities, compare your list with other members of your class (if applicable). At this point you should discuss the reasons you ranked the various categories as you did.

Optional Essay   On a separate sheet of paper, write a short paragraph-length essay on the topic: What is the most important reason for studying history?

Set A, Exercise 2   A major theme of this chapter was the *re-creative* nature of historical study. The past is real, but accounts of the past reflect the historian's interests,

---

[6] Nearly all the quotations in this exercise, and the companion exercise in Set B, were drawn from an extensive list compiled by Ferenc M. Szasz and published in *The History Teacher*, Vol. VII, No. 4 (August 1974); Vol. VIII, No. 1 (November 1974); Vol. VIII, No. 2 (February 1975); Vol. IX, No. 2 (February 1976).

priorities, values, abilities, and the like. A work of history is never *the* history of a subject, but *a* history of the subject—just one of many possible versions. In other words, any work of history has subjective elements. As a student of history you should try to notice the many ways the story you read is shaped by the hand of the historian.

Below are a number of statements drawn from history books, magazines, and newspapers (remember journalists are "historians"). Some of the statements are predominantly factual, that is they simply describe a person or event. Other statements reflect the writer's judgment or opinion. The opinion might be justified in light of the evidence, but it is an opinion nevertheless.

This exercise is designed to sharpen your awareness of how much historical writing depends on the interpretations and judgments of the historian. Label each passage below either FACT (F) or OPINION (O). If a passage contains both facts and judgments (opinions), write "FO," and *underline* the segment that you feel is the opinion or judgment. We have completed the first two to give you a start.

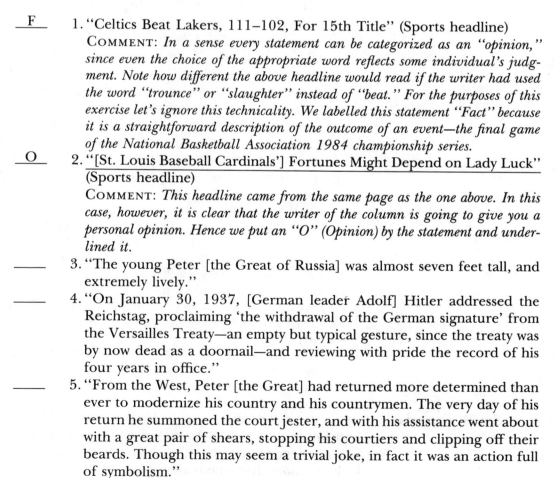

    F   1. "Celtics Beat Lakers, 111–102, For 15th Title" (Sports headline)
        COMMENT: *In a sense every statement can be categorized as an "opinion," since even the choice of the appropriate word reflects some individual's judgment. Note how different the above headline would read if the writer had used the word "trounce" or "slaughter" instead of "beat." For the purposes of this exercise let's ignore this technicality. We labelled this statement "Fact" because it is a straightforward description of the outcome of an event—the final game of the National Basketball Association 1984 championship series.*

    O   2. "[St. Louis Baseball Cardinals'] Fortunes Might Depend on Lady Luck" (Sports headline)
        COMMENT: *This headline came from the same page as the one above. In this case, however, it is clear that the writer of the column is going to give you a personal opinion. Hence we put an "O" (Opinion) by the statement and underlined it.*

    _____   3. "The young Peter [the Great of Russia] was almost seven feet tall, and extremely lively."

    _____   4. "On January 30, 1937, [German leader Adolf] Hitler addressed the Reichstag, proclaiming 'the withdrawal of the German signature' from the Versailles Treaty—an empty but typical gesture, since the treaty was by now dead as a doornail—and reviewing with pride the record of his four years in office."

    _____   5. "From the West, Peter [the Great] had returned more determined than ever to modernize his country and his countrymen. The very day of his return he summoned the court jester, and with his assistance went about with a great pair of shears, stopping his courtiers and clipping off their beards. Though this may seem a trivial joke, in fact it was an action full of symbolism."

    _____   6. "[The invasion of Normandy on D-Day, June 6, 1944, marked] the beginning of a new era. The largest military invasion in history laid the foundation for the Marshall plan, the recovery of Europe and the birth

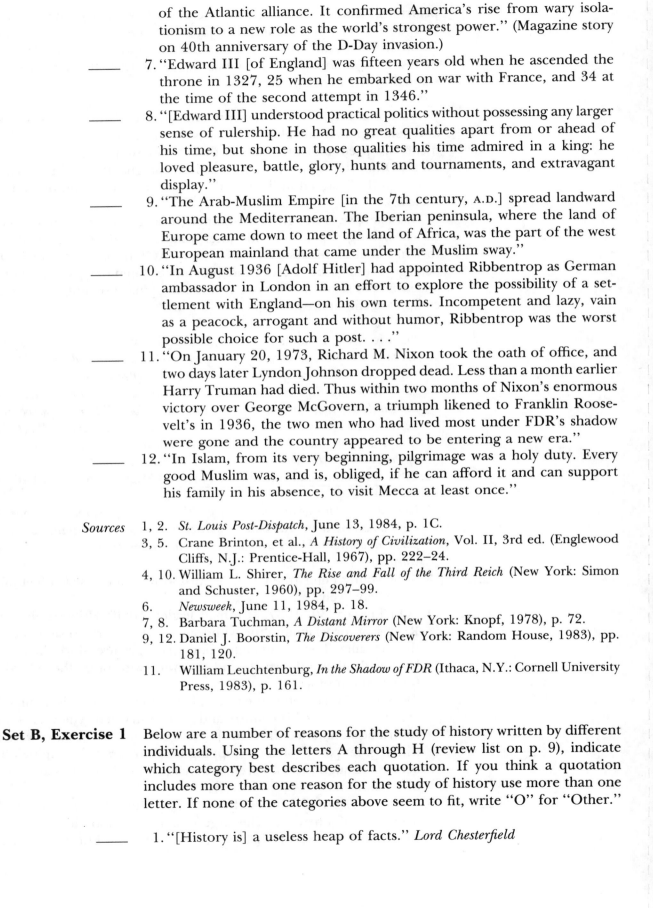

of the Atlantic alliance. It confirmed America's rise from wary isolationism to a new role as the world's strongest power." (Magazine story on 40th anniversary of the D-Day invasion.)

_____ 7. "Edward III [of England] was fifteen years old when he ascended the throne in 1327, 25 when he embarked on war with France, and 34 at the time of the second attempt in 1346."

_____ 8. "[Edward III] understood practical politics without possessing any larger sense of rulership. He had no great qualities apart from or ahead of his time, but shone in those qualities his time admired in a king: he loved pleasure, battle, glory, hunts and tournaments, and extravagant display."

_____ 9. "The Arab-Muslim Empire [in the 7th century, A.D.] spread landward around the Mediterranean. The Iberian peninsula, where the land of Europe came down to meet the land of Africa, was the part of the west European mainland that came under the Muslim sway."

_____ 10. "In August 1936 [Adolf Hitler] had appointed Ribbentrop as German ambassador in London in an effort to explore the possibility of a settlement with England—on his own terms. Incompetent and lazy, vain as a peacock, arrogant and without humor, Ribbentrop was the worst possible choice for such a post. . . ."

_____ 11. "On January 20, 1973, Richard M. Nixon took the oath of office, and two days later Lyndon Johnson dropped dead. Less than a month earlier Harry Truman had died. Thus within two months of Nixon's enormous victory over George McGovern, a triumph likened to Franklin Roosevelt's in 1936, the two men who had lived most under FDR's shadow were gone and the country appeared to be entering a new era."

_____ 12. "In Islam, from its very beginning, pilgrimage was a holy duty. Every good Muslim was, and is, obliged, if he can afford it and can support his family in his absence, to visit Mecca at least once."

Sources 1, 2. *St. Louis Post-Dispatch*, June 13, 1984, p. 1C.
3, 5. Crane Brinton, et al., *A History of Civilization*, Vol. II, 3rd ed. (Englewood Cliffs, N.J.: Prentice-Hall, 1967), pp. 222–24.
4, 10. William L. Shirer, *The Rise and Fall of the Third Reich* (New York: Simon and Schuster, 1960), pp. 297–99.
6. *Newsweek*, June 11, 1984, p. 18.
7, 8. Barbara Tuchman, *A Distant Mirror* (New York: Knopf, 1978), p. 72.
9, 12. Daniel J. Boorstin, *The Discoverers* (New York: Random House, 1983), pp. 181, 120.
11. William Leuchtenburg, *In the Shadow of FDR* (Ithaca, N.Y.: Cornell University Press, 1983), p. 161.

Set B, Exercise 1 Below are a number of reasons for the study of history written by different individuals. Using the letters A through H (review list on p. 9), indicate which category best describes each quotation. If you think a quotation includes more than one reason for the study of history use more than one letter. If none of the categories above seem to fit, write "O" for "Other."

_____ 1. "[History is] a useless heap of facts." *Lord Chesterfield*

_____ 2. "If History teaches any lesson at all, it is that there are no historical lessons." *Lucien Febvre*

_____ 3. "The value of history . . . is that it teaches us what man has done and thus what man is." *R. G. Collingwood*

_____ 4. "Everything has a history. At least part of the answer to any question about the contemporary world can come from studying the circumstances that led up to it." *Jules Benjamin*

_____ 5. "In an age when so much of our literature is infused with nihilism, and other social disciplines are driven toward narrow, positivistic inquiry, history may remain the most humanizing of the arts." *Richard Hofstadter*

_____ 6. "The function of history, as I see it, is to describe and make understandable the forces which have shaped the destiny of man and brought him to the present time equipped as he now is with these ideas and institutions." *Walter Prescott Webb*

_____ 7. "What man is, only history tells." *Wilhelm Dilthey*

_____ 8. "History enables bewildered bodies of human beings to grasp their relationship with their past, and helps them chart on general lines their immediate forward course." *Allan Nevins*

_____ 9. "The study of history is in the truest sense an education and a training for political life. . . . The most instructive or rather the only, method of learning to bear with dignity the vicissitudes of fortune is to recall the catastrophes of others." *Polybius*

_____ 10. "History is not (merely) the past. It is an intellectual process . . . the function of which is to cleanse the story of mankind from the deceiving visions of a purposeful past." *C. Vann Woodward*

Set B, Exercise 2

This exercise gives a slightly different twist to the Set A exercise on distinguishing between fact and opinion (judgment). When you did that exercise it should have occurred to you how difficult it is to find any passage longer than a sentence or two which is totally and unambiguously factual. The historian's judgments, perspectives, values and priorities are, in fact, an almost inseparable part of any piece of historical writing.

Contrary to the assertion of some commentators, facts do *not* "speak for themselves." The historian gives meaning to facts by tying them together with *generalizations* and *interpretations*—i.e., "opinions" of a sort but based on evidence. Perhaps it would be better to call them "considered judgments." Below you will find three types of historical statement:

1. *Type "G" (for "Generalization"):* These are almost wholly interpretive in nature. The historian is giving a generalization or interpretation with little or no factual support. (Note: There could be, and probably is, considerable factual support in the original work, but in *the particular excerpt listed below* the generalizations dominate.)
2. *Type "F" (for "Factual"):* These statements are overwhelmingly factual in nature with little or no interpretive comment.
3. *Type "GF" (a combination of 1 and 2):* These statements include both generalizations (interpretations) *and* some supporting factual material.

Using the labels "G," "F," or "GF" indicate which of the three types of statement *best* describes each of the passages below. We have done the first one as an example.

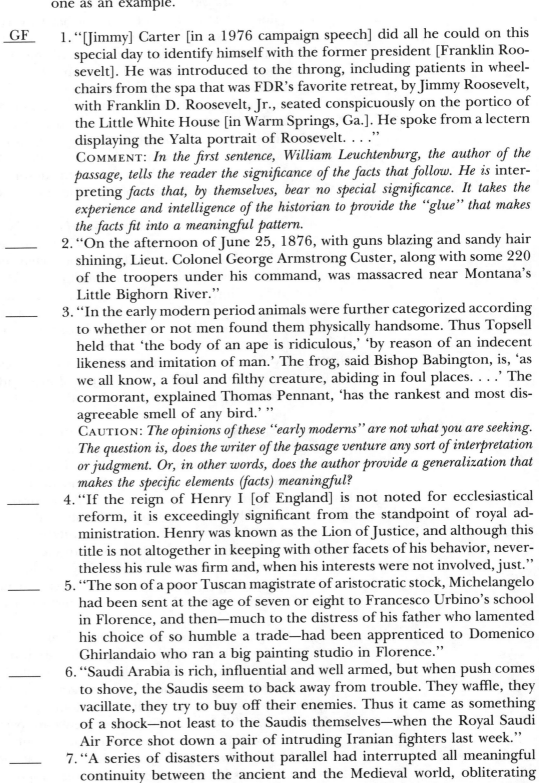

GF   1. "[Jimmy] Carter [in a 1976 campaign speech] did all he could on this special day to identify himself with the former president [Franklin Roosevelt]. He was introduced to the throng, including patients in wheelchairs from the spa that was FDR's favorite retreat, by Jimmy Roosevelt, with Franklin D. Roosevelt, Jr., seated conspicuously on the portico of the Little White House [in Warm Springs, Ga.]. He spoke from a lectern displaying the Yalta portrait of Roosevelt. . . ."
COMMENT: *In the first sentence, William Leuchtenburg, the author of the passage, tells the reader the significance of the facts that follow. He is interpreting facts that, by themselves, bear no special significance. It takes the experience and intelligence of the historian to provide the "glue" that makes the facts fit into a meaningful pattern.*

_____ 2. "On the afternoon of June 25, 1876, with guns blazing and sandy hair shining, Lieut. Colonel George Armstrong Custer, along with some 220 of the troopers under his command, was massacred near Montana's Little Bighorn River."

_____ 3. "In the early modern period animals were further categorized according to whether or not men found them physically handsome. Thus Topsell held that 'the body of an ape is ridiculous,' 'by reason of an indecent likeness and imitation of man.' The frog, said Bishop Babington, is, 'as we all know, a foul and filthy creature, abiding in foul places. . . .' The cormorant, explained Thomas Pennant, 'has the rankest and most disagreeable smell of any bird.' "
CAUTION: *The opinions of these "early moderns" are not what you are seeking. The question is, does the writer of the passage venture any sort of interpretation or judgment. Or, in other words, does the author provide a generalization that makes the specific elements (facts) meaningful?*

_____ 4. "If the reign of Henry I [of England] is not noted for ecclesiastical reform, it is exceedingly significant from the standpoint of royal administration. Henry was known as the Lion of Justice, and although this title is not altogether in keeping with other facets of his behavior, nevertheless his rule was firm and, when his interests were not involved, just."

_____ 5. "The son of a poor Tuscan magistrate of aristocratic stock, Michelangelo had been sent at the age of seven or eight to Francesco Urbino's school in Florence, and then—much to the distress of his father who lamented his choice of so humble a trade—had been apprenticed to Domenico Ghirlandaio who ran a big painting studio in Florence."

_____ 6. "Saudi Arabia is rich, influential and well armed, but when push comes to shove, the Saudis seem to back away from trouble. They waffle, they vacillate, they try to buy off their enemies. Thus it came as something of a shock—not least to the Saudis themselves—when the Royal Saudi Air Force shot down a pair of intruding Iranian fighters last week."

_____ 7. "A series of disasters without parallel had interrupted all meaningful continuity between the ancient and the Medieval world, obliterating creative science in the process. A singularly lucky combination of circumstances rekindled scientific thought around the twelfth century, and thereby gave birth to a new and continuous phase that has by no means yet reached its peak. So fortunate, in fact, was that historical constellation that it sparked the most spectacular scientific evolution history has ever seen so far.''

———— 8. "Japan's attack on Pearl Harbor brought post-haste from Monterey to Washington one of the unlikeliest officers of the United States army. Joseph Warren Stillwell—Warren to his family, already Vinegar Joe to subordinates and superiors who knew the whiplash of his tongue—was commanding III Corps on December 7, 1941.''

———— 9. "Three kings ruled England in the fourteenth century: Edward II (1307–1327), Edward III (1327–1377), and Richard II (1377–1399), and of these three, two had their reigns cut short by rebellion and deposition. Edward II was the weakest and least successful of them.''

———— 10. "All cultures, we know, place boundaries around the passions; they construct powerful defenses against murder and incest, to say nothing of derivative transgressions. In complex cultures like nineteenth-century Europe and America, these boundaries are sure to be complex as well. . . . Segments of culture, like religious denominations or classes, add prohibitions of their own.''

Sources
1. Leuchtenburg, *Shadow of FDR*, p. 177.
2. *Time*, May 28, 1984, p. 49.
3. Keith Thomas, *Man and the Natural World* (New York: Pantheon, 1983), p. 57.
4. C. Warren Hollister, *The Making of England*, 3rd ed. (Lexington, Mass.: D.C. Heath, 1976), p. 116.
5. Christopher Hibbert, *The House of Medici* (New York: Morrow Quill, 1980), p. 165.
6. *Newsweek*, June 18, 1984, p. 48.
7. Thomas Goldstein, *Dawn of Modern Science* (Boston: Houghton Mifflin, 1980), p. 43.
8. John Keegan, *Six Armies in Normandy* (Harmondsworth, Middlesex, England: Penguin, 1982), p. 22.
9. Hollister, *The Making of England*, p. 220.
10. Peter Gay, *The Bourgeois Experience, Victoria to Freud*, Vol. I. *Education of the Senses* (New York: Oxford Univ. Press, 1984), p. 107.

CHAPTER 2

**HISTORICAL-MINDEDNESS:
THE GOAL OF HISTORY STUDY**

"Nothing capable of being memorized is history."
R. G. Collingwood

In this chapter we'll be discussing historical-mindedness—the ways the historian's mind works when analyzing the past. For most of us, daily mental life passes from one distraction to another: a news broadcast, a bit of gossip, a problem at work, a joke, a soap opera, a phone call—whatever. In all of this our thinking is often quite shallow—as one writer put it we "keep watching the fence posts whiz by, not the broader panorama." To be able to see this "broader panorama," to have the ability to put passing events into perspective, adds a special dimension to the human mind, and is a major purpose of studying history.

In June of 1939 Admiral Isoroku Yamamoto was made Commander-in-Chief of the Combined Fleet of the Empire of Japan. An original thinker and instinctive gambler, Yamamoto was Japan's most distinguished military man, and knew how vulnerable America was in the western Pacific. He recognized that Japanese power could readily overrun the Philippines, Indo-China, Malaya, the Dutch East Indies, and many island chains to the south and the east. But Yamamoto was also a keen student of history, both of his own country and of the United States. He told his countrymen that easy early victories might prove too costly in the long run. They would arouse America's "fierce fighting spirit," shown in so many Civil War battles and in the naval actions of the Spanish-American War. He did not want to see that force, so evident in American history, unleashed against Japan. Again and again he urged caution upon his nation's rulers.[1]

By late 1940 the Japanese war party had become dominant; and soon Yamamoto was directed to prepare for war, though he told the Japanese premier, "If I am told to fight regardless of the consequences, I shall run wild for the first six months or a year, but I have utterly no confidence for the second or third year." It was the reluctant Yamamoto who conceived the bold Pearl Harbor attack plan (based on his historical awareness of the successful surprise attack against Port Arthur in the Russo-Japanese War of 1904), organized it, and brought it to completion on December 7, 1941. Yet so strongly did his sense of history enter into his thinking that while toasts to his great victory still lingered in the air, he remarked, "I fear that all we have done is awaken a slumbering giant and fill him with a terrible resolve."

Though he did not survive the war, Yamamoto's vision of what would happen in the Pacific proved prophetic as the Japanese navy began its long,

---

[1] Edwin P. Hoyt, *Japan's War, The Great Pacific Conflict* (New York: McGraw-Hill, 1986), pp. 187–93.

slow retreat in June 1942. Yamamoto was a prophet not because he could look directly into the future, but because he saw that a strong force active in the past could once again assert its shaping power. He had a sense of perspective; he saw the "broader panorama" rather than the "fence posts."

Most of us are aware, if only vaguely, how much more there is to education than factual information about a variety of subjects. We learn grammatical rules, geometric axioms, principles of government, computer literacy, and other segmented bits of knowledge. These are worthwhile, even crucial in some cases; but there is something much more important about education. This "something more" is a special quality of mind that develops through years of study—a cultivation, a breadth, an enlargement of one's intellectual perspective. This is not the exclusive product of any academic discipline, for it can be learned while pursuing many fields of study. But we believe, perhaps immodestly, that this special intellectual quality is best developed through the study of history. In fact, many historians would argue that the development of this quality of mind, known within the discipline as "historical-mindedness," is far more important than any sterile memorization of facts. Historical-mindedness is a precondition to historical literacy, and, in a sense, is what the study of history is all about.

Though terminology may vary from one historian to another, there is general agreement that historical-mindedness includes these elements:

—Sensitivity to how other times and places differ from our own.
—Awareness of basic *continuities* in human affairs over time.
—Ability to note and explain significant *changes*.
—Sensitivity to multiple causation.
—Awareness that all written history is a *reconstruction* that inadequately reflects the past as it really happened.

Each of these components requires elaboration.

The Elements of Historical-Mindedness

1. **Sensitivity to how other times and places differ from our own.** To one degree or another all of us have something of a "now mentality" which inclines us to think that present priorities, concerns, and values are permanent and valid for all time. Such attitudes make it difficult to journey mentally, and sympathetically, to another time or place. Yet in another way we make such journeys all the time in a fictional world, when we burrow down in the chair to read a horror story or suffer through the tribulations of a romance in a soap opera.

Historical-mindedness calls for something of this same vicarious projection of oneself into a somewhat different world—a willingness to accept, without prejudging, the values and attitudes of another time or place. At the same time, this projective frame of mind has as its companion a lurking critical spirit that suggests questions that must be asked and answered concerning that time and place. Put in a more concrete way, historical understanding involves more than, say, an appreciation of General Washington's courage at Valley Forge in 1777. It also involves raising questions leading to a recognition that his courage can only be *understood* in the context of such realities as the continual bickering among his officers, the undisciplined ways of his foot soldiers, and the instability of the fledgling rebel government.

2. **Awareness of basic continuities in human affairs over time.** Of all the intellectual tools that a historian uses, the concepts of *continuity* and *change* are by far the most important. We will be discussing them in separate sections, but you'll note that one can scarcely be discussed without the other.

If asked whether change or continuity is more dominant in our lives, most of us would probably say "continuity." We would then speak of the monotony of the things we do, including eating, working, sleeping, talking to friends, watching television, making monthly payments—all adding up to continuity. Life, as experienced on the day-to-day level, is inevitably routine so that most of us are drawn to the excitement of change, such as a major news event, some exciting gossip, or even a soap-opera crisis.

In contrast, when we open a history book, too often we find we are asked to enter a world where change is so constant it is almost overwhelming. Events are paraded before us, each representing a change from what preceded it. We get a sense of excessive movement and can easily lose our perspective. We know change doesn't happen so rapidly in our personal lives, and gradually we retreat from a historical world that seems so unreal.

This problem is often the fault of the historian not the reader. Historians are under an obligation to portray the past as it really was. However, in their preoccupation with the factors leading to change, they often forget that nearly every change is in some way a compromise and that in many ways life goes on pretty much as before. Many of us make a "change" every year with our New Year's resolutions, but in most cases the same old habits prevail. Medical breakthroughs occur, but doctors find that two-thirds of their patients' problems are best treated with traditional methods. Congress might enact new tax laws, but for most of us preparing an income tax return, the categories remain the same. The most effective historians remain conscious of the essentially conservative nature of human society and weave their stories with threads of both change and continuity. Thus, they follow the dictum so neatly phrased by British historian G. J. Renier: "All things flow, but they need not necessarily rush down a cataract."

3. **Ability to note and explain significant changes.** Someone once said, "The mountain has no history." Neither does the polar ice cap nor do oceans. Why? Because they never seem to change, at least not to our eyes. Geologists would disagree with this observation, but it serves to bring out a major point: There can be a "history" only when there is change. If everything remained the same—no history. In essence, history is the story of change.

Change is an ever-present part of our lives. We change clothes, courses, schools, jobs, apartments, none of which are of any great significance. But we use the same term to describe developments that are of potentially enormous importance, such as a new Congress, a sudden war, or a decisive shift in public attitude. There should be three or four different words to distinguish between minor and major changes. In this case, however, the English language, ordinarily so rich in vocabulary, fails us.

What history is concerned with is *significant* change. Sometimes this involves radically different conditions for society, such as those brought on by wars, revolutions, and plagues. At other times, a society remains the same structurally, but important changes still occur. For instance, in 1960s America there emerged major shifts in attitude toward country, clothes, sexual behavior, music, and politics. Perhaps more often history is concerned with gradual changes, such as population shifts that can affect the balance of political power or the economic advance of nations and peoples.

Some of the questions historians deal with in explaining change are: How much room did the existing societal structures (government, economy, social class, religion, etc.) allow for freedom to improvise and experiment?; Was there some decisive event (depression, war, rebellion, etc.) that set off a series of major changes?; Was there a backlash to changes that occurred, whereby major groups successfully conserved what was important and satisfying in the older structure?; Was there a long evolution of slow changes that suddenly telescoped into a short episode? All these questions suggest the variety of forms change can assume.

4. **Sensitivity to multiple causation.** Democratic political candidates through the 1930s, 1940s, and 1950s frequently set up Republican Herbert Hoover, president from 1929–1933, as a scapegoat for the ferocious depression of the 1930s. Republican candidates, taking a somewhat different approach, condemned Franklin D. Roosevelt's New Deal as the enemy of traditional American principles. Both claims are nonsense, violations of elementary historical-mindedness. Hoover, of course, had nothing to do with the onset of the depression. He was in office only seven months when it began and, acting according to his principles, did everything he could to alleviate its distresses. Roosevelt, far from destroying American principles, actually helped conserve them by refusing to go as far to the left as some of his advisors advocated. Such partisan behavior is the stuff of American politics, and it will not quickly disappear given the passionate nature of party competition.

But historians cannot be so narrow-minded, since important events rarely have simple or singular causes. Most historians, for instance, accept great men arriving on the scene but do not accept the "Great Man Theory," which attributes much that happens to some great man or his shadow. Or historians readily accept the importance of economic class rivalry but do not, like Karl Marx, interpret all events based on this singular focus. Historians realize the importance of ideas and ideals but generally do not regard them as the sole motivators of human behavior. The historian, knowing that bureaucracies sometimes decisively affect the course of events, is also aware that cleverness can and does surmount bureaucratic policy. In short, one who is historically minded must take a wider view of affairs than the politicians and their (sometimes) unquestioning followers. This wide-angled view of the historian will be discussed in detail in Chapter 7.

5. **Awareness that all written history is a reconstruction that inadequately reflects the past as it really happened.** Suppose you were asked about a basketball game you saw last night, one that in this case went into two overtimes. Most of us would respond with something like "great game—exciting all the way—wild finish," etc. But does such description get at the emotional fervor one felt, the great plays, the questionable coaching strategy, the half-time conversations with friends, the dumb calls by the referee, etc.? Of course not. No description, as we saw in Chapter 1, can ever bring back the full reality of the original event. Furthermore, the description—an effort at portraying or in a sense reconstructing the event—necessarily involves a subjective element.

In its most fundamental nature, history is a way of thought that ties together causes and results. It works with facts, but its essence is the effort to *explain* them; and it is *never* sure of its explanation. How can it be when it has to work with insufficient evidence, which in itself contains contradictions? When it has to speculate about motivations and make inferences from questionable premises? History is a way of thinking about connections between elements of the past. Because of the inherent difficulties of that undertaking, it *is* uncertain in its conclusions and *is* ambiguous in its perspectives.

This is not necessarily a liability. By its emphasis on multiple causation, history requires development of that wider vision necessary to understand the complex realities of modern life. By its very ambiguity and uncertainty, history encourages the flexibility of mind necessary to adapt more comfortably to changed intellectual environments. The study of history, like life, requires us to "reach the maximum conclusions with the minimum of evidence."

History, then, is a continuing *search*, not an unchanging compendium, of facts. (The origin of the word "history"—Greek for "inquiry"—attests to that.) History is also a *reconstruction*, a reconstruction often based on flawed sources of information. Obviously, the historian can never be sure if the search is complete or the reconstruction totally accurate. But at this point it is wise to remember that historical claims (statements, generalizations, interpretations) *are* based on evidence, and that the uncertainty inherent in historical writing is not absolute.

Historical claims are only as valid as the evidence used to support them, and clearly some statements are more convincing than others. To take an extreme example, one historian might say that President Franklin Roosevelt was a fool; another, that he was a charlatan; a third, that he was a shrewd politician. Each of these is a generalization, believable to the extent supported. The first generalization, that FDR was a fool, is not supported by the evidence; and no reputable historian would make such a statement. That Roosevelt was a charlatan is somewhat more credible, but the evidence is probably insufficient and questionable. That he was a shrewd politician is extremely believable, with a wealth of evidence attesting to such an interpretation. Any respectable piece of history, then, presents a generalization, a reconstruction, which is acceptable to the extent that it generalizes appropriately about related events.

In summary, to think historically you must be sensitive to all the elements discussed above. Historical-mindedness is a powerful instrument, a way of thought that explores not merely length and width but the larger geometry of depth. It enables one to deal effectively with the dimension of time, thus opening the mind to consideration of origins, to breadth of influences, to the varieties of motivation, to an appreciation of gradual change—in short, to a fuller comprehension of human nature.

The Stages of Historical Consciousness

After all that we have said about historical-mindedness, it should be clear that thinking historically is not as easy as it might at first appear. But remember, you can't become a good historical thinker overnight. Learning to think historically is a gradual process that involves a number of developmental stages. At minimum there are four stages through which students pass as they become more sophisticated in their understanding of the nature of historical studies. At what stage are you?

Stage I: History as Fact

To me (says the typical Stage I student) history is a bunch of facts—dates, names, events—that I have to memorize for the test. The books and lectures are full of facts, but I really don't see how they all fit together. I take history because I have to, and it bores me. Once I get my requirements out of the way, I plan to avoid history like the plague.

Too many people in our society never get beyond this view of history. (It is not always their fault. All too often history teachers teach the subject as if memorization of facts *were* the essence of historical study.) *Of course* such people are bored by history. They lack any sense of the causal relationships that give meaning to the study of the past, and certainly they don't have the faintest understanding of the role interpretation plays in history writing.

Stage II: History as Causal Sequence

I now see (says the student at Stage II) that history is more than facts. History provides a story of sequential developments over time, you know—event A leads to event B which leads to event C, and so forth. The stories are often interesting (my teacher tells some great anecdotes!), and it is satisfying to know why things happened as they did. More important, I am now beginning to see where I fit into the picture. I understand my own origins a bit better, and I know where those values they are forcing me to study came from. The only thing that bothers me is that my book and the teacher contradict each other sometimes. It's a shame that historians can't get their act together and come to some sort of agreement on the causes of events. Maybe in time they will.

Generally, a large number of people reach this stage. State II "consciousness" is still quite basic, but much beyond the very simplistic outlook of Stage I. People at Stage II can be fascinated by history and can understand cause and effect relationships. But they do not realize the complexity of such relationships and cannot accept the possibility of alternative interpretations. When they come across contradictions, they assume that one version is, of necessity, false and the other true. Or both could be false and the "truth" yet to be discovered. Put another way, what they seek from a history book is *the* truth, not *a* truth. Such people also have difficulty in perceiving the difference between fact and opinion.

Stage III:
History as
Complexity

I'm confused (says the Stage III student). History is a subject where there is so much to learn, I don't even know where to begin. There are too many variations in the accounts you read, even accounts of the same time and place! Some books (or lecturers) emphasize politics and war; others emphasize social life, or economics, or ideas, or art, or science and technology. Studying history is like looking in a kaleidoscope where the picture changes with each turn of the cylinder. History certainly isn't like math or chemistry, where you can get exact and certain answers. In history there seem to be so many ways of looking at the same event or period that I often don't know what I should be studying anymore.

People at this stage become (at last!) conscious of the relativistic character of history. The paradox of Stage III is that people who reach it often feel themselves to be more confused and ignorant than they did at Stages I and II. It is at Stage III that students realize how *complex* human affairs really are and how *much* there is to be learned about even tiny segments of the past. They also begin to realize how little they know compared to the immensity of what there is to know. But this feeling of helplessness is really a positive sign. The recognition of ignorance is the first step to real understanding and wisdom.

At this level people begin to think like historians. They finally realize that, due to the enormity and complexity of the historical record, accounts of even the smallest segment of the past are very selective and limited in what they cover. They understand, further, that individual historians are the ones who ultimately decide what to include and exclude. Historians tell different stories depending on their interests and points of view. This awareness is an important insight. Even at Stage III, however, people still lack a full appreciation of the inherently interpretive nature of history.

Stage IV:
History as
Interpretation

Last year (remarks the increasingly confident student at Stage IV) a professor said that "history" is as much a product of the historian who writes it as of the actual people who lived it. At the time I didn't understand the comment at all; now I do. Just as individual historians will choose their topics differently, and disagree on what evidence should be included or excluded [see Stage III], historians, of necessity, *interpret* their materials differently. Not only that, but I now realize that studying the various interpretations of an event, and how historians support and develop their interpretations, is much more interesting than just trying to memorize facts.

Students like this will derive the most intellectual satisfaction from the study of history. They have come to terms with the interpretive nature of written history. They understand that the evidence for any historical event is contradictory, complex, and incomplete. At the same time, paradoxically, there is far more evidence available (for most events) than the historian can handle comfortably. Moreover, historians will approach the evidence with different questions, different personalities, different value systems, and different abilities. The result: history as interpretation. These realizations are uncomfortable for individuals who crave moral certainty and loath ambiguity. However, the sooner they realize that history cannot provide absolute truth, the sooner they will be able to extract the maximum intellectual benefit from its study.

EXERCISES

Set A, Exercise 1   Not every piece of historical writing reflects the qualities of historical-mindedness as we have discussed them. Some writing presents no more than a sequence of facts loosely tied together. But with good historians these qualities do shine through their writing at many points.

Each of the passages below reflects, in some way, one or more of the elements of historical-mindedness. One passage, for example, shows that a given development is but part of a long tradition (continuity). Another reflects an aspect of "history as reconstruction," i.e., the use of narrative style to give the reader a sense of being there as the event unfolded. And so forth. There is also a passage that manifests two of the qualities of historical-mindedness.

In each of the six passages below your task is to decide which of the following categories is *most* visible. Each of the categories is represented, and one of the excerpts is an example of two categories. Give reasons for your selection in each case.

Categories:

A. Relatedness of the developments of a given period to an earlier time (continuity).
B. Presentation of a series of changes or developments occurring rapidly during a given time period.
C. Emphasis on "multiple causation," or of varied factors having influenced a given event.
D. Description of a way of life that differs clearly from our own, having a different life-style, and perhaps different values.
E. Reflects a "you are there" quality.

1.   Once the C.I.O. pierced the fortifications of G.M. [General Motors] and U.S. Steel, it was able to overrun much of the rest of industry. By the end of 1937, the U.A.W. [United Auto Workers] had brought every car manufacturer save Ford into line. The pace of organization moved so swiftly that workers outdistanced union leaders. "Many of us," reflected a Dodge unionist, "had the feeling we were like the kid that gets a little fire started in the hayfield." In a year, the U.A.W.'s membership jumped from 30,000 to 400,000. By early May, 1937, S.W.O.C. [Steel Workers' Organizing Committee] formed less than a year before, claimed 325,000 members; by the end of the month, it had signed up all the subsidiaries of U.S. Steel and such important independents as Jones and Laughlin, Wheeling Steel, and Caterpillar Tractor. As steel and auto went, so went much of the nation. After an eight-week strike in March and April, 1937, Firestone Tire & Rubber capitulated to the United Rubber Workers. By the end of 1937, General Electric, RCA-Victor, and Philco had recognized the United Electrical and Radio

Workers. The Textile Workers Organizing Committee, run by Sidney Hillman, brought into line industry titans like American Woolen in Lawrence; by early October, it boasted 450,000 members.

CATEGORY: _____

BASIS: _____

_____

_____

2.   Only a rugged, roughhewn, obstinate man could have shouldered his way to success in the circumstances—the looming figure of Luther makes the personal factor important in the causation of the Reformation. . . .

The circumstances were ready for the man, and his religious zeal furnished a focal point for the hitherto diffused causes for the Reformation. One may legitimately question if one single force, albeit as powerful as this one, could in itself have altered the course of history. From our perspective, at least, a number of social forces seem to converge upon the developing events and carry them forward.

We have seen gunpowder and the better ocean-going vessels make possible the expansion of the European into other parts of the world. The printing press, another technological advance, served as a tool of incalculable importance in the Reformation. Someone might argue very plausibly that no Reformation could have occurred had it not been for the invention of the printing press. Without this method of spreading ideas, the Lutheran doctrines could not have been disseminated so rapidly. . . .

Social forces emerging from economic motives, powerful as they were, must have exercised an important influence on these events. The kind of merchant that we encountered in Florence or in sixteenth-century England, and who was also active in Germany, would deplore the constant flow of money to Rome. Most people, indeed, would feel indignation at this continual drain on the national wealth, and any rebel against papal authority would find useful ammunition here. The incessant sniping at the wealth of the bishops and the monasteries was partly due to the unfortunate contrast with the early ideal of the Church, but the criticisms were also likely to remind people that their contributions were not always usefully applied. Especially would the growing middle class deplore the drag on productivity caused by the clerical possession of land, the numerous church festivals, and the presumed idleness of the monks. . . .

We know that the nobles were always eager to expand their holdings. They had long eyed the lands of the Church, and the Reformation, with its expropriation of clerical wealth, offered the awaited opportunity. . . .

CATEGORY: _____

BASIS: _____

_____

_____

3.   It was about 10 P.M. when Private Arthur B. "Dutch" Shultz of the 82nd Airborne Division (preparing to invade Europe in 1944) decided to get out of the crap game; he might never have this much money again. The game had been going on ever since the announcement that the airborne assault was off for at least twenty-four hours. It had begun behind a tent, next it had moved under the wing of a plane, and now the session was going full blast in the hangar, which had been converted into a huge dormitory. Even here it had done some traveling, moving up and down the corridors created by the rows of double-tiered bunks. And Dutch was one of the big winners.

How much he had won he didn't know. But he guessed that the bundle of crumpled greenbacks, English banknotes and fresh blue-green French invasion currency he held in his fist came to more than $2,500. That was more money than he had seen at any one time in all his twenty-one years. . . .

The young paratrooper felt good; he had taken care of everything—but had he? Why did the incident of the morning keep coming back, filling him with so much uneasiness?

CATEGORY: _____

BASIS: _____

_____

_____

4.   Carnegie's book [*How to Win Friends and Influence People*], despite the sneers of the literati, was squarely in the classical heritage of self-help literature. The essays of Francis Bacon and Montaigne, Castiglione's *Courtier*, and Lord Chesterfield's *Letters to His Son* gave advice to the ambitious young man who aimed to improve himself. In England, Samuel Smiles, with his *Lives of the Engineers*, and his cheery essays on Self-Help, Thrift, and Duty, had begun to adapt this literature to the wider audience and the sterner demands of an industrial age. The most popular and most frequently quoted passage of Benjamin Franklin's *Poor Richard's Almanac* was Father Abraham's Speech, entitled "The Way to Wealth." For most Americans who heard Ralph Waldo Emerson lecture and who read his books, Emerson was no transcendentalist, but the man who showed them the path to "Self-Reliance," and so to successful living. A bizarre latter-day American prophet of self-improvement was the pseudo-Bohemian Elbert Hubbard, whose leaflet *A Message to Garcia* (1899), a parable of the resourcefulness and self-reliance of an American lieutenant in the Spanish-American War, sold over forty million copies, mostly to industrial firms for circulation to their employees. While Dale Carnegie's work showed no literary distinction, it was written in the plain style and had the virtues of the most effective advertising copy. Brilliant in its psychological insights and its practicality, it long remained the most successful adaptation of the moralistic tradition of self-improvement to the special circumstances of twentieth-century America.

CATEGORY: _____

BASIS: _____

149.578

College of St. Francis Library
Joliet, Illinois

5.   Everywhere, in town and country, the worship of God was carried out with great splendour on Sundays and feast days. Work ceased and rest from work was enforced by civil sanctions. As a Synod of Salzburg (1456) insisted afresh, the city gates must be closed on Sundays and feast days so that the peace be not disturbed by travellers with their carts. Feast days, which varied from state to state, were numerous— about fifty in all. Thus, besides Sunday, there was on average one holiday of obligation each week. The days of the apostles and of commemoration of famous saints and martyrs and virgin-martyrs were all observed by cessation of labour. Then there were many local holidays. People took time to worship God: inns were open as a rule not for profit, but for necessary provisions, and most of the free time was devoted to worship. The centre of liturgical life was, as of old, the cathedral church with its canons and clergy.

CATEGORY: _____

BASIS: _____

_____

_____

6.   In November 1830 the evangelist Charles Grandison Finney faced an audience of merchants, master craftsmen, and their families at Third Presbyterian Church in Rochester, New York. The people at Third Church were inheritors of New England Calvinism, and they knew that the world was beyond their control. In 1815 the town's Presbyterians had declared themselves impotent before a God who "foreordained whatsoever comes to pass." Ten years later the founders of Second Church reaffirmed the belief that men could alter neither their individual spiritual states nor the shape of their society. Revivals had been eroding these beliefs since the 1790s, and there were people at Third Church who had rejected them altogether. But most Rochester Protestants still inhabited a world where events, in H. Richard Neibuhr's phrase, were a glove on the hand of God.

Finney had been fighting that idea since the middle 1820s, in revivals that had taken him throughout northern and central New York and, most recently, into Philadelphia and New York City. Now he turned to the audience at Third Church and completed the revolution. "God has made man a moral free agent," he declared. Evil was the product not of innate depravity but of choices made by selfish men and women. Sin and disorder would disappear when they chose good over evil and convinced others to do the same. Finney stared down from the pulpit and said flatly that if Christians united and dedicated their lives to the task, they could convert the world and bring on the millennium in three months. The evangelist finished, and his audience stirred. Then scores of people rose from their seats, many of them weeping, and pledged their lives to Jesus. With that act they left the imperfect and confining world that God had made for corrupt man, and entered a world where men worked ceaselessly to make themselves and others perfect.

CATEGORY: _____

BASIS: _____

_____

_____

Sources

1. William E. Leuchtenburg, *Franklin Roosevelt and the New Deal* (New York: Harper & Row, 1965), p. 240.
2. Carl G. Gustavson, *A Preface to History* (New York: McGraw-Hill Book Company, 1955), pp. 58–60.
3. Cornelius Ryan, *The Longest Day* (New York: Simon and Schuster, Inc., 1959), pp. 63–64.
4. Daniel Boorstin, *The Americans, The Democratic Experience* (New York: Vintage Books, 1974), p. 468.
5. J. A. Jungmann, *Pastoral Liturgy* (New York: Herder and Herder, 1962), p. 64.
6. Paul E. Johnson, *A Shopkeeper's Millennium* (New York: Hill and Wang, 1978), pp. 3–4.

Set A, Exercise 2   The following exercise is intended to deepen your awareness of history as an attempt to *reconstruct* the reality of a given past. An account of an event is dependent upon those elements the historian chooses to emphasize. In this exercise you are asked to make the sort of choices all historians have to make. First, read the brief account below:

> In early June, 1944, during World War II, supreme Allied commander General Dwight Eisenhower had to make a decision as to whether the invasion of Europe would be postponed or go on as scheduled. Despite adverse weather conditions, Eisenhower chose to go. On June 6 Allied forces landed on Normandy beaches and went on from there to victory over Germany eleven months later. After the war was over, Eisenhower remarked that the invasion decision was one of the most difficult he faced during the entire war.

As a historian, if you were asked to write a history of Eisenhower's decision, which factors would you emphasize? Listed below are a number of the factors that may or may not have entered in Eisenhower's decision. Indicate by number *in order of importance* the five factors you'd most like to have more information about before writing your story. Be prepared to defend your choices in class discussion. Note: We assume that you might not have sufficient background information to make an informed choice. The point is not to be "correct," but to choose those items that you think would be worth knowing more about.

_____ a. Exact content of weather reports
_____ b. Morale of Allied troops
_____ c. Basic invasion strategy
_____ d. Professional quality of army commanders who would lead invasion

_____ e. Advice given Eisenhower by closest advisors
_____ f. Difficulties of reversing invasion procedures already under way
_____ g. Eisenhower's independence of judgment
_____ h. Extent of enemy readiness
_____ i. Enemy expectations
_____ j. President Roosevelt's view of Eisenhower as supreme commander
_____ k. State of readiness of Allied forces
_____ l. Political pressures exerted by Allied leaders, Franklin Roosevelt and Winston Churchill

Set A, Exercise 3 The six documents that follow deal with the beginnings of American fur trade on the upper Missouri River. This trade had great potential economic value, since animal furs and hides were regarded as *the* major resource of the developing West. The events described in the documents took place within what was legally American territory (Louisiana Purchase, 1803). One must remember, however, that for more than a hundred years British fur traders had operated successfully throughout the forest and mountain areas of North America, no matter who owned them. Your task in reading these pieces is to write a brief historical essay (two to four fully developed paragraphs will do) that explains why this first American fur trading effort turned out as it did. Or, alternatively, develop any other theme which in your opinion emerges strongly from these documents. Remember, the documents (along with these preliminary remarks) are *all* you have to work with. Give your essay a title that summarizes the theme of your essay.[2] These documents are taken from *The West of William H. Ashley*, edited by Dale L. Morgan (Denver: Old West Publishing Co., 1964), pp. 17, 22, 29–31, 33, 36–37. Published with permission. Original spelling has been retained.

> John C. Calhoun, Secretary of War, to William Clark, Superintendent of Indian Affairs at St. Louis, Washington, July 1, 1822
>
> Sir,
>   . . . I have received a letter from Major O'Fallon, in which he states that he understands a licence has been granted to Gen. Ashley and Major Henry, to trade, trap, & hunt, on the upper Missouri, and expresses a hope that limits have been prescribed to their trapping and hunting on Indian lands, as, he says, nothing is better calculated to alarm and disturb the harmony so happily existing between us and the Indians in the vicinity of the Council Bluffs.
>   The license which has been granted by this Department by order of the President to Gen. Ashley & Major Henry confers the privilege of trading with the Indians only, as the laws regulating trade and intercourse with the Indian tribes do not contain any authority to issue licenses for any other purpose. The privilege thus granted to them they are to exercise conformably to the laws and regulations that are or shall be made for the government of trade and intercourse with the Indians, for the true and faithfull observance of which they have given bonds

---

[2] The concept for this exercise was drawn from Harold D. Woodman, "Do Facts Speak for Themselves?" *Perspectives*, AHA, 25 (April, 1987): 18–20.

with sufficient security; consequently, it is presumed, they will do no act not authorized by such laws and regulations, which would disturb the peace and harmony existing between the government and the Indians on the Missouri, but rather endeavor, by their regular and conciliatory conduct, to strengthen and confirm them.

Missouri Republican, St. Louis, March 12, 1823

Two keel-boats belonging to general Ashley, left this place on Monday [March 10] for the Yellow Stone, having on board about 100 men. They have started to join the establishment commenced by that gentleman last year, above the mouth of the Yellow Stone, for the purposes of hunting and trapping. If enterprise could command success, it would certainly await upon the exertions of the head of these expeditions.

We understand a man fell overboard from one of the boats, on Monday morning, and was drowned.

William H. Ashley to a Gentleman in Franklin, Missouri

On board the keel boat *Rocky Mountains*, opposite the mouth of the Shegan River [a tributary of the Missouri River], June 7, 1823.

As I ascended the river I was informed by some gentlemen of the Missouri Fur Company, that in a reccent affray which they had had with a war party of the Rickaree Indians, two of the Indians were killed, and that their conduct during the last winter, had shewn a hostile disposition towards the Americans. I therefore used all the precaution in my power for some days before I reached their towns; not one of them, however, did I see until my arrival there on the 30th of May, when my boats were anchored about the middle of the river. I took with me two men & went on shore, where I was met by some of the principal chiefs, who professed to be very friendly disposed, and requested me to land some goods for the purpose of trading with them. I had just received an express from Maj. Henry, desiring me to purchase all the horses I could get; consequently I proposed to exchange goods for horses, intending to send a party of forty men by land to the Yellow Stone River. I requested that the principal chiefs of the two towns would first meet me on the sand beach, where there should be a perfect understanding relative to the principles of our barter. After some consultation, the chiefs made their appearance at the place proposed. I then stated to them what I had heard below relative to their conduct, and the impropriety of repeating it. They said they much regretted the affray between some of their nation and the Americans, and confessed that they had been much displeased with us, but that all those angry feelings had left them; that then they considered the Americans their friends, and intended to treat them as such.

The next morning I commenced the purchase of horses, and on the evening of the 1st inst [of the present month, hence June] was ready to proceed on my voyage, intending to set out early the next morning. Late in the afternoon an Indian came down with a message to me from the principal chief (the Bear) of one of the towns, requesting that I would come and see him. After some hesitation (as I did not wish to let them know that I apprehended the least danger from them) I went to the lodge of the chief, where I was treated with every appearance of friendship.—The next morning, about half past 3 o'clock, I was informed that Aaron Stephens, one of my men, had been killed by the Indians, and that in all probability the boats would be attacked in a few minutes. The boats were anchored in the stream, about 90 feet from the shore. My party consisted of ninety men, forty of whom had been selected to go by land, and were encamped on the sand beach, to whose charge the horses were entrusted. The men on the beach were placed as near as possible between the two boats.

At sunrise the Indians commenced a heavy and well directed fire from a line extending along the picketing of one of their towns, and some broken land adjoining, about six hundred yards in length. Their aim was principally at the men on shore. The fire was returned by us, but, from their advantageous situation, I presume we did but little execution. Discovering the fire to be destructive to the men on shore, the steersmen of both boats were ordered to weigh their anchors and lay their boats to shore; but, notwithstanding every exertion on my part to enforce the execution of the order, I could not effect it—the principal part of the boatmen were so panic struck, that they would not expose themselves in the least. Two skiffs, one sufficient to carry twenty men, were taken ashore for the embarcation of the men, but, from a predetermination on their part not to give way to the Indians as long as it was possible to do otherwise, the most of them refused to make use of that opportunity of embarking, the large skiff returned with four, two of them wounded, and was immediately started back, but unfortunately one of the oarsmen was shot down, and by some means the skiff set adrift. The other was taken to the opposite side of the river by two men, one mortally wounded; some swam to the boats, others were shot down in the edge of the water and immediately sunk, and others who appeared to be badly wounded sunk in attempting to swim. To describe my feelings at seeing these men destroyed, is out of my power. I feel confident that if my orders had been obeyed I should not have lost five men.

If our government do not send troops on this river, as high as the mouth of the Yellow Stone, or above that place, the Americans must abandon the trade in this country—The Indians are becoming more formidable every year. The Rickarees are about six hundred warriors, three fourths of whom, I think, are armed with London fusils, which carry a ball with considerable accuracy and force—others have bows and arrows, war axes, &c. [etc.]. They are situated in two towns about three hundred yards apart.—Immediately in front of them is a large sand bar, nearly in the shape of a horse-shoe. On the opposite side of the river the ground is very high and commanding, and at the upper end of the bar they have a breastwork made of dry wood. The river there is narrow, and the channel near the south side.

From the situation of my men and boats, when the men had embarked, I concluded to fall back to the first timber, and place them in a better state of defence, then to proceed on my voyage; but to my great mortification and surprise, I was informed, after my men had been made acquainted with my intentions, that they positively refused to make another attempt to pass the towns, without a considerable reinforcement. I had them paraded, and made known to them the manner in which I proposed fixing the boats and passing the Indian villages. After saying all that I conceived necessary to satisfy them, and having good reason to believe that I should be, with but very few exceptions, deserted in a short time by all my men, as some of them had already formed a resolution to desert, I called on those disposed to remain with me under any circumstances, until I should hear from Maj. Henry, to whom I would send an express immediately, and request that he would descend with all the aid he could spare from his fort at the mouth of the Yellow Stone.—Thirty only have volunteered, among whom are but few boatmen; consequently I am compelled to send one boat back, having secured [some of] her cargo here [opposite the mouth of the Cheyenne]. I am determined to descend no lower until I pass the Rickarees, should it be in my power so to do.

Hugh Glass to the Parents of John S. Gardner

[June, 1823]

Dr Sir,

My painfull duty it is to tell you of the deth of yr Son wh befell at the hands of the indians 2nd June in the early morning. He lived a little while after he was shot and asked me to inform you of his sad fate We brought him to the ship where he soon died. Mr Smith a young man of our company made a powerful prayr wh moved us all greatly and I am persuaded John died in peace. His body we buried with others near this camp and marked the grave with a log. His things we will send to you. The savages are greatly treacherous. we traded with them as friends but after a great storm of rain and thunder they came at us before light and many were hurt. I myself was hit in the leg. Master Ashley is bound to stay in these parts till the traitors are rightly punished.

Y^r Obt Svt
Hugh Glass

Letter by One of Ashley's Men to a Friend in the District of Columbia

Fort Kiawa, ten miles below the Big Bend of the Missouri, June 17th, 1823.

. . . We retreated down the river about 20 miles, intending to fortify ourselves until we could get assistance from the Bluffs [a military post]; the French boatmen were so panic-struck they would listen to no terms—they would return and forfeit their wages sooner than remain. Ashley paraded his men, told them his situation, and called for volunteers; one third, being twenty-five, only remained, and of these one half are boatmen, who intend returning when Henry's boat comes down. Out of one hundred men, the number he left St. Louis with, I question much whether he will arrive at the Yellow Stone with more than ten, (and of this number I hope to be one;) finding he could not obtain men enough to remain with sufficient to man both boats, he determined to fortify his own [the *Rocky Mountains*]—take all those on board who were willing to stay, and those goods only that might be wanted—send the balance of the goods to this place and the large boat to St. Louis. With the goods, I was left in charge, and shall remain here until I hear from him or Henry. . . .

Council Bluffs is 600 miles below this, a very injudicious place for a military post. Here, and above this, is the spot where the Indians have always been most troublesome. You will hardly believe it, but I assure you it is a fact, our Indian Agent has never been above the Bluffs. He has never made himself known to the Indians in this quarter. They have been told of troops, &c. &c. at the Bluffs, but they do not believe it; they have never seen more of the white people than the few traders that come among them; and each tribe thinks we are less numerous than they—they have reason to think so, having never been punished for the numerous robberies and murders committed by them. . . .

I have been told, though I cannot vouch for its authenticity, although I think it highly probable, from their determined hostility, that they [the British] have erected trading establishments within our territories. One thing is certain, they are not willing we should rival them in this valuable trade. All the injury they can do us they will do. The hostility of the Ricarees, Black-feet, Snake, Chiaus [Cheyennes], and Assiniboines, is entirely owing to the influence of the Northwest or Hudson Bay Company [a British Company]. The late act [of May 6, 1822] prohibiting the sale of spirituous liquors to the Indians has not that good effect which the framers of it had in view. It was passed without mature deliberation and a knowledge of the circumstances. No act that Congress could have passed could have such a tendency to aggrandize the North-West Company. In consequence of this, most of those tribes that formerly frequented the river have now left it, and more contemplate doing so, should that act not be repealed or amended. From the English they can get what liquor they want, and the distance is nothing to an Indian, when he has in view the gratification of his passions. Among the Ricarees I saw several English medals, and some of British manufacture.

The government must remedy these abuses; she mut divest herself of that appalling slowness that attends all her operations. She must show more energy than she has done, if she wishes to preserve the fur trade; otherwise, our traders may as well abandon the business. The risque is too great for individual enterprise when unaided and unassisted by the government. Adieu. For myself I am determined to have revenge for the loss of two young men to whom I became very much attached, and I never will descend this river until I assist in shedding the blood of some of the Ricarees. It would give me pleasure beyond the power of language to express, could I personally extend my hand and greet you, &c.

Benjamin O'Fallon, U.S. Indian Agent, Upper Missouri Agency, to William Clark, Superintendent of Indian Affairs at St. Louis, Fort Atkinson, June 24, 1823

Dear Sir,

I arrived at this place [from St. Louis] on the 6.ᵗʰ instant after a long and disagreeable trip of more than twenty days and have been anxiously waiting an opportunity to write you a long letter on many subjects, but more particularly on the subject of Indian affairs—But I now take up my pen to announce to you a circumstance, which not only wounds my national pride, but grieves my heart greatly—it is the defeat of Gen. Ashleys Expedition by the Aricharars [i.e., Rickarees]—One of his boats arrived here on the 18ᵗʰ. instant with forty three men including five wounded, who are now in the Hospital, bringing me a letter from the General which I herewith enclose, giving a more detailed account of the affair, than I without reference to it would be enabled to do—From his hurried account and that of the most inteligent of his men with whom I have conversed it appears to have been the most shocking outrage to the feelings of humanity ever witnessed by Civilized men—unexampled in the annals of the world—

As those inhuman monsters will most probably be made to atone for what they have done by a great effusion of their blood, I shall (however painful it may be) endeavour to restrain my feelings, and defer (untill a later period) giving you a gloomy picture of a scene, which if justly portrayed would from a man of your sensibility extract tears of blood—Although young in years, and without a polished or even a common education, I have for a long time been endeavouring to Arouse the better feelings, and excite the Sympathy of my Country in favour of the most daring, the most energetic, and enterprising portion of the community. I mean those of our fellow Citizens, who from our forbearance are dayly exposed, and falling victims to the tomihauk and sculping knife of the Indians

On being apprised of this unfortunate circumstance, which has not only put in Jeopardy upwards of two hundred of our Citizens, who are legally engaged in the fur trade above this, but threatens to arrest for a long time the individual enterprise of the fairest portion of the western country Co. Levenworth and myself consulted, and considering the best interests of our Country, was not slow to determine what steps should be taken, consequently, he lost no time in organizing and fitting out an Expedition of upwards of two hundred regular troops, exclusive of Officers, which set out on the 22nd. ins^t. accompan[i]ed by M^r. Pilcher, several other Partners of the Missouri fur Company and about fifty of their men . . . This expedition, when it reaches the A'richarar Village, will including trading [traders?] and trading men, consist of upwards of three hundred effective white men, and about five hundred Souix Indians I expect will join them at or near the grand Bend—enough to look down all opposition—no Indian force can posibly resist them—

This unprovoked and dreadful massacre of white men, by the A'rickarar nation of Indians (men, women and Children Concerned) has awakened the peaceful natives of the land It has directed the attention of all the neighboring tribes, who are suspending their opinion of us untill they hear the result of this expedition—Now, say the Indians "all will see what the white people intend to do—We will see the extent of their forbearance—We will also see (if they have any) the extent of their spirit of resentment—"For a long time we have been presuming upon the forbearance of the whites, slowly bleeding their veins, and they have born it patiently, for we have heard but the murmer of a single man—"But now the A'richarars have by sticking and sticking made a deep incision—They have made a dreadful wound, in which even their men, women, and children have stained their hands with blood—"

This expedition (as your experience of the Indian character will tell you) is big with great events The peace, and tranquility of this Country depends upon its success, which, with great anxiety I calculate on surely—The Indian nations about here continue as friendly as usual—The Ottoes & Missouris are here and now assembling to council with me

Set B, Exercise 1   Your task is to identify which of the following categories each passage represents. Give the basis for your selection in each case. Note: One category is represented twice.

Categories:

A. Relatedness of historical developments to an earlier time (continuity).
B. Presentation of a series of changes or developments occurring rapidly during a given time period.
C. Emphasis of "multiple causation," or of varied factors having influenced a given event.
D. Description of a way of life that differs clearly from our own, having a different life-style, and perhaps different values.
E. Reflects a "you are there" quality.

1.   For the world and for the United States, 1940 was a momentous year. During the early fall of 1939 the German war machine overran Poland, and that country was divided between Germany and Russia. A short time later Russia invaded Finland and eventually dictated a peace. In the following month, Germany invaded neutral Denmark and Norway and occupied Holland. These events helped tumble Neville Chamberlain from power in Britain. But Winston Churchill's new government was powerless to stop the tide of German might. By June the British had achieved their incredible evacuation of Dunkirk, but the army came back to Britain defeated, dispirited, disorganized, and without equipment. France fell, and Mussolini entered the war to grab the jackal's share of the spoils. On August 12, three superb mechanized German armies was poised on the Channel in view of England, while overhead the Luftwaffe of 1,800 planes struck at the Royal Air Force in the Battle of Britain. Against these formidable men and machines, the British fought with an outnumbered air force, the fleet, the indomitable spirit of the people, and the leadership of Winston Churchill.

CATEGORY: _____

BASIS: _____

_____

_____

2.   Christianity took over several priceless characteristics from its original environment. It had the Jewish scriptures, of course, that superhuman source of truth. With these, like the Hellenized Judaism it had supplanted, it proposed to meet the Greek longing for salvation by mystical knowledge. . . . Further, Christianity took over from the Jewish religion its deep moral purpose, combined with the lofty ethical teaching of the Stoics. Were the Greeks teaching that man should so school himself that he would ask little of life, and be happy under any misfortune? The Christians took them at their word, and amazed the Roman world by being able to live out such a doctrine. . . . It was a Jewish-Greek morality, Jewish in its patient steadfastness, Greek in its flouting of external goods, but still uniquely Christian in its emphasis upon love and humility, and in the abandoned enthusiasms with which it was practiced.

And one other great thing Christianity had from Judaism: it had what has recently been called the sense of having a 'cause' for which to live and die. . . .

CATEGORY: _____

BASIS: _____

_____

_____

3. The men of the two feudal ages were close to nature—much closer than we are; and nature as they knew it was much less tamed and softened than we see it today. The rural landscape, of which the waste formed so large a part, bore fewer traces of human influence. The wild animals that now only haunt our nursery tales—bears and, above all, wolves—prowled in every wilderness, and even amongst the cultivated fields. So much was this the case that the sport of hunting was indispensable for ordinary security, and almost equally so as a method of supplementing the food supply. People continued to pick wild fruit and to gather honey as in the first ages of mankind. In the construction of implements and tools, wood played a predominant part. The nights, owing to the wretched lighting, were darker; the cold, even in the living quarters of the castles, was more intense. In short, behind all social life there was a background of the primitive, of submission to uncontrollable forces, of unrelieved physical contrasts. There is no means of measuring the influence which such an environment was capable of exerting on the minds of men, but it could hardly have failed to contribute to their uncouthness.

CATEGORY: _____

BASIS: _____

_____

_____

4. In the dark early-morning hours scores of torpedo planes, bombers, and fighters soared off the pitching flight decks of their carriers to the sound of "Banzai!" Soon 183 planes were circling the carriers and moving into formation. At about 6:30 they started south. Emerging from the clouds over Oahu an hour later, the lead pilots saw that everything was as it should be—Honolulu and Pearl Harbor bathed in sunlight, quiet and serene, the orderly rows of barracks and aircraft, the white highway wriggling through the hills—and the great battlewagons anchored two by two along the mooring quays of Pearl Harbor. It was a little after 7:30 A.M., December 7, 1941. It was the time for war.

On the American ships this Sunday morning sailors were sleeping, eating breakfast, lounging on deck. Some could hear the sound of church bells. A bosun's mate noticed a flight of planes orbiting in the distance but dismissed it as an air-raid drill. Then the dive bombers screamed down, and the torpedo bombers glided in. Explosions shattered the air; klaxons squalled general quarters; a few antiaircraft guns began firing. . . .

CATEGORY: _____

BASIS: _____

_____

_____

5.   In retrospect there seem to have been many reasons for the stock market crash and the Great Depression. Among the more important were the major economic maldistributions arising out of World War I; a chaotic international financial policy, to which the United States contributed markedly by its insistence upon high tariffs and upon repayment of war debts, after it had become the world's creditor; the speculative urge, which was probably as rabid on the European exchanges as it was in New York; the overextension of credit, which applied to families buying appliances, as well as to businessmen and stock speculators; the downright dishonesty of some financial and business leaders, whose practices in America as elsewhere were little above those of the cardsharp; and the rigidity of the world and national price structure for industrial goods as compared to that for primary goods or raw materials.

CATEGORY: _____

BASIS: _____

_____

_____

6.   There have survived writings in classic, or ancient, Greek, dating very roughly from 750 B.C. to 1000 A.D., which cover almost the whole range of thinking men have done in the fields of noncumulative knowledge. Greek philosophers, Greek observers of human nature, Greek historians, Greek men of letters have expressed in some form or other almost all the kinds of intellectual and emotional experience Western men have recognized and named. This may seem an extreme statement, and is not of course a denial of the force, weight, beauty, wisdom, and in many senses, originality of medieval or modern achievement in these fields.

      You can test this assertion in almost any field. In literature, the Greeks tried all of what we call the genres, including, toward the end, something very close to the novel. Especially in epic, lyric, and dramatic poetry and in history they set standards never yet surpassed—some would say, never yet equaled. In philosophy, their schools put all the Big Questions—being and becoming, the one and the many, mind and body, spirit and matter—and gave all the big answers. . . . Finally, in science or cumulative knowledge the Greeks, building in part on earlier achievements in Egypt and Mesopotamia, carried to high development the theoretical side of mathematics and astronomy and did creditably in physics and in medicine; the Romans, building in part on Greek achievements, attained high standards in engineering. In political and economic life, this culture attained great complexity. These people, in short, were fully "civilized."

CATEGORY: _____

BASIS: _____

_____

_____

Sources
1. George E. Mowry, *The Urban Nation* (New York: Hill and Wang, 1965), pp. 141–42.
2. Erwin Goodenough, *The Church in the Roman Empire* (New York: Henry Holt and Company, 1931), pp. 20–21.
3. Marc Bloch, *Feudal Society* (Chicago: University of Chicago Press, 1961), p. 72.
4. James McGregor Burns, *Roosevelt: The Soldier of Freedom, 1940–45* (New York: Harcourt Brace Jovanovich, 1970), pp. 161–62.
5. Mowry, *The Urban Nation*, p. 71.
6. Crane Brinton, *Ideas and Men: The Story of Western Thought* (Englewood Cliffs: Prentice-Hall, Inc., 1950), pp. 29–30.

Set B, Exercise 2
The following exercise is intended to deepen your awareness of history as an attempt to *reconstruct* the reality of a given past. An account of an event is dependent upon those elements the historian chooses to emphasize. In this exercise you are asked to make the sort of choices all historians have to make. First, read the brief account below:

> Early in 1961 new president John F. Kennedy approved a plan to have 1200 Cuban exiles invade their homeland, which several years earlier had fallen under communist control. The invasion took place a few months later in April, and the result was an unmitigated disaster. The exile force was destroyed on the beaches, and the new Democratic administration suffered a major disgrace.

As a historian you are asked to write a history of Kennedy's decision. Below are listed a number of the factors that may or may not have entered into Kennedy's deliberations. Indicate by number *in order of importance* the five factors you'd most like to have more information about before writing your story. Be prepared to defend your choices in class discussion. Note: We assume that you might not have sufficient background information to make an informed choice. The point is not to be "correct," but to choose those items that you think would be worth knowing more about.

_____ a. Military prowess of the invasion force
_____ b. Status of Soviet-American relations
_____ c. Extent of danger to American citizens still in Cuba
_____ d. Quality of information supplied by the CIA
_____ e. Kennedy's conception of America's relationship to Latin America
_____ f. Relationship between Russia and Cuba
_____ g. Kennedy's popularity
_____ h. Advice given Kennedy by closest advisors
_____ i. Traditional American policy toward Latin American nations

_____ j. American strength in the Caribbean
_____ k. Estimates of Cuban government's military readiness
_____ l. Extent of Cuban subversive activity in the United States
_____ m. Cuban domestic attitudes toward the Castro regime

Set B, Exercise 3 Using the documents dealing with the Kent State incident (chapter 8, pp. 155–158) or, if the instructor prefers, the documents that describe the first skirmish of the American Revolution (chapter 8, pp. 164–166), write a brief historical essay (two to four fully developed paragraphs will do) that *explains* what happened and why. Remember, these documents are *all* you have to work with. Give your essay a title that summarizes the theme of your essay.

CHAPTER 3

THE SEARCH FOR INFORMATION

*"I have always imagined that Paradise will be a
kind of library."*

Jorge Luis Borges

Today's students are more technologically sophisticated than ever before. Many are totally at home with computers, hand calculators, videotape cameras, cassette recorders, microfilm readers, and other magical machines. Yet all too many students never master (some never attempt to master) the largest and most complex piece of "equipment" that colleges possess—the library. This is a shame; the library is the most important educational resource on the campus. The library not only houses the books, journals, films, and documents that serve as the lifeblood of learning, it is often a pleasant (and increasingly colorful) place to browse, study, and think. Also, its potential for providing a companion for the Saturday night party should not be overlooked.

Historically, libraries were simply places to store books. Access was difficult and often limited to members of ruling aristocracies. In recent decades, however, this picture has changed radically. The storage of books has taken a back seat to providing services for people. The library exists for human beings not just books; if it is not used, it serves no real purpose beyond being a mere repository for materials. The student who fails to take advantage of the library misses out on one of the most practical lessons a college education can provide.

It is not the purpose of this section to make you experts on using the library. One can no more learn to use a library by reading about it than one can learn to ride a bicycle by reading an article on bike racing. *The only way to learn how to use a library properly is to use one.* This is true even for seasoned scholars who may be quite ignorant of sections of the library they rarely use. Jaroslav Pelikan, the eminent historian of Christian doctrine, once dumbfounded a Yale University library employee by asking where the periodicals room was. Pelikan knew, he explained, "where the incunabula" [rare books] were, but since he never used recent magazines in his research, he had no idea where the periodicals room was located. Like Pelikan, you will learn how to use library resources as the need arises. It is the modest aim of this chapter to help you get enough of a toehold to function as an educated beginner.

There are three basic things you must know to begin:

1. How your library is laid out, and how its books are classified.
2. How to initiate a search for the information you need.
3. Whom to ask for help if you reach a dead end.

Layout of the Library   First, play the role of a tourist in your own library. Wander around and note where certain important items are located. One old hand insists that pinpointing the rest rooms should be the first priority. Without criticizing such a practical suggestion, we propose that it is equally important to locate the following:

1. The card catalog (or computer terminals)
2. The main desk
3. The reference room or reference area along with the general placement of the major indexes and encyclopedias
4. The book stacks
5. The reserve room or reserve shelves

When you have finished your tour (or even before you begin), ask for any informational guides or pamphlets that might be available.

As overwhelming as a library may seem at first glance, remember that everything in it is classified according to a system. Those who understand the system ultimately understand how to make the library work for them. You should, therefore, find out what classification system your library uses and endeavor to master its basic features.

The two dominant systems of classification are: (1) The Dewey Decimal system and (2) the Library of Congress system. The *Dewey Decimal system* is based on numbers divisible by ten (hence "decimal"). There are ten general categories numbered with hundreds (100, 200, 300, etc.), nine subcategories for each general category (910, 920, 930, etc.), and nine more sub-subcategories for each of these (931, 932, 933, etc.). When further sub-categories are needed, they are designated by the addition of one, two, or sometimes three numbers following a decimal point (e.g., 909.6, 909.7, 909.8). Much of this is irrelevant to anyone but a librarian, but a knowledge of the "hundreds" will give you an immediate overview of the major branches of knowledge and where they are located in the library. They are:

000s	General Works	500s	Pure Sciences
100s	Philosophy	600s	Applied Sciences
200s	Religion	700s	Arts and Recreation
300s	Social Sciences	800s	Literature
400s	Linguistics	900s	History, Geography

In history the major subcategories are as follows:

910	Geography	960	African History
920	Biography	970	North American History
930	Ancient World History	980	South American History
940	European History	990	History of Oceania
950	History of Asia		

The *Library of Congress system* is more broadly based and hence preferred by many large university research libraries. Even many smaller libraries already use, or are converting to, the Library of Congress system. In this system twenty-one letters of the alphabet are assigned to general categories.

A. General Works
B. Philosophy/Religion
C. Auxiliary Sciences of History
D. Universal History
E–F. American History
G. Geography/Anthropology
H. Social Sciences
J. Political Science
K. Law
L. Education
M. Music
N. Fine Arts
P. Language and Literature
Q. Science
R. Medicine
S. Agriculture
T. Technology
U. Military Science
V. Naval Science
Z. Bibliography/Library Science

Innumerable subcategories can be created by adding a second letter to the general designation.

It is, of course, unnecessary to memorize either system; but you should know the classification numbers for your own field of study. Also, do not ignore the pleasures and benefits of simply browsing at random through the stacks. Not only does browsing make the "system" more comprehensible, it is a satisfying and intellectually rewarding activity for anyone who finds bookstores a congenial place to shop.

The Library Catalog: Initiating the Search

Understanding your library's classification system will help you locate the relevant book collections. To find specific works on specific topics, however, you must turn to the *library catalog*. The catalog is the most important research tool in the library. It is essentially a complete, cross-indexed bibliography of all the materials in the library. Libraries whose collections have not been entered on a computer rely on the traditional card catalog. *The card catalog is arranged alphabetically, and each book is listed in at least three ways—on an author card, a title card, and a subject card.* Thus you can find a book even if you are lacking a vital piece of information, such as the name of the author.

Looking up the works of a given author or a specific title is relatively easy. Finding all the relevant books on a given subject or topic, however, is not always so simple. The problem arises when your idea of what a proper subject heading should be differs from the subject heading actually in use in the catalog. For instance, books on the history of England are not found under "England" but under "Great Britain." Even more perplexing, library materials on Revenue Sharing will be found under the subject heading "Intergovernmental Fiscal Relations"—a category that neither logic nor imagination could supply. If you run into a dead end, consult the publication entitled *Library of Congress Subject Headings*. Finally, do not hesitate to ask the librarian for help; not even the most sophisticated library users know all the tricks of card-catalog use.

Another consideration in locating resources is to search for *additional* subject headings that might yield results. For instance, if you are interested in the history of witchcraft, it is not enough to look under "witchcraft"; additional works might be found under such headings as "magic," "occult sciences," "demonology," "Inquisition," "sorcery," "Salem," and so on. Likewise, the catalog cards on medieval and early modern history should not be overlooked as guides to books that might have something to say on the subject of witchcraft. Often the catalog itself will include cards that refer you to other potentially useful subject headings. And, as noted above, don't ignore the benefits of browsing if the book stacks are open to you. Once you have found some relevant sections of the library by using the card catalog, you can often find more useful sources by actually looking over the shelves for titles you might have missed in your catalog search.

Finally, do not overlook the cards themselves as useful sources of information. Each card contains a wealth of information. In addition to the classification number, the card will tell you the number of pages in a book, whether the book is illustrated, the date of publication, and, often, some of the topics covered. A typical author card is reproduced below.

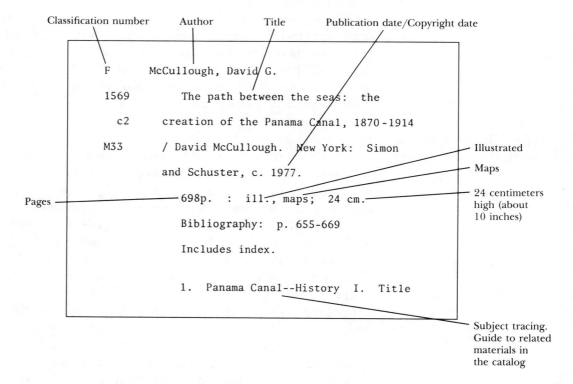

All this is basic and traditional. Card catalogs and classification systems have been around for a long time. Not so the computer. As you read these words the library business is being revolutionized by the computer. Information systems based on paper and ink are gradually giving way to those based on "invisible electronic charges in silicon chips."[1] Already most academic libraries catalog their books via computer networks that connect thousands of libraries together. Many libraries are already replacing the traditional card catalog with computer-based catalog systems, and most libraries will follow suit in the near future.

The brave new world of the computer will offer countless shortcuts in the tedious process of accumulating sources and information. The indexes and abstracts so useful to students and other researchers are now available in data base form. A search for relevant books and articles that formerly took many hours can be done far more quickly and efficiently by computer. Further, even small libraries will now have access to information and services that, until now, could only be found in the largest and most sophisticated libraries.

Whether these changes fill you with joy or horror, one basic point should not be overlooked. The advent of the computer does not herald the death of the book and other printed materials. The computer will change the way in which you discover the materials you need for your research; it will not change (at least not soon) the nature of the materials you use and the way in which you use them. You, the researcher, will still have to do the hard work of reading, taking notes, thinking, and writing. Computers are tools, not synthetic humans.

The Reference Section

The library catalog is certainly *the* place to begin any research project. It is only the first step, however. In addition to the catalog there are literally hundreds of indexes and printed bibliographies that can help you locate books and articles relevant to your particular topic.[2] As Montaigne noted, without much exaggeration, "There are more books upon books than upon all other subjects." Unfortunately, books that list other books are not especially exciting reading. They don't even have pictures. They are necessary, however, if you want to find the sources that will make your research productive and meaningful.

The guides, indexes, and bibliographies that we have mentioned are usually found in a special reference room or reference area in your library. This is a section of the library you should get to know well. It would take literally hundreds of pages simply to list the materials that might be found in the larger reference collections. Even small libraries often house an impressive array of reference works. With the advent of the computerized index and data services mentioned above, the potential of small libraries can be quite impressive.

An addendum to this chapter will provide a short and select list of some key reference works for the history student. For now, the only volumes that merit special mention are the *periodical indexes*, which do for journal (magazine) literature what the library catalog does for books. The most important

---

[1] S. D. Neill, "Libraries in the Year 2010," *The Futurist* (October, 1981), p. 47.

[2] Remember, even though your card catalog lists all the books in *your library*, your library (in most cases) will not have all the possible books on a topic. Printed catalogs and bibliographies will acquaint you with sources you may wish to order through interlibrary loan or seek in another library.

are (1) the *Readers' Guide to Periodical Literature* and (2) the publication known variously as the *International Index* (to 1965), the *Social Sciences and Humanities Index* (to 1974), and now published separately as the *Social Sciences Index* and the *Humanities Index*.

The *Readers' Guide* and the *Social Sciences Index* list articles alphabetically by author and under one or more subject headings. The abbreviations used to save space in these mammoth volumes are confusing at first but easily understood after a brief look at the key in the front. Reference books and indexes always have a preface that explains their use. The system is well worth mastering, because these indexes are invaluable resources for countless topics. The more current the information you seek, the more will you need to consult such indexes and the periodical articles they list.

Beyond these guides to articles in magazines and journals, the reference section of your library houses a vast array of other works (indexes and bibliographies) designed to help you find the actual books and articles you will need to research your topic.

These works are the books that list *other* books; they don't actually contain the historical information you are seeking. However, the reference section will also possess countless additional volumes that contain summaries of all sorts of historical information. Included in this group are encyclopedias, dictionaries, statistical compilations, biography collections, and other sources too numerous to list. Simply remember that somewhere in your reference collection there is a book that contains the answer to virtually any informational question you might have. For instance, in the category of dictionaries alone there are historical dictionaries, pronunciation dictionaries, slang dictionaries, and rhyming dictionaries. There are dictionaries of forgotten words, new words, common words, foreign words, technical words, crossword-puzzle words, uncouth words, and even criminal words.[3]

Faced with such overwhelming diversity, you may well ask, "How do I begin?" Of course, the card catalog will list all the reference works in your library. Browsing through the reference collection is an even better way to get a feel for the scope and diversity of the holdings.

Perhaps the best way to get started, however, is to ask the reference librarian to help you. Usually reference librarians will bend over backward to aid the student in need. But don't expect them to do your work for you. Seek guidance, not ready-made answers.

One manual on using the library lists some rules for seeking help from reference librarians. In essence they are:

1. Don't be afraid to approach a reference librarian. Reference librarians are there to help library users.
2. Don't expect reference librarians to answer your research questions for you. Their function is primarily to lead you to likely sources and not to do your research.

---

[3] A good example of how specialized some dictionaries can be is Eric Partrige's *A Dictionary of the Underworld.* It is subtitled: "Being the vocabularies of crooks, criminals, racketeers, beggars and tramps, convicts, the commercial underworld, the drug traffic, the white slave traffic, [and] spivs." The dictionary is 886 pages long! If you want to know what a "spiv" is, look it up in this dictionary. Even then the list is not exhausted.

3. Be specific in your questions and requests. Don't say, "I want to find out something about China" when you mean, "I want to find out how the Chinese cook rice." You'll find what you want a lot more rapidly if you make your request as specific as possible.
4. Don't be afraid to come back if you don't find what you want in the first source the librarian recommends.[4]

In sum, remember, the only way to learn to use the library is to *use the library*. Good luck.

Some Places to Begin This section is optional. We don't want you to waste your time reading, and promptly forgetting, lists of reference works unless you are actively engaged in a research project of some sort. You should quickly skim the items below, however, so you know what resources are listed. Then, when you need some assistance to begin a research project, you can return to this section.

Indexes and Bibliographies: Finding Your Source Materials

This is a brief list of some of the best places to *begin* compiling a few of the sources you will use on your research project. Remember, any such preliminary list is just that—a preliminary list. You should update your bibliography as you get further into your subject and discover new, potentially useful sources.

American Historical Association: Guide to Historical Literature. New York: Macmillan, 1961. A bit dated but still a good beginning.

A Reader's Guide to Contemporary History. Chicago: Quadrangle Books, 1972. Bernard Krikler and Walter Laqueur, eds.

Harvard Guide to American History. 2 vols. Cambridge, Mass.: Harvard University Press, 1974. Frank Freidel and Richard Showman, eds. This is a specialized bibliography for United States history. There are many specialized bibliographies for other regions of the world. Ask your reference librarian to help you find an appropriate subject bibliography for these areas.

Historical Abstracts, 1775–1945: Bibliography of the World's Periodical Literature. Santa Barbara, Cal.: Clio Press, 1955–present. Eric H. Boehm, ed. Begun in 1955, this publication lists, and *gives summaries of,* scholarly articles covering much modern history (i.e., the period 1775–1945). Good for finding articles relevant to your research and for getting a preview of the content.

Reader's Guide to Periodical Literature. New York: H. W. Wilson, 1900–present. An excellent source; discussed above on page 44. Note, however, that this index covers popular magazines (e.g., *Time, Newsweek,* etc.) rather than scholarly literature.

International Index, Social Sciences and Humanities Index, Social Sciences Index/

---

[4] These rules were drawn from Robert W. Murphey, *How and Where to Look It Up* (New York: McGraw-Hill, 1958), p. 29. In addition, our sections on library layout and the catalog drew some ideas from William Coyle, *Research Papers,* 2nd ed. (Indianapolis, Ind.: Odyssey Press, 1965), pp. 1–5.

Humanities Index. New York: H. W. Wilson, 1907–present. Discussed above, page 44. One of *the* best guides for the student of history and politics. This index concentrates on more scholarly, specialized periodicals than does the *Reader's Guide.*

New York Times Index. New York: New York Times, 1913–present. Excellent source for the beginner. This index covers the *Times* from its founding in 1851. Most libraries have the *New York Times* in some form or another.

Dictionaries and Encyclopedias: Finding General Information

The same advice given above still applies. The few titles listed below will help you get an initial overview of any topic you are researching. These sources are useful for getting started and for filling in the odd fact here and there that eludes you. They are much too general, however, to serve as the core sources for your research. Such references allow you to *begin*; alone they are not sufficient.

In addition to the standard encyclopedias—*Britannica, Americana*—the following reference works are often excellent resources for the student of history.

An Encyclopedia of World History. Boston: Houghton Mifflin Company, 1972. William Langer, ed.

Encyclopedia of American History. New York: Harper and Row, 1970. Richard B. Morris, ed.

International Encyclopedia of the Social Sciences. New York: Macmillan, 1968. Articles in the realm of political science, economics, anthropology, law, sociology, and psychology. Much historical research touches on these related disciplines. Since history is the mother of the social sciences, it is quite appropriate to dip into such materials.

Statesman's Yearbook. New York: Macmillan, 1864–present. Up-to-date political information on governments and leaders.

Dictionary of American Biography. New York: Charles Scribner's Sons, 1928–1958, including supplements. Excellent multi-volume source for biographical information on prominent Americans who died before 1945.

Dictionary of National Biography. Oxford: Oxford University Press, 1922. Leslie Stephan and Sidney Lee, eds. Supplement, Boston: G. K. Hall, 1966. This is the British equivalent of the *Dictionary of American Biography.* The lack of any national designation often confuses American students. The *DNB* (as it is known) was the first such biographical dictionary, and everyone knew which "nation" was referred to in the title. (British postage stamps, likewise the first in the field, also do not carry the name of the country of origin.)

Oxford English Dictionary. Oxford: Clarendon Press, 1888–1928. James A. H. Murray et al., eds. A comprehensive multi-volume English-language dictionary that traces the historical evolution of the meanings of words. When reading and interpreting documents from previous centuries it is important to know how that age understood certain words, rather than how we understand them. Look up the word "enthusiasm" in the *OED* and see what we mean.

Guidebooks to Other Useful References

The above list is abbreviated. Much more definitive listings and descriptions of all sorts of bibliographies, indexes, and informational references may be found in:

Jules R. Benjamin, *A Student's Guide to History*. 4th ed. New York: St. Martin's Press, 1987. See especially "Appendix A: Basic Reference Sources for History Study and Research."

Helen J. Poulton, *The Historian's Handbook: A Descriptive Guide to Reference Works*. Norman, Okla.: University of Oklahoma Press. Especially valuable for the history student are chapter 3, "Guides, Manuals, and Bibliographies of History," and chapter 4, "Encyclopedias and Dictionaries."

EXERCISES

Set A, Exercise 1   Using a diagram and/or words, note the location of the following in your library. Use a separate sheet of paper.

Card catalog	U.S. history collection
Main desk	European history collection
Reference room/area	The *Social Sciences Index*
Reserve room/area	Encyclopedia sets
Periodical room/area	Audio/visual section

Set A, Exercise 2[5]   On a separate sheet of paper, answer the following questions about your college library:

1. What are the regular opening and closing hours on weekdays?
2. Who is the chief reference librarian?
3. Who is the head librarian?
4. Is the library open on Sundays? What hours?
5. Where do you go to discover the periodicals in your library's collection?
6. What is the policy for checking out books?

Set A, Exercise 3   The card catalog, or computer terminal, is the logical place to begin a search for research materials. To get the full benefit of a catalog search, however, you should check the widest variety of possible subject headings. For instance, we indicated earlier that a person researching the topic of "witchcraft" should look for books not only under that heading but also under headings such as "magic," "sorcery," and "occult sciences."

For each of the general topics below, list four or more sections of the catalog in which relevant materials might be listed. Don't guess! Go to the catalog and investigate the categories yourself. Note: In the "History" sections of the catalog (for countries, regions, etc.) there are broad chronological subdivisions within which books are listed alphabetically by author.

---

[5] For the concept of Exercises 2 and 3 (and some of the questions in Exercise 2) the authors are indebted to Coyle, *Research Papers*, pp. 103–06.

1.   THE ORIGINS OF WORLD WAR I

World War I was fought during the years 1914–1918, predominantly in Europe. The major contestants on one side were Great Britain, France, Russia, and, later, the United States; and on the other side were Germany, Austria-Hungary, and Italy. Italy later changed sides. Remember, the topic is the origins of World War I, hence *your focus should be on the period before 1914*. For example, "Germany—History, 1871–1918," or "Europe—History, 1871–1914" would be two relevant categories. Find four more.

Catalog Subject Headings:

_____   _____

_____   _____

2.   NAT TURNER'S REBELLION

Nat Turner was the leader of an 1831 slave rebellion in Virginia.

Catalog Subject Headings:

_____   _____

_____   _____

3.   THE DEVELOPMENT OF THE FIRST ATOMIC BOMB

In July 1945 near Alamogordo, New Mexico, the United States exploded the world's first atomic bomb. That bomb had been developed by a group of scientists at Los Alamos, New Mexico, after the U.S. entered the Second World War in late 1941.

Catalog Subject Headings:

_____   _____

_____   _____

4.   CHIVALRY IN THE MIDDLE AGES

Chivalry was the code of values (at least in theory) of the feudal aristocracy—the knightly class—during the late Medieval period in Europe, ca. 1100–1500.

Catalog Subject Headings:

_____   _____

_____   _____

5.   THE AMERICAN WOMEN'S SUFFRAGE MOVEMENT—EARLY 20th CENTURY

Catalog Subject Headings:

_____   _____

_____   _____

Set A, Exercise 4 Using the reference collection, answer the following questions and list the source you used for each answer. *Do not use general encyclopedias. Do not use any single source for more than one answer.* The object of this exercise is to acquaint you with as wide a variety of sources as possible.

You might want to review the list of possible references on pp. 45–46. In addition to the specific sources listed on those pages, the following categories of reference works might be helpful:

Atlases (maps plus geographic and demographic information)
Dictionaries of Famous Quotations
Book Review Indexes (summaries of reviews of important books)
Guides to Government Publications
Almanacs and Yearbooks (information on the year just past plus many statistics)
Dictionaries of Dates

Questions

1. Locate a book review of Daniel Boorstin's *The Discoverers* (1983). Simply provide the citation for the magazine or journal in which the review appeared, including the author of the review and the date.

_____

SOURCE: _____

2. What mountain is the highest in Colorado?

_____

SOURCE: _____

3. Which baseball team won the National League pennant in 1933?

_____

SOURCE: _____

4. On what date was President Theodore Roosevelt born? What years did he serve as president?

_____

SOURCE: _____

5. Locate a magazine article about the 1980 Winter Olympics written in 1980 (list author, title, date, name of periodical).

_____

SOURCE: _____

6. Who wrote: "A good book is the precious lifeblood of a master spirit"?

_____

SOURCE: _____

7. Locate an article in *a scholarly historical journal* written in 1981 or 1982 about World War I. Cite the title, author, journal, and date.

SOURCE: _____

8. When and where was the Battle of the Bulge fought?

SOURCE: _____

9. What did the residents of England mean by the word "enthusiasm" in the eighteenth century?

SOURCE: _____

10. What is the library classification number for Winston Churchill's *The Gathering Storm*?

SOURCE: _____

11. When was Benjamin Disraeli prime minister of Britain?

SOURCE: _____

12. Which schools in your state have graduate programs in Management or Business Administration?

SOURCE: _____

Set B

Questions   1. What is the longest river in Asia?

SOURCE: _____

2. What or who is a "cony catcher"?

SOURCE: _____

3. Who wrote: "Power tends to corrupt and absolute power corrupts absolutely"?

SOURCE: _____

4. Locate an article on American slavery written after 1980 and appearing in a historical journal. Cite the title of the article, author, journal, and date.

_____

SOURCE: _____

5. When did Nigeria become an independent nation?

_____

SOURCE: _____

6. When was the Taiping Rebellion? Where did it take place?

_____

SOURCE: _____

7. What was the population of Great Britain (England, Scotland, Wales) in 1861?

_____

SOURCE: _____

8. Locate and provide a citation for a book review of Barbara Tuchman's _A Distant Mirror_ (1978).

_____

SOURCE: _____

9. Who was the women's 100-meter run champion in the 1968 Olympics?

_____

SOURCE: _____

10. When did Charles Dickens die (day of the week, date, year)?

_____

SOURCE: _____

CHAPTER 4

READING HISTORY

"Books are not made to be believed, but to be subjected to inquiry."
William of Baskerville in Umberto Eco's
The Name of the Rose

Books are the historian's lifeblood, providing as they do a path to new knowledge, the ideas of other minds, and experiences that would otherwise be out of reach. A great frustration for all historians—for all serious readers—is the knowledge that books (just in one's own field of interest) are being published far more rapidly than any mere mortal can read them. Likewise, serious students often feel that they have too much to read in too short a time, especially when confronted with the extensive background reading needed to do a sound research project. Such being the case, it seems obvious that there are tangible rewards for those who become more effective readers. It is not the purpose of this chapter to turn you into a speed reader with a photographic memory—a virtual impossibility in any case. We will, however, explore some techniques that will allow you to get the most out of the reading you do.

History books (along with articles and essays) are both reservoirs of information and works of explanation and interpretation. The key words here are *explanation* and *interpretation*. Many students hold the unfortunate (and mistaken) opinion that history books are no more than dry collections of facts to be memorized. Of course, no student of history can ignore facts, for the study of history is ultimately based upon our knowledge of what actually happened in the past. It is one of the historian's most important obligations to present the facts as clearly and as accurately as possible. But the presentation of the facts, important though it may be, is only one part of a larger whole. *The real objective of the historian is to offer an* explanation *of how the relevant facts are related to one another*. It is the historian's job to explain *how and why* things happened as they did. Francis Parkman, the famous nineteenth-century American historian, put it well: "Facts may be detailed with the most minute exactness, and yet the narrative, taken as a whole, may be unmeaning or untrue."

The facts, then, do not "speak for themselves"; they must be interpreted properly before they yield a true picture. For instance, a staple scenario of television detective shows is the story of the innocent bystander (usually with a criminal record) happening upon a murder victim and then running from the scene of the crime. The police of course jump to the conclusion that flight implies guilt. At this point the lead character, usually a private detective with razor-sharp instincts (and occasionally dubious morals), saves the day by unmasking the real killer. The original suspect, it turns out, fled from fear not guilt. The police had interpreted the "facts" one way; the private detective, on the basis of further inquiry, saw the facts in quite a different light. Historians, like the fictional detective, must be ever vigilant that their interpretations do full justice to the facts.

In real life, however, the solution of historical mysteries is rarely as tidy as in television detective dramas. Many times the known facts will bear the weight of more than one interpretation. That is one of the reasons why historians keep writing and *rewriting* the history of a single event or period. They are not writing simply to regurgitate facts that have already been recorded in other books. They are writing to explore alternative explanations (interpretations), firmly based on the evidence, of why and how things happened the way they did, and perhaps to introduce new evidence not included in previous studies.

Another reason for rewriting the history of many events is that over the generations our perspectives and interests change, and hence the questions we choose to ask about the past. It is common for new interpretations of the past to grow out of present-day passions and preoccupations. It was, for instance, no accident that the explosion of interest in the history of women and blacks paralleled the increased activism of both groups in the 1960s and 1970s. Nor should it be surprising that Americans became increasingly interested in the history of Southeast Asia during the Vietnam War.

The study of history, therefore, involves not only learning the events of the past, but learning (from written histories) how others before you have tried to explain the interrelationships among those events. "History," wrote Pieter Geyl, "is an argument without end."

All good history is interpretation, but not all interpretation is good history. The fact that historical explanation involves an element of subjective judgment should not be taken to mean that "one opinion is as good as another." Interpretations based on shoddy scholarship or faulty reasoning should be exposed and rejected. It all boils down to one concept: While there is room for much honest disagreement among historians, in certain cases it must be recognized that some interpretations fit the facts better than others. All history, indeed all scholarship, must be judged with the critical eye of the skeptic. Reading history is not a passive task where you simply absorb "knowledge"; it is a pursuit that requires active participation on the part of the reader.

How to Read Historical Literature

How, you may ask yourself, can I actively participate in the books I read? As with anything worth doing, time and effort are essential. Unfortunately, no one has yet invented a labor-saving device to make learning effortless. You can save time and energy, though, if you know what you should be looking for when reading nonfiction.

The basic point to remember is that when you read a book or article your main goal should be to understand the author's major explanatory conclusions. Of course, you will come across much new factual material, and you should master the most important of the new facts. But it is equally important to master the author's *interpretation of how the facts relate to one another and to understand the author's value system and point of view.* It is common, as we all know, to forget facts relatively soon after we have learned them. There was once a noted expert on fish who became a college president. He vowed to memorize the name of every student on campus but soon abandoned the effort, complaining, "I found that every time I learned the name of a student, I forgot the name of a fish." Many of us share the college president's forgetfulness for facts. However, we are much better able to remember neatly summarized generalizations or conclusions; in the long run it is far more profitable to do so. An author's interpretation is what makes a book or article distinctive, and it is this we should try to imprint on our memories.

The Thesis The first thing to look for is the author's *thesis or central argument*. When asked to state the thesis of a book or article, many students respond, "This book is about . . ." and proceed to tell the events the book describes. **This is wrong**. The *topic* of the book (the material the book covers) and the *thesis* (the interpretation applied to that material) are *not* one and the same. There are many examples of books that share the same general topic (i.e., cover many of the same events) but differ markedly in interpretation (thesis).

In the late 1920s, for example, both Sidney Fay and Bernadotte Schmitt wrote lengthy studies of the origins of World War I.[1] Both authors had access to the same evidence, but each interpreted that evidence in a different way. Schmitt assigned to Germany most of the responsibility for starting the war, whereas Fay minimized German war guilt by distributing blame more widely among a number of countries. Thus, the *topics* of the books were almost identical—both books examined the events leading to the outbreak of hostilities in 1914. But their *theses* (interpretations) were radically different.

If you are still not sure whether you understand the difference between the topic *of a book and the* thesis, *read the preceding paragraph again.*

Usually the thesis of a book can be discovered quickly. If it can't, either the book is poorly constructed (not uncommon) or you are missing something. Many times the author states the thesis explicitly ("My thesis is . . ."); on other occasions you must do the work yourself. Most authors summarize their central arguments in a preface, introduction, or first chapter, and recapitulate the main points again at the end of a book or article. *These are the sections of a book you should read first.* (In the case of an article, read the first few paragraphs and the last few in order to isolate the thesis.) Don't be afraid to read the last chapter before those in the middle; a history book is not a murder mystery where the reader needs to be kept in suspense until the end.

It is important to identify the thesis early so that as you read the rest of the book you need not read every detail with equal diligence. The facts in the book should support and illustrate the thesis. If you have identified that thesis from the beginning, you will be better able to concentrate on how the author builds the case rather than on trying to memorize a chaotic assortment of individual facts. As you become more and more familiar with

---

[1] Sidney B. Fay, *The Origins of the World War*, 2 vols. (New York: Macmillan, 1928); Bernadotte E. Schmitt, *The Coming of the War, 1914*, 2 vols. (New York: Scribners, 1930).

a given topic, each new book you read on that topic can be mastered more efficiently. With the essential facts already at your command, you will be able to concentrate on the book's interpretation and how that interpretation differs from others you have read. You will be thinking creatively, not just absorbing masses of information.

Finally, although the thesis is the most important single element in a book, you should by no means ignore the rest of it. As you read you should take note of the important generalizations made in each chapter or subsection of the book. You should also make a mental (or preferably written) note of what factual material is covered. This is not to say you should memorize all the facts. You should, however, have a clear idea of what the book does and does not contain. That way, if you need a specific piece of information in the future you will know where to find it.

Reading a book is like mining for precious gems—the valuable stones must be separated from the surrounding rocks. A useful technique for "mining" historical literature is *skimming*. After you have read carefully to establish the thesis, the rest of the book can be digested rapidly. A well-constructed book will contain regular patterns that can be used as shortcuts by the astute reader. For instance, an author's major points are usually summarized at the beginning or end (or both) of each chapter. Similarly, central ideas in individual paragraphs are often contained in a topic sentence; usually, but not always, the first sentence in the paragraph. Once you have established where a particular author tends to locate the ideas he or she considers most important, it is easy to concentrate on those key ideas and skim over much of the supportive or illustrative factual material. Be aware, however, that this technique is only valuable for books on *topics for which you already have a basic textbook knowledge*. Skimming is not recommended when reading a book on a brand-new subject. Further, we are not talking here about "speed-reading" (a questionable and highly overrated technique) but about "selective" reading. The advice given above is intended to help you discriminate between the sections of a book that should be read with relative care and those that can be read less intensively.[2]

The Author's Values: Hidden Agendas

"What I like in a good author," wrote Logan Pearsall Smith, "is not what he says, but what he whispers." Indeed, the "whispers" in a work of history— what we can read "between the lines"—are frequently as important as the author's explicit statements. In every history book the author makes countless value judgments and decisions that are not explicitly identified but nevertheless influence the tone, organization, point of view, and conclusions. Therefore, it is important for the reader to identify the author's underlying assumptions and values. There is no absolutely foolproof way to do so. To some extent each book and each author is unique, and the historian-detective must use any and all clues to penetrate below the surface. At a bare minimum the following questions should be asked of every book you read:

---

[2] We are indebted for the discussion of thesis-finding and skimming techniques to Norman E. Cantor and Richard I. Schneider, *How to Study History* (New York: Thomas Y. Crowell, 1967), especially Chapter Five.

1. **Does the book reflect an identifiable bias or point of view, and how might the author's bias have influenced the book's subject matter or conclusions?** Books often reflect—usually unintentionally—the political, national, religious, or ideological values of their authors. For instance, in many cases books on the religious upheavals of the Reformation era (the sixteenth century) clearly reveal the religious convictions of the authors. Similarly, British accounts of the American Revolution often differ quite markedly from American accounts. Critical readers should look for clues to an author's biases in order to weigh more intelligently the arguments made in the books. A word of caution is appropriate here. The intrusion of bias does not automatically discredit an author's thesis. The test of a historical interpretation is how well it conforms to and explains *all* the evidence.

2. **How does the author approach the subject?** Put another way, which of the varieties of history does the book represent? Most authors choose to emphasize some aspects of past experience more than others. A writer may concentrate on economic relationships (economic history); political issues (political/institutional history); the single individual (biography); the role of social groups (social history); the evolution of ideas (intellectual history); war (military history); diplomacy (diplomatic history); everyday life (social history again); or any number of other facets of past life. In any event, the approach an author chooses in writing history reflects a conscious decision—perhaps to examine the subject from an economic as opposed to a political perspective. You should always be aware of an author's choices. Whenever you read a history book, try to identify the author's "approach" to the particular subject matter.

3. **How does the author organize the book?** The author also decides whether to organize a book according to chronological/narrative principles or topical/analytical principles. Actually, the two forms of organization are usually combined by alternating the chronological narration of events with periodic analyses of specific issues or topics. Taken as a whole, though, most books will conform predominantly to one organizational scheme or the other. A look at the table of contents may help you determine whether a book is organized topically or chronologically. Usually, however, you will have to dip into the work itself to get a firm sense of how the author has organized the material.

NOTE: Books organized *chronologically* present material the same way many college survey courses do—year by year or period by period. Books organized *topically* or *analytically* have chapters or sections based on thematically similar materials. Such books might cover the same chronological periods again and again, but each time the actual "topic" being discussed will be different. A good example of a book organized topically is Clinton Rossiter's *The First American Revolution* (1956). Each chapter of Rossiter's book covers the same period of American history (the colonial period before 1776); but each chapter focuses on a different aspect of the period—the economy, religion, politics, social structure, etc.

4. **What are the author's sources and how well are they used?** Here you are concerned with the author's research apparatus. Are there extensive footnotes? Few? None? Is the bibliography large? Small? Missing altogether? This sort of information can give you a clue as to the seriousness and perhaps the credibility of the book, although it would be a mistake automatically to equate extensive sources with quality. Also, a lack of such research apparatus does not necessarily mean that the book is worthless. It could have been the author's intention to write an introductory study (like this one) intended for a general audience.

You should also note what sources the author used. Are the sources appropriate to the subject matter? For instance, a history of American slavery using only material written by southern plantation owners would be highly suspect, as would a history of the labor movement based only on the observations of the factory owners. Further, did the author use extensive primary sources or was the book written on the basis of secondary literature? The answer to this question can help you discover whether the author was attempting to break new ground by examining original sources or attempting to synthesize the research findings of a number of other historians.

5. **Who is the author?** To answer all of the above questions it helps to know something about the author both personally and professionally. Is the author a scholar? Journalist? Politician? What is the author's political persuasion? Religion? Nationality? Sex? If a scholar, is the person a historian? Political scientist? Economist? Sociologist? Psychologist? What kind of reputation does the author have in academic circles? Many times such information (or some of it) can be found on jacket covers or in a brief biographical sketch in the book itself. (The reference librarian will also be able to guide you to pertinent biographical dictionaries.) If you know of some other books the author has written it might be helpful to read some reviews of those works.

6. **When was the book first published?** This piece of information can provide many clues to the quality and orientation of a book. A history of World War II written in 1946 might be less objective and less substantive than one written in 1980, although you should not assume that automatically. Certainly, though, the 1980 author would have had the opportunity to study evidence that had come to light since 1946.

A Note on Writing Book Reviews

The book review is one of the most common, and most commonly misunderstood, assignments in college. All too often students simply summarize the contents of a book. From what we have said above, however, it should be clear that a good book review should provide critical commentary on the quality of the book: the thesis and major arguments, the organization and style, the scholarly apparatus, and the author's values and assumptions. A good book review does, of course, indicate (briefly!) what a book covers— i.e., the contents. The review should pay far more attention, however, to *evaluating* the strengths and weaknesses of the book. The book review should ultimately answer the question: "Is this a good book that would be worth reading?"

Use the following checklist as a guide for writing critical book reviews. A good review should answer the following questions, not necessarily in the order listed.

1. What material does the book cover? (Should be summarized briefly.)
2. What is the author's thesis and major supporting arguments? How well does the author support the thesis? (The author's use of evidence and the soundness of the author's reasoning are relevant here.)
3. How is the book organized? (Chronologically or topically?)
4. What is the author's "approach"? That is, would you classify the work as political history, social history, economic history, intellectual history, etc.?
5. Who is the author and what are the author's biases?
6. What are the literary qualities? Is the book well-written or does it read like a badly written insurance policy?
7. What did the book add to *your* understanding of the subject? Did you enjoy the book? Why or why not?
8. If you have read other books on the same general topic, how does this book compare? Most important, how does the interpretation (thesis) of this book differ from that of the others?

Again, these questions need not be answered in any specific order, but all of them should be addressed, however briefly, somewhere in the review. Finally, a book review, like any piece of writing, should observe the basic requirements of literary discourse. There should be an introduction (in this case an overview of *your* thesis concerning the book you are reviewing— "This was a good book because . . ."), a middle section in which you develop your argument, and a brief conclusion. As always, clarity and grammatical precision are important if you want your reader to understand what you are saying.

EXERCISES

Set A, Exercise 1: Thesis-Finding

Above, a distinction was made between the *contents* or *topic* of a book (the subject matter the book discusses) and the *thesis* of a book (the major arguments or interpretations used by the author to explain the events under discussion). In the thesis the author will usually identify those forces, individuals, and relationships that he/she considers most useful for explaining the events in question.

Below are a number of brief abstracts of some books in European history.[3] These abstracts, or summaries, were written by the authors themselves or by editors. Some of the abstracts emphasize the material the book covers (the *topic* or *contents*); others talk more about the author's interpretation of that material (the *thesis*); still others discuss both topic (contents) and thesis.

---

[3] *The Journal of Modern History*, Vol. 51, Nos. 2, 3, and 4 (June 1979, September 1979, December 1979). Abstract No. 7 is taken from a publisher's advertising brochure.

Identify those abstracts that *primarily* summarize the *contents* of the book by placing a "C" in the appropriate space. Identify those that emphasize the author's interpretation or *thesis* by writing a "T." For passages that describe both contents and thesis write a "CT." For all passages labelled "T" or "CT" *underline the sentence or sentences that best represent the author's central thesis.* Before doing this exercise you might want to review the discussion of topic and thesis on page 54. The first item is completed for you as an example.

   <u>CT</u>   1. *Electoral Reform in War and Peace, 1906–18.* By Martin Pugh. London and Boston: Routledge & Kegan Paul, 1978.

Overview of content

The book is the first attempt to explain the major turning point of the Fourth Reform Act which extended the vote to 13 million men and over 8 million women. It does so partly by examining the relationship between reform of the franchise and reform of the electoral system. In analyzing the prewar debate over proportional representation and the alternative vote it sheds new light on the Liberal-Labour relationship.

Thesis statement

<u>The book attacks the status traditionally accorded to the militant suffragettes and shifts attention to the role of the moderates. It demonstrates how reform grew out of prewar conditions and provides a salutory corrective to the assumption that twentieth-century warfare had a democratizing effect on British society.</u>

<u>Finally, wartime politics are reinterpreted as a struggle over the timing of the General Election,</u> and the author explains how the Liberal and Labour parties exposed themselves to twenty years of Conservative hegemony under the mass franchise.

   _____   2. *The Metamorphosis of Greece since World War II.* By William H. McNeill. Chicago: University of Chicago Press, 1978.

The thesis of this book is that contrary to universalizing theories of modernization, especially those using economists' terminology, the transformation of Greek society since 1945 diverges significantly from Anglo-American norms due to the survival of distinctive values and habits deriving from a rural past of very long standing. Urbanization and the Greek diaspora, though seemingly congruent with Anglo-American models of "modernization," disguised but did not erase these heritages. Recent Greek experience is thus a metamorphosis not a modernization.

   _____   3. *Germany, 1866–1945.* By Gordon A. Craig. London and New York: Oxford University Press, 1978.

This is a full-scale history of Germany from the battle of Königgrätz in July 1866 to the collapse of the Third Reich. It devotes equal space to the Bismarck period, the reign of William II, the Weimar Republic, and Hitler's Reich, and includes three substantial chapters (out of twenty) on religion, education, and the arts, and one each on the wars of 1914–18 and 1939–45. It is decidedly more critical of Bismarck than earlier books in the field and more attentive to the role and problems of women. It is also perhaps more systematic in its demonstration of the reciprocal relationship between domestic and foreign affairs and of the way in which, in each of the four periods covered, cultural tendencies and the attitudes and activities of intellectuals reflected social and political realities.

_____ 4. *Protest and Punishment: The Story of the Social and Political Protesters Transported to Australia, 1788–1868.* By George Rude. Oxford: Clarendon Press, 1978.

This book is a study of the political and social protesters who were transported to Australia from Britain, Ireland, and Canada between 1788 and 1868. The protesters comprised 2 to 3 percent of the total convict population, and this work is the first attempt to distinguish them from the common-law criminals with whom they were transported. The author begins with a brief account of crime and protest in the three countries and shows how they were repressed. He then analyzes the different types of protesters; examines the lives they led in the colonies; and asks, finally, what sort of men were the protesters who were transported.

_____ 5. *In Command of France: French Foreign Policy and Military Planning, 1933–1940.* By Robert J. Young. Cambridge, Mass.: Harvard University Press, 1978.

This work, based extensively on recently released archival material in Britain and France, is one of the first to combine a detailed survey of French foreign policy during the Nazi period with an examination of France's corresponding military planning and preparation. This combination of diplomatic and military perspectives has led the author to a revisionist interpretation of the French response to Nazi Germany, an interpretation which credits the civilian and military command in France with more vision, more determination, more competence than generally has been recognized. Rich in unpublished material and new in interpretation, the work also introduces the reader to some of the leading personalities of the day, soldiers and statesmen whose names have come close to fading from our view.

_____ 6. *Social Reform in England, 1780–1880.* By John Roach. New York: St. Martin's Press, 1978.

This book attempts to study the reasons for change in English society between 1780 and 1880. During this period a new society developed, based on movement rather than stability, cash rather than status. The changes which were to produce the social pattern of modern industrial England began in the 1780s. They were inspired by an individualistic philosophy which produced a certain accommodation with state power which endured until about 1880. Much recent study of this period has begun either with the administration or with economic conditions. These aspects have obviously been considered, but the book does not begin from either of these standpoints. It sees social history primarily as the working out of ideas under the pressure of events. Much attention is given to the Utilitarians, to the mid-Victorian debates about individual freedom and collective claims, to religious themes, and to self-help and philanthropy.

——— 7. *Women, Nazis and Universities.* By Jacques R. Pauwels. Westport, Conn.: Greenwood Press, 1984.

> Hitler's view that "a woman must be a cute, cuddly, naive little thing—tender, sweet, and stupid" was reflected in the policies of the National Socialist party, whose discouragement of female academic aspirations was supposed to result in young women's concentration on their "biological duties"—marriage and motherhood. The intrinsically misogynic nature of the Nazi party, bolstered by the reality of Germany's economic plight in the early 1930s, underscored the expectation that German women would be academically disfranchised. However, this expectation was not fulfilled. Preparations for war created a serious labor shortage, and a rise in the birthrate eventually undermined the eugenic argument.

Set A, Exercise 2 Often, when sitting down with a new book, we are tempted to skip the preface or foreword and begin reading the first chapter. This is a mistake. Frequently the preface (or introduction) contains vital information that can help us understand the book more easily. The author will often state the reason for writing the book, the thesis, the point of view, the approach, etc. In short, a preface can be a gold mine of information, and you should always read such introductory sections very carefully.

Read the preface below, and in the spaces provided list any important points you can find concerning the *contents* (what the book covers) and the *thesis* (the author's interpretation) of the book in question. Also, does the preface give you any clues as to the author's "approach" (the sub-type of history he will be writing), his intended audience, the type of sources he is using, etc.?

Lynn White, Jr., *Medieval Technology and Social Change.* London: Oxford University Press, 1962. Reprinted by permission.

> Voltaire to the contrary, history is a bag of tricks which the dead have played upon historians. The most remarkable of these illusions is the belief that the surviving written records provide us with a reasonably accurate facsimile of past human activity. 'Prehistory' is defined as the period for which such records are not available. But until very recently the vast majority of mankind was living in a subhistory which was a continuation of prehistory. Nor was this condition characteristic simply of the lower strata of society. In medieval Europe until the end of the eleventh century we learn of the feudal aristocracy largely from clerical sources which naturally reflect ecclesiastical attitudes: the knights do not speak for themselves. Only later do merchants, manufacturers, and technicians begin to share their thoughts with us. The peasant was the last to find his voice.
>
> If historians are to attempt to write the history of mankind, and not simply the history of mankind as it was viewed by the small and specialized segments of our race which have had the habit of scribbling, they must take a fresh view of the records, ask new questions of them, and use all the resources of archaeology, iconography, and etymology to find answers when no answers can be discovered in contemporary writings.

Since, until recent centuries, technology was chiefly the concern of groups which wrote little, the role which technological development plays in human affairs has been neglected. This book has a triple intention. First, it presents three studies of technology and social change in the European Middle Ages: one on the origins of the secular aristocracy; one dealing with the dynamism of the early medieval peasantry; one with the technological context of early capitalism. Second, it shows the kinds of sources and the means which must be used if the unlettered portions of the past (which involve far more than technological history) are to be explored. Third, it demonstrates that, long before Vasco da Gama, the cultures of the eastern hemisphere were far more osmotic than most of us have believed. To understand the sources and ramifications of developments in medieval Europe one must search Benin, Ethiopia and Timor, Japan and the Altai.

Since lately many people have become interested in the relation between technology and the alteration of social forms, I have tried to keep the text of this book fairly brief and fluid, hoping thus to make it useful to the general student. As a result, the notes are not only a documentation but often an orchestration, developing arguments for the specialist which would have slowed the pace of the text, or exploring bypaths into obscure regions which eventually must be mapped monographically. I hope most ardently that readers may be both provoked to correct errors and stimulated to amplify inadequacies, and that they will do me the favour of sharing their learning with me.

IMPORTANT POINTS FROM PREFACE:

_____

_____

_____

_____

_____

_____

_____

_____

Set A, Exercise 3: Optional Essay

It is important to be able to translate the ideas of others (whether those of a lecturer or author) into your own words. This skill will help you take effective notes in class or useful review notes for books you have read. Effective summarizing techniques will also save you a good deal of time. If you can reduce lecture or written material into a brief summary you will avoid tedious verbatim copying. You will also (and this is important) be forced to think actively about what you have heard or read. If you find that you are unable to summarize something in your own words, it may indicate that you did not fully understand it in the first place. Effective summarizing skills are among the most useful you can possess.

For this exercise, on a separate sheet of paper, write a brief summary of the major points of the preface you have just read. You may reread the preface, but try to write your summary without referring to it directly. Also, don't just *list* the major points. Write a cohesive paragraph (perhaps four or five sentences) that captures the essence of the preface. You may wish to review the abstracts in Exercise 1 to get an idea of how some authors have summarized their own books.

Set A, Exercise 4: Analysis of Article

Although most of our discussion on how to read historical literature was focused on the reading of books, in this exercise you will be asked to analyze a brief article using the criteria described on pages 56–57. Remember, however, that books differ from articles only in length and depth of detail, not in their basic nature. The same analytical principles can be applied to both.

For the articles reprinted at the end of this chapter you will be asked to describe in a few short sentences: (1) the topic, (2) the central thesis and major subpoints (i.e., major components of the thesis), (3) the dominant organizational scheme, (4) the author's "approach" to the subject matter, and (5) the nature and quality of the sources used. You will also be asked to respond to a number of specific short-answer questions.

Read Lowell Tozer's article "A Century of Progress, 1833–1933: Technology's Triumph Over Man" (pp. 64–67) and answer the questions below. You may refer back to the article as many times as necessary.

1. *Topic of the article (i.e., the subject matter; the material the article covers):*

   _____

   _____

2. *Central thesis (the author's interpretation or argument):*

   _____

   _____

   _____

   NOTE: Indicate paragraph number(s) where the thesis is most clearly summarized.

3. *Major subpoints that support the thesis:*
   a. *Example: The traditional American view held that Technology was a tool for achieving human purposes. (Paragraph 3)*

   b. _____

   c. _____

   d. _____

   e. _____

4. *Predominant mode of organization (topical/analytical or chronological/narrative):*

   _____

   _____

5. *Author's "approach" to the subject (i.e., is the emphasis on political history, intellectual history, cultural history, social history, etc.?):*

_____

_____

Explain your choice:

_____

_____

_____

6. *Use of sources (discuss both the type of sources used and the thoroughness of the documentation—i.e., footnotes or endnotes):*

_____

_____

_____

_____

Lowell Tozer, "A Century of Progress, 1833–1933: Technology's Triumph Over Man," *American Quarterly*, IV (Spring, 1952). Copyright 1952, American Studies Association.

¶ 1 IN the Hall of Science at the Chicago Century of Progress International Exposition in 1933 stood a large sculptural group containing a nearly life-sized man and woman, hands outstretched as if in fear or ignorance. Between them stood a huge angular robot nearly twice their size, bending low over them, with an angular metallic arm thrown reassuringly around each.[1]

¶ 2 The significance of the sculptural group was missed by most visitors, although the exposition was focused upon change. The Fair was held to celebrate Chicago's centennial, and to display the progress made since 1833. The theme was "progress through the application of science to industry," that is, through Technology. But of the many changes that had occurred between 1833 and 1933, the important one symbolized by the robot statue was not recognized. The relative positions of Man and Technology had become reversed in the American mind: in 1833 Technology was understood as one of Man's tools; by 1933 it had become his acknowledged master.

¶ 3 The traditional concept states that Man has an intelligence and a will, and that Technology is a tool that he uses in effecting his purposes. Most Americans before 1865 either held this view explicitly, or spoke and acted *as if* they did. Franklin's attitude, for example, is suggested by the first words of his famous prophecy of 1780:

> . . . it is impossible to imagine the Height to which may be carried, in a thousand years, the Power of Man over Matter.[2]

In 1829 Jacob Bigelow said in his *Elements of Technology* that the mark of modern times is the application of science to "the arts of life."[3] And as late as 1855, even the forward-looking Thomas Ewbank was still clearly within the tradition:

> The original and all-comprehending injunction, "replenish the earth and subdue it," was given before "the fall." In it, the true relationship of man to the earth, and the business of his life, are compressed in half-a-dozen words. On agriculture and the arts his powers, mental and physical, were to be concentrated. No intimation of limits to his progress in them is conveyed.[4]

¶ 4 The Century of Progress exposition demonstrated in two ways a radical shift from the orthodox view: attention was focused on what Technology can do rather than on what Man needs or wants, and Technology was acknowledged to be in a position to dictate to Man.

¶ 5 The exposition placed great emphasis on geographical mobility. The outstanding virtue of the Lama Temple was that it had been brought "halfway around the world." Most of the buildings at the Fair were mobile. They were flimsy, made mostly of plasterboard "clipped" to frameworks, so they could be easily dismantled and moved away. This was partly for economy, and for the special needs of an exposition, but other motives emerge in the following statement by the Secretary of the Architectural Commission of the Fair:

> If this exposition will demonstrate that serviceable and attractive buildings can be erected without the enormous expenditure now involved in present-day building methods and that these buildings will last as long as buildings need to last in this ever-changing civilization of ours, the exposition will have proved itself vastly worth while.[5]

¶ 6 The Fair presented an almost overwhelming display of motion for its own sake. Practically nothing stood still. Every scientific exhibit that could possibly be made to move did so, even if it only bubbled. Most of the hundreds of vehicles on display were up on blocks with their wheels spinning. At night the Fair was alive with searchlights, and most of them were kept moving restlessly about the sky, even playing on the dirigibles and airplanes that circled overhead, and on the continuously shuttling cars of the famous Sky-Ride.

The people at the Fair were delighted by Technology's ability to produce in greater size and quantity than had been previously possible. The dome of the Travel and Transport building was "bigger than the dome of St. Peter's or that of the capitol in Washington," and the twin towers of the Sky-Ride were "taller than any building in Chicago." One of the official claims of the exposition was the following:

> During the period from June 1 to November 1 of this year [1933] there will be more colored lights visible at night on the Exposition grounds than in any equal area or even in any city of the world.[6]

If there were any benefits to Man to be derived from greater size and quantity, they were not specified.

¶ 7 Technology was also admired for doing things in a "new way." A driverless farm tractor wandered about an enclosed field at the exposition. The desirability of a remotely controlled tractor was not questioned. Neon and other kinds of "tube" lights were a sensation at the Fair, but no one mentioned how they were *better*. Some of the "new ways" have since proved useful; others have not. The important point is that anything developed by Technology was *assumed* to be good.

¶ 8   The development of the artificial and the illusory was Technology's fourth achievement. Dazzling color was used to hide shoddy and ridiculous design. Human preferences were, in general, either ignored or deceived. This was Technology's day, and the only concession made was camouflage. At night, colored lights were used to "build," so that it was difficult to tell where buildings ended and sheets of light began. Vertical shafts of light were used extensively in an attempt to lift squatty buildings off the flat, filled-in land of Chicago's Lake Front by means of Arc Light Gothic. When Technology failed to satisfy, it dazzled Man into acquiescence.

¶ 9   Finally, Man's defeat was stated officially in plain words: SCIENCE FINDS—INDUSTRY APPLIES—MAN CONFORMS.[7]

¶ 10   The triumph of Technology over Man was celebrated blatantly at the Fair. The symbols of victory were of two main types: architectural and iconographical.

¶ 11   The architectural style of the buildings was unmistakably dedicated to Technology. It was of two motifs: Streamlined and Machineryesque. Among the Streamlined were the Hall of Science, which seems built from parts of the superstructure of a yacht; the Federal Building, which looks like the tail of a rocket protruding from the ground; and the Electrical building, which is a jumble of Assyrian temples and airplane parts. Some examples of Machineryesque are the Administration building, whose front suggests the grille of a 1942 Buick; the Foods and Agriculture building, which resembles an inverted ore boat; and the Travel and Transport building, the rotunda of which looks like a building permanently under construction, and whose attached hall resembles an elongated generator housing. The Streamlined and Machineryesque motifs were the architectural symbols of the triumph of Technology.

¶ 12   The iconographic symbols of victory came close to suggesting the deification of Technology. The robot sculpture represented the first step. The progression continued. In high relief on an outside wall of Communications Hall stood a figure perhaps twenty-five feet tall; his feet rested on a geared wheel, and in his hands he held the lightning. The climax is represented by the twin figures, Science and Industry, which flanked the main entrance of the Administration building. The two herculean figures were about forty feet tall, and were coated with aluminum leaf. Arms folded across their chests, they frowned majestically down upon the people below.

¶ 13   These figures boldly symbolized an attitude that was expressed with varying degrees of subtlety by the whole exposition. But regardless of the form it took, the idea aroused almost no comment. It surprised no one. The Fair expressed a fact: in the American mind, Technology was now accepted as Man's master, and Man did indeed "conform." The tool had come a long way, since 1833.

Notes   1. The best single source for pictures of the exposition is Chicago Century of Progress International Exposition, *The Official Pictures of A Century of Progress Exposition, Chicago, 1933–1934* (New York: Encyclopaedia Britannica, Inc., 1933).

2. *The Writings of Benjamin Franklin*, ed. Albert H. Smyth (New York: The Macmillan Company, 1905–7), VIII, 10.

3. (Boston: Hilliard, Gray, Little and Wilkins), pp. 4–5.

4. *The World a Workshop* (New York: D. Appleton and Company, 1855), pp. 183–84.

5. F. Crissey, "Why the Century of Progress Architecture?" *Saturday Evening Post*, CCV (June 10, 1933), 63. With A. D. Albert, Secretary of the Architectural Commission.

6. Chicago Century of Progress International Exposition, *Official Book of the Fair*, Giving Pre-Exposition Information, 1932–1933 (Chicago: A Century of Progress, Inc., 1932), p. 21.

7. Chicago Century of Progress International Exposition, *Official Guidebook of the Fair* (Chicago: A Century of Progress, Inc., 1933), p. 11.

Set B, Exercise 1: Thesis-Finding

Below are a number of brief abstracts of some recently published books in European history.[4] These abstracts, or summaries, were written by the authors themselves or by editors. Some of the abstracts emphasize the material the book covers (the *topic* or *contents*); others talk more about the author's interpretation of that material (the *thesis*); still others discuss both topic (contents) and thesis.

Identify those abstracts that *primarily* summarize the *contents* of the book by placing a "C" in the appropriate space. Identify those that emphasize the author's interpretation or *thesis* by writing "T." For passages that describe both contents and thesis write a "CT." For all passages labelled "T" or "CT" *underline the sentence or sentences that best represent the author's central thesis.* Before doing this exercise you might want to review the discussion of topic and thesis on page 54.

1. *War in European History.* By Michael Howard. London, Oxford, and New York: Oxford University Press, 1976.

> This is a study of warfare as it has developed in Western Europe from the Dark Ages until the present day. In it I show not only how the techniques of warfare changed, but how they affected or were affected by social, economic, and technological developments in the societies that employed them. I trace the growth and decay of the feudal organization of Western Europe for war; the rise of mercenary troops and their development into professions as the framework of the state became strong enough to keep them permanently employed; the connection between war and the development of European trade overseas; and the impact of the French Revolution on the military system of the *ancien régime*. I go on to show how the development of industrial technology and the social tensions within industrial states culminated in the two world wars, and end by summarizing the military situation of a continent kept at peace by a balance of nuclear terror.

2. *John Stuart Mill and Representative Government.* By Dennis F. Thompson. Princeton, N.J.: Princeton University Press, 1976.

> This book is the first major study of John Stuart Mill's *Considerations on Representative Government*, a work that Mill regarded as a mature statement of his theory of democracy. I analyze the structure of that theory,

[4] *The Journal of Modern History*, 49 (March 1977, June 1977).

drawing on the whole corpus of the writings of Mill and his contemporaries. Contrary to most interpreters, I argue that Mill strikes a balance between participatory and elitist visions of democracy and that his theory is more coherent and systematic than has generally been assumed. At the same time, this study appraises Mill's arguments from the perspective of recent work in social science and democratic theory. The book has extensive footnotes and a twenty-five-page bibliography.

_____ 3. *Colonial Self-Government: The British Experience, 1759–1856.* By John Manning Ward. Toronto: University of Toronto Press, 1976.

I offer a double reinterpretation of self-government in the British colonies, 1759–1856. (1) British ministers were usually willing, if imperial supremacy were maintained, that colonies should have a form of government resembling that in Britain, but the degree of resemblance permitted varied partly with the extent to which a colony was expected to reproduce English polity. Different forms of self-government were established at the same time. The possibilities varied further with changes in the constitution, politics, and attitudes of Britain to overseas colonies of settlement. (2) Imperial historians have misunderstood the British constitution, anachronistically assuming that "responsible" government (government by parliamentary ministers depending for office on the confidence of the Commons, not the sovereign) must have existed when Durham wrote his famous report. Colonial developments slightly affected British constitutional growth. The book treats principally Britain, Canada, Australia, and the West Indies, referring also to South Africa and New Zealand.

_____ 4. *Britain's Imperial Century, 1815–1914: A Study of Empire and Expansion.* By Ronald Hyam. New York: Harper & Row; Barnes & Noble Import Division, 1976.

This study integrates the formal British empire and areas of informal influence such as China, Japan, and Latin America. The Victorian drives toward expansion—economic, strategic, diplomatic, and cultural—are considered, with Palmerston cast in a key role. Part 1 establishes an overall chronological framework for the whole century of . . . activity and analyzes the way the empire was run. Part 2 consists of seven regional chapters. Territorial acquisition is regarded as the result of an interlocking between two different levels of motive: a metropolitan level, concerned with high politics and prestige, and a local one, more concerned with selfish interests. At both levels the export of surplus sexual energy (often sublimated) is seen to be more important than the export of surplus capital; the private lives of empire builders are investigated. Other topics explored include relations with the United States, Asian and African resistance, sport, freemasonry, and the racial attitudes and educational theories of the British political elite. The book is based on close references to monographic material old and new, and for the period 1880–1914 (seen as "the search for stability") draws also on my own research.

—— 5. *Adolf Hitler*. By John Toland. Garden City, N.Y.: Doubleday & Co., 1976.

In an attempt to uncover the Hitler that lies behind the polemic cartoon-monster portrayals and present a realistic full-length biography, I conducted more than 250 interviews with those who knew Hitler intimately—with his inner circle, his doctors, his favorite architects, his military leaders, and the women he most admired.

Significant new documents, reports, and studies have also been utilized to unravel the mystery of Hitler: the dossiers of the U.S. Army Intelligence Command, including one agent's interview with the Fuhrer's sister Paula; documents in the National Archives such as a secret psychiatric report on Hitler in 1918; and unpublished diaries, notes, and memoirs including the revealing recollections of Hitler's youngest secretary. My book (the result of five and one-half years' work) has no thesis, and any conclusions to be found in it were reached only during the writing, perhaps the most meaningful being that Hitler was far more complex and contradictory than I had imagined.

—— 6. *The Origins of the Marshall Plan*. By John Gimbel. Stanford, Calif.: Stanford University Press, 1976.

Based on American and German primary sources, this study argues that the Marshall Plan is traceable to certain decisions on German recovery that George C. Marshall and Ernest Bevin made in April 1947, during the Moscow Council of Foreign Ministers. The larger European recovery program, called forth by Marshall on June 5, 1947, was an effort to gain political acceptance for those decisions in Europe and America. Current theories about the open door, multilateralism, and containment of Russia notwithstanding, the Marshall Plan was a series of pragmatic political and bureaucratic compromises to solve the economic problems of the German occupation. In the end, Americans provided economic aid—either directly or through Germany—to many of the nations that had expected to use German reparations and cheap German exports for their postwar recovery programs. As after the First World War, the United States helped Germany to settle its reparations obligations.

Set B, Exercise 2: Analysis of Article

Read Edmund S. Morgan's article, "The Puritans and Sex," (pages 70–80) and complete the questions below. You may refer back to the article as many times as necessary.

1. *Topic of the article (i.e., the subject matter; the material the article covers):*

_____

_____

2. *Central thesis (the author's interpretation or argument):*

_____

_____

NOTE: Indicate paragraph number(s) where the thesis is most clearly summarized.

3. *Major subpoints that support the thesis:*

a. _____

b. _____

c. _____

d. _____

e. _____

4. *Predominant mode of organization (topical/analytical or chronological/narrative):*

_____

_____

5. *Author's "approach" to the subject (i.e., is the emphasis on political history, intellectual history, cultural history, social history, etc.?):*

_____

_____

Explain your choice:

_____

_____

_____

6. *Use of sources (discuss both the type of sources used and the thoroughness of the documentation—i.e., footnotes or endnotes):*

_____

_____

_____

_____

Edmund S. Morgan, "The Puritans and Sex," *The New England Quarterly*, XV (December 1942), pp. 591–607. Reprinted by permission.

¶ 1 Henry Adams once observed that Americans have "ostentatiously ignored" sex. He could think of only two American writers who touched upon the subject with any degree of boldness—Walt Whitman and Bret Harte. Since the time when Adams made this penetrating observation, American writers have been making up for lost time in a way that would make Bret Harte, if not Whitman, blush. And yet there is still more truth than falsehood in Adams's statement. Americans, by comparison with Europeans or Asiatics, are squeamish when confronted with the facts of life. My purpose is not to account for this squeamishness, but simply to point out that the Puritans, those bogeymen of the modern intellectual, are not responsible for it.

¶ 2 At the outset, consider the Puritan's attitude toward marriage and the role of sex in marriage. The popular assumption might be that the Puritans frowned on marriage and tried to hush up the physical aspect of it as much as possible, but listen to what they themselves had to say. Samuel Willard, minister of the Old South Church in the latter part of the seventeenth century and author of the most complete textbook of Puritan divinity, more than once expressed his horror at "that Popish conceit of the Excellency of Virginity."[1] Another minister, John Cotton, wrote that

> Women are Creatures without which there is no comfortable Living for man: it is true of them what is wont to be said of Governments, *That bad ones are better than none:* They are a sort of Blasphemers then who dispise and decry them, and call them *a necessary Evil,* for they are *a necessary Good.*[2]

These sentiments did not arise from an interpretation of marriage as a spiritual partnership, in which sexual intercourse was a minor or incidental matter. Cotton gave his opinion of "Platonic love" when he recalled the case of

> one who immediately upon marriage, without ever approaching the *Nuptial Bed,* indented with the *Bride,* that by mutual consent they might both live such a life, and according did sequestring themselves according to the custom of those times, from the rest of mankind, and afterwards from one another too, in their retired Cells, giving themselves up to a Contemplative life; and this is recorded as an instance of no little or ordinary Vertue; but I must be pardoned in it, if I can account it no other than an effort of blind zeal, for they are the dictates of a blind mind they follow therein, and not of that Holy Spirit, which saith *It is not good that man should be alone.*[3]

¶ 3 Here is as healthy an attitude as one could hope to find anywhere. Cotton certainly cannot be accused of ignoring human nature. Nor was he an isolated example among the Puritans. Another minister stated plainly that "the Use of the Marriage Bed" is "founded in mans Nature," and that consequently any withdrawal from sexual intercourse upon the part of husband or wife "Denies all relief in Wedlock vnto Human necessity: and sends it for supply vnto Beastiality when God gives not the gift of Continency."[4] In other words, sexual intercourse was a human necessity and marriage the only proper supply for it. These were the views of the New England clergy, the acknowledged leaders of the community, the most Puritanical of the Puritans. As proof that their congregations concurred with them, one may cite the case in which the members of the First Church of Boston expelled James Mattock because, among other offenses, "he denied Coniugall fellowship vnto his wife for the space of 2 years together vpon pretense of taking Revenge upon himself for his abusing of her before marryage."[5] So strongly did the Puritans insist upon the sexual character of marriage that one New Englander considered himself slandered when it was reported, "that he Brock his deceased wife's hart with Greife, that he wold be absent from her 3 weeks together when he was at home, and wold never come nere her, and such Like."[6]

¶ 4 There was just one limitation which the Puritans placed upon sexual relations in marriage; sex must not interfere with religion. Man's chief end was to glorify God, and all earthly delights must promote that end, not hinder it. Love for a wife was carried too far when it led a man to neglect his God:

> . . . sometimes a man hath a good affection to Religion, but the love of his wife carries him away, a man may bee so transported to his wife, that hee dare not bee forward in Religion, lest hee displease his wife, and so the wife, lest shee displease her husband, and this is an inordinate love, when it exceeds measure.[7]

Sexual pleasures, in this respect, were treated like other kinds of pleasure. On a day of fast, when all comforts were supposed to be foregone in behalf of religious contemplation, not only were tasty food and drink to be abandoned but sexual intercourse, too. On other occasions, when food, drink, and recreation were allowable, sexual intercourse was allowable too, though of course only between persons who were married to each other. The Puritans were not ascetics; they never wished to prevent the enjoyment of earthly delights. They merely demanded that the pleasures of the flesh be subordinated to the greater glory of God: husband and wife must not become "so transported with affection, that they look at no higher end than marriage it self." "Let such as have wives," said the ministers, "look at them not for their own ends, but to be fitted for Gods service, and bring them nearer to God."[8]

¶ 5 Toward sexual intercourse outside marriage the Puritans were as frankly hostile as they were favorable to it in marriage. They passed laws to punish adultery with death, and fornication with whipping. Yet they had no misconceptions as to the capacity of human beings to obey such laws. Although the laws were commands of God, it was only natural—since the fall of Adam—for human beings to break them. Breaches must be punished lest the community suffer the wrath of God, but no offense, sexual or otherwise, could be occasion for surprise or for hushed tones of voice. How calmly the inhabitants of seventeenth-century New England could Contemplate rape or attempted rape is evident in the following testimony offered before the Middlesex County Court of Massachusetts:

> The examination of Edward Wire taken the 7th of october and alsoe Zachery Johnson, who sayeth that Edward Wires mayd being sent into the towne about busenes meeting with a man that dogd hir from about Joseph Kettles house to goody marches. She came into William Johnsones and desired Zachery Johnson to goe home with her for that the man dogd hir. accordingly he went with her and being then as far as Samuell Phips his house the man over tooke them. which man caled himselfe by the name of peter grant would have led the mayd but she oposed itt three times: and coming to Edward Wires house the said grant would have kist hir but she refused itt: wire being at prayer grant dragd the mayd between the said wiers and Nathanill frothinghams house. hee then flung the mayd downe in the streete and got atop hir; Johnson seeing it hee caled vppon the fellow to be sivill and not abuse the mayd then Edward wire came forth and ran to the said grant and took hold of him asking him what he did to his mayd, the said grant asked whether she was his wife for he did nothing to his wife: the said grant swearing he would be the death of the said

wire. when he came of the mayd; he swore he would bring ten men to pul down his house and soe ran away and they followed him as far as good[y] phipses house where they mett with John Terry and George Chin with clubs in there hands and soe they went away together. Zachy Johnson going to Constable Heamans, and wire going home. there came John Terry to his house to ask for beer and grant was in the streete but afterward departed into the towne, both Johnson and Wire both aferme that when grant was vppon the mayd she cryed out severall times.

Deborah hadlocke being examined sayth that she mett with the man that cals himselfe peeter grant about good prichards that he dogd hir and followed hir to hir masters and there threw hir downe and lay vppon hir but had not the use of hir body but swore several othes that he would ly with hir and gett hir with child before she got home.

Grant being present denys all saying he was drunk and did not know what he did.[9]

¶ 6 The Puritans became inured to sexual offenses, because there were so many. The impression which one gets from reading the records of seventeenth-century New England courts is that illicit sexual intercourse was fairly common. The testimony given in cases of fornication and adultery—by far the most numerous class of criminal cases in the records—suggests that many of the early New Englanders possessed a high degree of virility and very few inhibitions. Besides the case of Peter Grant, take the testimony of Elizabeth Knight about the manner of Richard Nevars's advances toward her:

The last publique day of Thanksgiving (in the year 1674) in the evening as I was milking Richard Nevars came to me, and offered me abuse in putting his hand, under my coates, but I turning aside with much adoe, saved my self, and when I was settled to milking he agen took me by the shoulder and pulled me backward almost, but I clapped one hand on the Ground and held fast the Cows teatt with the other hand, and cryed out, and then came to mee Jonathan Abbot one of my Masters Servants, whome the said Never asked wherefore he came, the said Abbot said to look after you, what you doe unto the Maid, but the said Never bid Abbot goe about his businesse but I bade the lad to stay.[10]

¶ 7 One reason for the abundance of sexual offenses was the number of men in the colonies who were unable to gratify their sexual desires in marriage.[11] Many of the first settlers had wives in England. They had come to the new world to make a fortune, expecting either to bring their families after them or to return to England with some of the riches of America. Although these men left their wives behind, they brought their sexual appetites with them; and in spite of laws which required them to return to their families, they continued to stay, and more continued to arrive, as indictments against them throughout the seventeenth century clearly indicate.

Servants formed another group of men, and of women too, who could not ordinarily find supply for human necessity within the bounds of marriage. Most servants lived in the homes of their masters and could not marry without their consent, a consent which was not likely to be given unless the prospective husband or wife also belonged to the master's household. This situation will be better understood if it is recalled that most servants at this time were engaged by contract for a stated period. They were, in the language of the time, "covenant servants," who had agreed to stay with their masters for a number of years in return for a specified recompense, such as transportation to New England or education in some trade (the latter, of course, were known more specifically as apprentices). Even hired servants who worked for wages were usually single, for as soon as a man had enough money to buy or build a house of his own and to get married, he would set up in farming or trade for himself. It must be emphasized, however, that anyone who was not in business for himself was necessarily a servant. The economic organization of seventeenth-century New England had no place for the independent proletarian workman with a family of his own. All production was carried on in the household by the master of the family and his servants, so that most men were either servants or masters of servants; and the former, of course, were more numerous than the latter. Probably most of the inhabitants of Puritan New England could remember a time when they had been servants.

¶ 8   Theoretically no servant had a right to a private life. His time, day or night, belonged to his master, and both religion and law required that he obey his master scrupulously.[12] But neither religion nor law could restrain the sexual impulses of youth, and if those impulses could not be expressed in marriage, they had to be given vent outside marriage. Servants had little difficulty in finding the occasions. Though they might be kept at work all day, it was easy enough to slip away at night. Once out of the house, there were several ways of meeting with a maid. The simplest way was to go to her bed-chamber, if she was so fortunate as to have a private one of her own. Thus Jock, Mr. Solomon Phipps's Negro man, confessed in court

> that on the sixteenth day of May 1682, in the morning, betweene 12 and one of the clock, he did force open the back doores of the House of Laurence Hammond in Charlestowne, and came in to the House, and went up into the garret to Marie the Negro.
>
> He doth likewise acknowledge that one night the last week he forced into the House the same way, and went up to the Negro Woman Marie and that the like he hath done at severall other times before.[13]

Joshua Fletcher took a more romantic way of visiting his lady:

> Joshua Fletcher . . . doth confess and acknowledge that three severall nights after bedtime, he went into Mr Fiskes Dwelling house at Chelmsford, at an open window by a ladder that he brought with him. the said windo opening into a chamber, whose was the lodging place of Gresill Juell servant to mr. Fiske. and there he kept company with the said mayd. she sometimes having her cloathes on, and one time he found her in her bed.[14]

Sometimes a maidservant might entertain callers in the parlor while the family were sleeping upstairs. John Knight described what was perhaps a common experience for masters. The crying of his child awakened him in the middle of the night, and he called to his maid, one Sarah

Crouch, who was supposed to be sleeping with the child. Receiving no answer, he arose and

> went down the stayres, and at the stair foot, the latch of doore was pulled in. I called severall times and at the last said if shee would not open the dore, I would breake it open, and when shee opened the doore shee was all undressed and Sarah Largin with her undressed, also the said Sarah went out of doores and Dropped some of her clothes as shee went out. I enquired of Sarah Crouch what men they were, which was with them. Shee made mee no answer for some space of time, but at last shee told me Peeter Brigs was with them, I asked her whether Thomas Jones was not there, but shee would give mee no answer.[15]

In the temperate climate of New England it was not always necessary to seek out a maid at her home. Rachel Smith was seduced in an open field "about nine of the clock at night, being darke, neither moone nor starrs shineing." She was walking through the field when she met a man who

> asked her where shee lived, and what her name was and shee told him, and then shee asked his name, and he told her Saijing that he was old Good-man Shepards man. Also shee saith he gave her strong liquors, and told her that it was not the first time he had been with maydes after his master was in bed.[16]

¶ 9 Sometimes, of course, it was not necessary for a servant to go outside his master's house in order to satisfy his sexual urges. Many cases of fornication are on record between servants living in the same house. Even where servants had no private bedroom, even where the whole family slept in a single room, it was not impossible to make love. In fact many love affairs must have had their consummation upon a bed in which other people were sleeping. Take for example the case of Sarah Lepingwell. When Sarah was brought into court for having an illegitimate child, she related that one night when her master's brother, Thomas Hawes, was visiting the family, she went to bed early. Later, after Hawes had gone to bed, he called to her to get him a pipe of tobacco. After refusing for some time,

> at the last I arose and did lite his pipe and cam and lay doune one my one bead and smoaked about half the pip and siting vp in my bead to guie him his pip my bead being a trundell bead at the sid of his bead he reached beyond the pip and Cauth me by the wrist and pulled me on the side of his bead but I biding him let me goe he bid me hold my peas and folks wold here me and if it be replyed come why did you not call out I Ansar I was posesed with fear of my master least my master should think I did it only to bring a scandall on his brothar and thinking thay wold all beare witness agaynst me but the thing is true that he did then begete me with child at that tim and the Child is Thomas Hauses and noe mans but his.

In his defense Hawes offered the testimony of another man who was sleeping "on the same side of the bed," but the jury nevertheless accepted Sarah's story.[17]

¶ 10 The fact that Sarah was intimidated by her master's brother suggests that maidservants may have been subject to sexual abuse by their masters. The records show that sometimes masters did take advantage of their position to force unwanted attentions upon their female servants. The case of Elizabeth Dickerman is a good example. She complained to the Middlesex County Court,

> against her master John Harris senior for profiring abus to her by way of forsing her to be naught with him: . . . he has tould her that if she tould her dame: what cariag he did show to her shee had as good be hanged and shee replyed that shee would run away and he sayd run the way is befor you: . . . she says if she should liwe ther shee shall be in fear of her lif.[18]

The court accepted Elizabeth's complaint and ordered her master to be whipped twenty stripes.

¶ 11 So numerous did cases of fornication and adultery become in seventeenth-century New England that the problem of caring for the children of extramarital unions was a serious one. The Puritans solved it, but in such a way as to increase rather than decrease the temptation to sin. In 1668, the General Court of Massachusetts ordered:

> that where any man is legally convicted to be the Father of a Bastard childe, he shall be at the care and charge to maintain and bring up the same, by such assistance of the Mother as nature requireth, and as the Court from time to time (according to circumstances) shall see meet to Order: and in case the Father of a Bastard, by confession or other manifest proof, upon trial of the case, do not appear to the Courts satisfaction, then the Man charged by the Woman to be the Father, shee holding constant in it, (especially being put upon the real discovery of the truth of it in the time of her Travail) shall be the reputed Father, and accordingly be liable to the charge of maintenance as aforesaid (though not to other punishment) notwithstanding his denial, unless the circumstances of the case and pleas be such, on the behalf of the man charged, as that the Court that have the cognizance thereon shall see reason to acquit him, and otherwise dispose of the Childe and education thereof.[19]

As a result of this law a girl could give way to temptation without the fear of having to care for an illegitimate child by herself. Furthermore, she could, by a little simple lying, spare her lover the expense of supporting the child. When Elizabeth Wells bore a child, less than a year after this statute was passed, she laid it to James Tufts, her master's son. Goodman Tufts affirmed that Andrew Robinson, servant to Goodman Dexter, was the real father, and he brought the following testimony as evidence:

> Wee Elizabeth Jefts aged 15 ears and Mary tufts aged 14 ears doe testyfie that their being one at our hous sumtime the last winter who sayed that thear was a new law made concerning bastards that If aney man wear aqused with a bastard and the woman which had aqused him did stand vnto it in her labor that he should bee the reputed father of it and should mayntaine it Elizabeth Wells hearing of the sayd law she sayed vnto vs that If shee should bee with

Child shee would bee sure to lay it vn to won who was rich enough abell to mayntayne it wheather it wear his or no and shee farder sayed Elizabeth Jefts would not you doe so likewise If it weare your case and I sayed no by no means for right must tacke place: and the sayd Elizabeth wells sayed If it wear my Caus I think I should doe so.[20]

A tragic unsigned letter that somehow found its way into the files of the Middlesex County Court gives more direct evidence of the practice which Elizabeth Wells professed:

der loue i remember my loue to you hoping your welfar and i hop to imbras the but now i rit to you to let you nowe that i am a child by you and i wil ether kil it or lay it to an other and you shal have no blame at al for I haue had many children and none have none of them. . . . [i.e., none of their fathers is supporting any of them.][21]

¶ 12 In face of the wholesale violation of the sexual codes to which all these cases give testimony, the Puritans could not maintain the severe penalties which their laws provided. Although cases of adultery occurred every year, the death penalty is not known to have been applied more than three times. The usual punishment was a whipping or a fine, or both, and perhaps a branding, combined with a symbolical execution in the form of standing on the gallows for an hour with a rope about the neck. Fornication met with a lighter whipping or a lighter fine, while rape was treated in the same way as adultery. Though the Puritans established a code of laws which demanded perfection—which demanded, in other words, strict obedience to the will of God, they nevertheless knew that frail human beings could never live up to the code. When fornication, adultery, rape, or even buggery and sodomy appeared, they were not surprised, nor were they so severe with the offenders as their codes of law would lead one to believe. Sodomy, to be sure, they usually punished with death; but rape, adultery, and fornication they regarded as pardonable human weaknesses, all the more likely to appear in a religious community, where the normal course of sin was stopped by wholesome laws. Governor Bradford in recounting the details of an epidemic of sexual misdemeanors in Plymouth, wrote resignedly:

it may be in this case as it is with waters when their streames are stopped or damned up, when they gett passage they flow with more violence, and make more noys and disturbance, then when they are suffered to rune quietly in their owne chanels. So wickednes being here more stopped by strict laws, and the same more nerly looked unto, so as it cannot rune in a comone road of liberty as it would, and is inclined, it searches every wher, and at last breaks out wher it getts vente.[22]

¶ 13 The estimate of human capacities here expressed led the Puritans not only to deal leniently with sexual offenses but also to take every precaution to prevent such offenses, rather than wait for the necessity of punishment. One precaution was to see that children got married as soon as possible. The wrong way to promote virtue, the Puritans thought, was to "ensnare" children in vows of virginity, as the Catholics did. As a result of such vows, children, "not being able to contain," would be guilty of "unnatural pollutions, and other filthy practices in secret: and too oft of horrid Murthers of the fruit of their bodies," said Thomas Cobbett.[23] The way to avoid fornication and perversion was for parents to provide suitable husbands and wives for their children:

> Lot was to blame that looked not out seasonably for some fit matches for his two daughters, which had formerly minded marriage (witness the contract between them and two men in *Sodom*, called therfore for his Sons in Law, which had married his daughters, Gen. 19. 14.) for they seeing no man like to come into them in a conjugall way . . . then they plotted that incestuous course, whereby their Father was so highly dishonoured. . . .[24]

¶ 14   As marriage was the way to prevent fornication, successful marriage was the way to prevent adultery. The Puritans did not wait for adultery to appear; instead, they took every means possible to make husbands and wives live together and respect each other. If a husband deserted his wife and remained within the jurisdiction of a Puritan government, he was promptly sent back to her. Where the wife had been left in England, the offense did not always come to light until the wayward husband had committed fornication or bigamy, and of course there must have been many offenses which never came to light. But where both husband and wife lived in New England, neither had much chance of leaving the other without being returned by order of the county court at its next sitting. When John Smith of Medfield left his wife and went to live with Patience Rawlins, he was sent home poorer by ten pounds and richer by thirty stripes. Similarly Mary Drury, who deserted her husband on the pretense that he was impotent, failed to convince the court that he actually was so, and had to return to him as well as to pay a fine of five pounds. The wife of Phillip Pointing received lighter treatment: when the court thought that she had overstayed her leave in Boston, they simply ordered her "to depart the Towne and goe to Tanton to her husband." The courts, moreover, were not satisfied with mere cohabitation; they insisted that it be peaceful cohabitation. Husbands and wives were forbidden by law to strike one another, and the law was enforced on numerous occasions. But the courts did not stop there. Henry Flood was required to give bond for good behavior because he had abused his wife simply by "ill words calling her whore and cursing of her." The wife of Christopher Collins was presented for railing at her husband and calling him "Gurley gutted divill." Apparently in this case the court thought that Mistress Collins was right, for although the fact was proved by two witnesses, she was discharged. On another occasion the court favored the husband: Jacob Pudeator, fined for striking and kicking his wife, had the sentence moderated when the court was informed that she was a woman "of great provocation."[25]

¶ 15   Wherever there was strong suspicion that an illicit relation might arise between two persons, the authorities removed the temptation by forbidding the two to come together. As early as November, 1630, the Court of Assistants of Massachusetts prohibited a Mr. Clark from "cohabitacion and frequent keepeing company with Mrs. Freeman, vnder paine of such punishment as the Court shall thinke meete to inflict." Mr. Clark and Mr. Freeman were both bound "in XX £ apeece that Mr. Clearke shall make his personall appearance att the nexte Court to be holden in March nexte, and in the meane tyme to carry himselfe in good behaviour towards all people and espetially towards Mrs. Freeman, concerneing whome there is stronge suspicion of incontinency." Forty-five years later the Suffolk County Court took the same kind of measure to protect the husbands of Dorchester from the temptations offered by the daughter of Robert Spurr. Spurr was presented by the grand jury

> for entertaining persons at his house at unseasonable times both by day and night to the greife of theire wives and Relations &c The Court having heard what was alleaged and testified against him do Sentence him to bee admonish't and to pay Fees of Court and charge him upon his perill not to entertain any married men to keepe company with his daughter especially James Minott and Joseph Belcher.

In like manner Walter Hickson was forbidden to keep company with Mary Bedwell, "And if at any time hereafter hee bee taken in company of the saide Mary Bedwell without other company to bee forthwith apprehended by the Constable and to be whip't with ten stripes." Elizabeth Wheeler and Joanna Peirce were admonished "for theire disorderly carriage in the house of Thomas Watts being married women and founde sitting in other mens Laps with theire Armes about theire Necks." How little confidence the Puritans had in human nature is even more clearly displayed by another case, in which Edmund Maddock and his wife were brought to court "to answere to all such matters as shalbe objected against them concerning Haarkwoody and Ezekiell Euerells being at their house at unseasonable tyme of the night and her being up with them after her husband was gone to bed." Haarkwoody and Everell had been found "by the Constable Henry Bridghame about tenn of the Clock at night sitting by the fyre at the house of Edmond Maddocks with his wyfe a suspicious weoman her husband being on sleepe [*sic*] on the bedd." A similar distrust of human ability to resist temptation is evident in the following order of the Connecticut Particular Court:

> James Hallett is to returne from the Correction house to his master Barclyt, who is to keepe him to hard labor, and course dyet during the pleasure of the Court provided that Barclet is first to remove his daughter from his family, before the sayd James enter therein.

These precautions, as we have already seen, did not eliminate fornication, adultery, or other sexual offenses, but they doubtless reduced the number from what it would otherwise have been.[26]

¶ 16 In sum, the Puritan attitude toward sex, though directed by a belief in absolute, God-given moral values, never neglected human nature. The rules of conduct which the Puritans regarded as divinely ordained had been formulated for men, not for angels and not for beasts. God had created mankind in two sexes; He had ordained marriage as desirable for all, and sexual intercourse as essential to marriage. On the other hand, He had forbidden sexual intercourse outside of marriage. These were the moral principles which the Puritans sought to enforce in New England. But in their enforcement they took cognizance of human nature. They knew well enough that human beings since the fall of Adam were incapable of obeying perfectly the laws of God. Consequently, in the endeavor to enforce those laws they treated offenders with patience and understanding, and concentrated their efforts on prevention more than on punishment. The result was not a society in which most of us would care to live, for the methods of prevention often caused serious interference with personal liberty. It must nevertheless be admitted that in matters of sex the Puritans showed none of the blind zeal or narrow-minded bigotry which is too often supposed to have been characteristic of them. The more one learns about these people, the less do they appear to have resembled the sad and sour portraits which their modern critics have drawn of them.

Notes

1. Samuel Willard, *A Compleat Body of Divinity* (Boston, 1726), 125 and 608–613.

2. John Cotton, *A Meet Help* (Boston, 1699), 14–15.

3. *A Meet Help*, 16.

4. Edward Taylor, Commonplace Book (manuscript in the library of the Massachusetts Historical Society).

5. Records of the First Church in Boston (manuscript copy in the library of the Massachusetts Historical Society), 12.

6. Middlesex County Court Files, folder 42.

7. John Cotton, *A Practical Commentary . . . upon the First Epistle Generall of John* (London, 1656), 126.

8. *A Practical Commentary*, 126.

9. Middlesex Files, folder 48.

10. Middlesex Files, folder 71.

11. Another reason was suggested by Charles Francis Adams in his scholarly article, "Some Phases of Sexual Morality and Church Discipline in Colonial New England," *Proceedings* of the Massachusetts Historical Society, XXVI, 477–516.

12. On the position of servants in early New England see *More Books*, XVII (September, 1942), 311–328.

13. Middlesex Files, folder 99.

14. Middlesex Files, folder 47.

15. Middlesex Files, folder 52.

16. Middlesex Files, folder 44.

17. Middlesex Files, folder 47.

18. Middlesex Files, folder 94.

19. William H. Whitmore, editor, *The Colonial Laws of Massachusetts. Reprinted from the Edition of 1660* (Boston, 1889), 257.

20. Middlesex Files, folder 52.

21. Middlesex Files, folder 30.

22. William Bradford, *History of Plymouth Plantation* (Boston, 1912), II, 309.

23. Thomas Cobbett, *A Fruitfull and Usefull Discourse touching the Honour due from Children to Parents and the Duty of Parents toward their Children* (London, 1656), 174.

24. Cobbett, 177.

25. Samuel E. Morison and Zechariah Chafee, editors, *Records of the Suffolk County Court, 1671–1680, Publications* of the Colonial Society of Massachusetts, XXIX and XXX, 121, 410, 524, 837–841, and 1158; George F. Dow, editor, *Records and Files of the Quarterly Courts of Essex County, Massachusetts* (Salem, 1911–1921), I, 274; and V, 377.

26. *Records of the Suffolk County Court*, 422–443 and 676; John Noble, editor, *Records of the Court of Assistants of the Colony of Massachusetts Bay* (Boston, 1901–1928), II, 8; *Records of the Particular Court of Connecticut, Collections* of the Connecticut Historical Society, XXII, 20; and a photostat in the library of the Massachusetts Historical Society, dated March 29, 1653.

CHAPTER 5

HOW TO MANAGE INFORMATION: CLASSIFICATION

"Order and simplification are the first steps toward mastery of a subject—the actual enemy is the unknown."
Thomas Mann

So far we have discussed the resources of the library and, more particularly, how to read intelligently the articles and books found there. Regular, thoughtful reading, of course, contributes greatly to academic and professional success, and thoughtful reading requires mental discipline. Likewise, effective *use* of the facts and ideas gained from reading requires a disciplined and systematic procedure for ordering and classifying (i.e., managing) information. That is the subject of this chapter.

Anyone who plays cards knows that the first step after receiving the dealt cards is to arrange them by suit. We are thus able to "read" a hand, and we begin to develop a strategy for playing it. In making a diagnosis a doctor does the same thing, searching for symptoms and examining bodily functions to classify the illness and begin treatment. Classification of data is one of the most basic mental functions we perform. At the simplest level it involves the *systematic* grouping or categorizing of items according to the attributes they possess, such as color—black, brown, red, white. At higher cognitive levels, it involves dealing with things whose attributes are less obvious.

Classification is of the utmost importance in the study of history. The past, as a whole, is so complex and confusing that it is incomprehensible unless broken into small, digestible pieces. But more than small pieces is required; the pieces must be *organized* into patterns that make sense to the researcher. Just as books in a huge library are of little use without a clear classification scheme to help you find the book you need, the "facts" of history are useless without a similar system of classification.

The library analogy is worth examining in a bit more detail. The purpose of the library classification systems we discussed in chapter 3 is to help readers find the books they need on a given topic. That is, books are classified in a way that helps readers *use* the library. In this manner, book classification systems are powerful tools that allow us to find the information we need as quickly as possible. Similarly, in history, classification schemes are vital intellectual tools that allow historians to use the information they collect.

Simple enough. But there is a further point ultimately more important. Whether classifying books or historical data, the choice of a classification system is often quite arbitrary. The needs and perceptions of the classifier determine the most appropriate classification system. For instance, libraries organize their collections by subject, but many other plans are equally possible. Many people organize their own libraries according to the size of the books. Others arrange them by the name of the authors. We know a literature professor who organizes his sizeable collection according to the year of the author's death! (We've never been totally clear how he arranges books of authors who are still alive.) Certainly some classification systems are more logical (and useful) than others, but the point remains that they reflect the purposes and idiosyncrasies of the human beings who create them. They are artificial constructs that serve the needs of the moment.

You will confront the problem of classification within the first few minutes of research. Let us suppose, for example, that you are examining the historical situation that led to the choice of John F. Kennedy as the Democratic presidential candidate in 1960. You soon find that there were a great many individuals involved, including Kennedy himself, his brother Robert, Lyndon Johnson, Hubert Humphrey, Adlai Stevenson, Clark Clifford, Lawrence O'Brien, and a host of others. That discovery is only the beginning. In addition to studying the role of the individual participants, you will want to investigate the role of organizations, the press, public opinion, behind-the-scenes political maneuvering, specific issues—well, you get the point. In dealing with this great mass of details, you will have to separate them into manageable categories, i.e., classify the data in some way.

Although every researcher would use a slightly different classification system, the following list shows the categories one student used to organize her materials as she proceeded with her research. (The list below is not an outline of the final paper but a set of categories used to organize research materials.)

I. Major Contenders
    Kennedy
        Stance on issues
        Campaign effectiveness
        Relationship with press
        Major advisors/supporters
            Campaign advisors
            Contributors
            Intellectuals/Idea Sources
    Johnson
        (See above)
    Humphrey
        (See above)

II. Campaign Developments
    Primaries
    Public opinion polls
    Candidate successes/failures

III. The State Delegations
    How chosen
    Contacts with national campaign organizations

IV. The Los Angeles Convention

We want to make several points about the classification scheme above, or any classification scheme for that matter. First, classification systems are built piece by piece rather than being imposed from the start. At the very beginning of most research projects the historian is a "stranger in a strange land," hesitant and uncertain about the themes and categories that *must* be established if the project is to be made manageable. Just as a stranger eventually gets his bearings in a new place, so, too, does a researcher gradually identify suitable ways to organize information. There is no easy way; the key ingredients are time and mastery of one's topic.

A second point to be made about classification systems is that they are trial-and-error undertakings. As we proceed from ignorance to comprehension most of us find ourselves using tentative categories or names that later prove to be inexact or imprecisely phrased. We take notes using such categories and later on find that we must rename or reclassify some of the notes. Almost everyone has this experience in major research projects, so when it happens to you, consider the situation normal.

A third point concerning classification schemes is this: in one way or another any good scheme makes use of a "part–whole" mentality. That is, somewhere along the way the researcher reaches the point of establishing the major categories (often three or four), along with subdivisions appropriate to each. Suppose, for example, that someone is investigating the impact of the Great Depression of the 1930s on Jackson County, Missouri. After some amount of research it appears that the following headings are the most appropriate: "Economic Impact," "Social Impact," "Political Impact." But each category could be further broken down into a number of component parts. The "Political Impact" section might, for instance, be subdivided into sections on state agencies, county agencies, municipal agencies. Each of these categories could also be broken down into subsections, and so on. The point is that through such classification efforts there gradually emerges a picture of the whole in relation to its parts.

We will approach our final point concerning classification schemes a bit indirectly. A fan of old Hollywood movies has provided a list of stars popular at some time between 1930 and 1970.

Marilyn Monroe	Greta Garbo
Betty Grable	James Mason
Shirley MacLaine	Judy Garland
Cary Grant	Andy Griffith
Jayne Mansfield	Paul Muni
Stewart Granger	Fred MacMurray

As an informal exercise, quickly now, how would you group them? (The names are the "evidence" you have to work with.)

Students of the 1980s would probably know little about some of these stars. They might use some basic classification schemes arising from surface features of the "evidence," such as sex, length of name (three five-letter names, etc.), or alphabet (six "M" names, six "G" names). People who have more knowledge of the period, however, would likely classify the stars according to some more subtle (and personal) criteria, such as box office success, acting ability, number of marriages, frequency of gossip column mention, or whatever.

What we are restating here is that all classification systems have an artificial, arbitrary quality about them. Each of us "sorts out" the world according to the features of evidence, but also, more significantly, according to the *frame of reference* dominating our mind at a given time. (Your "frame of reference" very often reflects your interests of the moment. If you are interested in acting ability you will use a different classification scheme for the names above than if you are interested in box-office appeal.) A Russian Marxist would look at the events preceding the American Revolution differently than would, say, a British monarchist, while an American nationalist would have still another perspective. Thinking about the past does not take place in a vacuum but in a container called the human mind, with all of its ideas, attitudes, values, and biases. G. J. Renier effectively summarizes the importance of frame of reference in the following passage:

> While it is not the historian's task to formulate a philosophy of history, no historian approaches his task without certain preconceived and systematic generalizations about the course of the human past. He may owe these notions to his membership of a church, to his approval of the doctrines of a political party, he may, instead, base them entirely upon his own reflections strengthened by his reading. He may derive them from both sources. The essential factor is that his philosophy is *a prioristic*, held before he set out upon his task of historical research, and that it provides him with a ready-made system for serializing into a story the events detected by research. But the conscientious historian must never forget that he is not writing to prove a theory or to make a contribution to the philosophy of history.[1]

Obviously the presence of a frame of reference has its dangers, for you run the risk of finding only what you want to find. The other extreme, approaching historical data with a totally blank mind, is also unsatisfactory (not to mention impossible), as you lack the beginnings of a classification system to make the data manageable. Since you cannot totally eliminate the influence of personal values and biases when creating a classification scheme, at least you can avoid the twin dangers mentioned above if you take to heart the words of Barzun and Graff: "*To be successful and right, a selection* [i.e., pattern or scheme of classification] *must face two ways: it must fairly correspond to the mass of evidence, and it must offer a graspable design to the beholder.*"[2]

In concluding this section we want to emphasize that classification, with all that it involves, is a highly useful mental skill, with many applications beyond academic research. It can be used as an aid to memory in studying. If you were trying to master Adolf Hitler's military campaigns, it might be convenient to classify them geographically (Russian, Mediterranean, Western European) or chronologically (1939–1941 [Blitzkrieg], 1942–1943 [re-

---

[1] G. J. Renier, *History: Its Purpose and Method* (New York: Harper and Row, 1965), p. 219.

[2] Jacques Barzun and Henry Graff, *The Modern Researcher*, rev. ed. (New York: Harcourt, Brace & World, 1970), p. 179.

treat], 1944–1945 [D-Day to surrender]). Good classification skills are useful at examination time. Many students find that outlining their response *before* beginning to write pays large dividends. (One colleague of ours regards such organization of thought as so important that he gives high grades whenever he encounters it, even if it is, as he says, "organized nonsense.") Finally, skill in classification can be an important ingredient in professional success. For instance, few would deny the importance of public speaking in many management positions—at conferences, workshops, instructional sessions, and the like. Many people are terrified at the thought of giving a speech, but it isn't so hard if one divides a presentation into its component parts: introduction, thesis statement, development, conclusion, with appropriate subcategories for each part.

Periodization

Classification often involves division of the past into time units, usually called periods. Periodization is of fundamental importance in the study of history and must be clearly understood.

To begin with, periodization—the division of the past into time units—is a starting point and no more. To set off the years 1930–1939 from the rest of the twentieth century does not tell us anything other than these years somehow "belong" together. To give that period a name, in this case "The Depression Thirties," helps but not much. The name provides only a general theme which may or may not be entirely applicable. Much more needs to be done in order to advance our understanding and insight of this particular decade.

Second, period limits, like the classification systems already discussed, are in most cases artificial. They are an invention of a historian, the beginning and ending of which are invariably fuzzy. The first tick of the clock on January 1, 1930, did not usher in a totally new era called "The Depression Years," nor did the final days of 1939 end the patterns of life as they had existed throughout the 1930s. There are no absolute openings and closings in history. To think there are is fundamentally anti-historical—remember what was said about change and continuity. Historical pots generally boil slowly, and so the assigned dates of a historical "period" must be treated with flexibility.

Third, and this is the most important point of all, periods vary widely as to the unity that characterizes them. At one end of the spectrum we find "periods" that seem to have the quality of a three-ring circus, with lots of events which have little relationship to each other. Still, a textbook (or a professor) might give us such a time unit just to break down the task of learning into digestible pieces. Division of a segment of twentieth-century American history into a 1910–1920 period might be regarded as such a case. In that time span there was little relationship between diplomatic developments, economic achievements, government policies, and ideological attitudes. At the other end of the spectrum there are periods that seem to have deep and pervasive cultural unity. In these periods, politics, the arts, economic life, religion, ideology, and social structure are profoundly affected by some powerful underlying current and are therefore interrelated in identifiable ways. The fifth century B.C. in Greece might be cited as an excellent example and so, too, the American South of the 1850s.

Between these two ends of the spectrum are periods that have a good deal of integrity. The main events share similar attributes, making it fruitful to study the period following strong thematic lines. In fact, the Depression Thirties are a good example of this middle type.

Yet looking at this whole matter of periods, whether we use the term tightly or loosely, it must be said that no period ever has total unity. In the many corners of any society, life forever goes on pretty much as before: ministries may fall, armies may march, churches may decay, but still the cows must be milked, roofs mended, and the baby fed. Still, periods are important in the study of history. In fact, one can almost never think seriously about any event without an awareness of the surrounding culture, that is, its particular time and place. The larger framework in which an event occurs is called its "context"—a concept developed more fully in Chapter 6.

Classification is a natural inclination of the mind; but, like any other human capability, this inclination must be disciplined and thus expanded. Such is the purpose of the exercises that follow. You will be asked to make some classifications, often on a superficial basis. This is necessary. But please remember that the only valid basis for classifying anything is extensive knowledge of a subject.

EXERCISES

Set A, Exercise 1   In this chapter we discussed the importance of classification in the study and understanding of history. To think historically implies the ability to perceive and create categories that make the past more comprehensible. To some extent historical categories (periods, the various "types" of history, etc.) grow out of the material itself; and to some extent the patterns are chosen by the historians in order to facilitate their work.

In this exercise your task is to create a system of classification for the book titles listed below. In fact, we want you to divide all the titles into two categories (columns) *according to two entirely different sets of criteria.* Example: You could divide the movie stars on page 83 into two categories (columns) by separating the men from the women. You could create an entirely different classification scheme based on the first letter of the last name. We hope you will be a bit more sophisticated in your classification of the titles below. But, in the end, any scheme that is consistent and fits the "evidence" (the book titles/subjects) is legitimate. Both fiction and non-fiction titles are included. Works of fiction are labelled with an "F."

Dorothy George, *London Life in the 18th Century*
Barbara Tuchman, *The Guns of August* [1914]
Bertolt Brecht, *Galileo* (F)
Isaac Asimov, *The Universe*
C. Warren Hollister, *The Making of England, 55BC to 1399*
Gore Vidal, *1876* (F)
Joseph Needham, *Science in Traditional China*
Friedrich Durrenmatt, *The Physicists* (F)

George Sarton, *A History of Science*
Margaret Mitchell, *Gone with the Wind* (F) [Novel on American Civil War]
Regna Darnell, *Readings in the History of Anthropology*
J. Robert Wegs, *Europe Since 1945*
Marie Boas, *The Scientific Renaissance*
George Bernard Shaw, *The Doctor's Dilemma* (F)
Carolyn Wood Sherif, *Orientation in Social Psychology*
Ira Sharkansy, ed., *Policy Analysis in Political Science*
Paul Samuelson, *Economics*
Donald McQuarrie & Peter Rock, *General Chemistry*
Gordon Wood, *The Creation of the American Republic, 1776–1787*
Frederick Cartwright, *A Social History of Medicine*
Helen Cam, *England Before Elizabeth*
Josephine Tey, *Daughter of Time* (F) [Novel on age of Richard III of England]
Charles Dickens, *A Tale of Two Cities* (F) [Novel on French Revolution period]

Classification Scheme I:

Indicate the basis for your classification of the books into two groups. List the books that belong to each group by writing down the titles. Underneath your categories list those books that do not fit your scheme of classification. *Note: You do not have to fit all the books into your classification scheme,* but each one should be valid for the majority of the titles.

Basis for Classification:

_____
_____
_____

Group 1   Group 2

_____   _____
_____   _____
_____   _____
_____   _____
_____   _____
_____   _____
_____   _____
_____   _____
_____   _____

Titles That Do Not Fit Classification Scheme:

_____

_____

_____

_____

Classification Scheme II:

Using a completely different set of criteria, divide the same titles into two different categories. Again, give the basis of your classification system, list the titles in each category, and indicate which books do not fit the system. All books do not have to fit into your scheme, but most of them should if your system is to be convincing.

Basis for Classification:

_____

_____

_____

Group 1   Group 2

_____   _____

_____   _____

_____   _____

_____   _____

_____   _____

_____   _____

_____   _____

_____   _____

_____   _____

Titles That Do Not Fit Classification Scheme:

_____

_____

_____

_____

Set A, Exercise 2   We want you to classify this list of titles in two separate ways: 1) divide them into two groups using a *geographic* principle and 2) divide the same titles into two, or not more than three, groups using a *chronological* principle.

Soldier and Civilian in the Later Roman Empire (R. MacMullen)
Indians Before Columbus (P. S. Martin)
Franklin D. Roosevelt and the New Deal, 1932–40 (W. Leuchtenburg)
Florentine Politics and Society, 1343–1378 (G. Brucker)
German-Soviet Relations (E. H. Carr)
Ancient Civilization of Mexico and Central America (H. J. Spinden)
Crisis of the Aristocracy, 1588–1641 (L. Stone)
The American Colonies in the Eighteenth Century (H. L. Osgood)
English Men and Manners in the 18th Century (A. S. Turberville)
Herbert Hoover's Latin American Policy (A. De Conde)
Affairs of State: The Eisenhower Years (R. Rovere)
The Grandeur That Was Rome (J. C. Stobart)
The Great Depression (J. K. Galbraith)
English History 1914–1945 (A. J. P. Taylor)
Ancient Mexico (F. A. Peterson)

Geographic Division:

First Category (Give name):   Second Category (Give name):

_____   _____

Specific Items (list titles):   Specific Items (list titles):

_____   _____

_____   _____

_____   _____

_____   _____

_____   _____

_____

Chronological Division:

First Category (Give period):   Second Category (Give period):

_____   _____

Specific Items (list titles):   Specific Items (list titles):

_____   _____

_____   _____

_____   _____

_____   _____

_____   _____

_____   _____

Third Category (if used):

_____

Specific Items (list titles):

_____

_____

_____

_____

_____

Set A, Exercise 3   In the study of history, chronology is a great help to the researcher. If all else fails you can organize your materials in chronological order. However, chronology alone has its limitations as a classification tool. Even writers who are planning to write a strictly chronological historical narrative find they have to organize materials *topically* as well as chronologically. Topical organization involves dividing your materials according to thematic similarity (i.e., "topics").

In this exercise you are asked to classify book titles by listing them under one of the following four topical categories. (If you think a given title fits in more than one category, list it as such and be prepared to defend your answer. But remember, you should be trying to find *the best* category for a given title.)

1. **Political**: Relating to government, elections, relations between governmental branches, diplomacy, the process of legislation, etc.
2. **Economic**: Relating to the production, distribution, and sale of goods and services. Also finance, business management, labor-management relations, and the like.
3. **Social**: Relating to popular customs, leisure activities, behavior, social values, problems, life styles, etc.
4. **Ideological/Intellectual**: Relating to the major ideas that influence society, to public opinion and attitudes, to major systems of belief, and so forth.

Titles:

The WPA and Federal Relief Policy (D. S. Howard)
Crestwood Heights: The Culture of Suburban Life (J. R. Seeley, et. al.)
America's Capacity to Produce (E. G. Nourse, et. al.)
Propaganda Technique in the World War (H. Lasswell)
The History of Photography (B. Newhall)
American Minds (S. Persons)

Prohibition: The Era of Excess (A. Sinclair)
The New Radicalism in America (C. Lasch)
The United States and the Spanish Civil War (F. J. Taylor)
Railroads: Rates and Regulations (W. Z. Ripley)
The California Progressives (G. Mowry)
The Modern Corporation and Private Property (A. A. Berle, Jr., and G. C. Means)
1600 Pennsylvania Avenue (W. Johnson)
Labor on the March (E. Levinson)
The Liberal Imagination (L. Trilling)
The Supreme Court From Taft to Burger (A. T. Mason)

Classification: (Please use two or three key words from the above titles)

Political:	Economic:	Social:	Ideological/ Intellectual:
———————	———————	———————	———————
———————	———————	———————	———————
———————	———————	———————	———————
———————	———————	———————	———————
———————	———————	———————	———————

Set A, Exercise 4   The following is a list of headlines taken from the *New York Times* (August 14–28, 1983). Using a basis of your own choosing, classify them into two groups. Then divide each of the two groups into three subclassifications, providing two or three illustrative headlines. Though you need not fit *every* headline into your classification scheme, try to find themes into which all, or nearly all, of the items can be fitted legitimately. Note the spaces provided.

BRAZILIANS DEBATE CURBS ON SALARIES

CAMPSITES AT YELLOWSTONE MAY GO TO PROTECT GRIZZLIES

SOCIAL SECURITY, TO AVOID FRAUD, TO CHANGE OFFICIAL CARD'S PAPER

TURKEY'S GENERALS EXCLUDE THE OPPOSITION FROM NOVEMBER ELECTION

TAIWAN OFFERS HAVEN TO PILOT FROM CHINA

PIRATES' CANDELARIA DEFEATS EXPOS, 2–0

PAPANDREOU RENEWING GREECE'S TRADITIONAL TIES WITH U.S.

PHILADELPHIA SEES UNDERDOGS BATTLE

REAGAN REAFFIRMS HIS MIDEAST PLAN

ISRAEL IS QUIETLY EXPANDING LINKS WITH NATIONS THROUGHOUT AFRICA

YOUNG WEST GERMANS HAVE SHAKEN OFF THE PAST

4 DEMOCRATS ATTACK REAGAN AT ANTIARMS FORUM IN IOWA

NEW EVIDENCE LEADS POLICE TO THINK AUTHOR WAS SLAIN

3 NATURE GROUPS ACCEPT POWER LINE IN MONTANA

REAGAN PRAISES WEINBERGER FOR MILITARY SPENDING CURB

PANAMA, OUT OF PRACTICE, PREPARES TO ELECT PRESIDENT

SOVIET NAMES ATOM-SAFETY CHIEF

BONN LEADER SAY REAGAN LETTER FAVORS A MEETING WITH ANDROPOV

LAYOFFS OF POLICE BARRED IN CHICAGO

JUDGE IN CONNECTICUT CURBS USE OF THE INSANITY DEFENSE

REDSKINS HOLD OFF BENGALS AND WIN

SEVEN CHILEANS KILLED IN NEW PROTESTS

INDIA PLANS TO BUILD A 2,500-MILE FENCE AROUND BANGLA-DESH

RELIEF, DELIGHT AND A HUGH CLEANUP AS LIGHTS GO ON AGAIN IN MIDTOWN

CONTRACT TALKS TO RESUME TODAY IN STRIKE AT NEW YORK CITY OPERA

RIGHTS MARCHERS ASK NEW COALITION FOR SOCIAL CHANGE

UP TO A FIFTH OF U.S. WORKERS NOW RELY ON PART-TIME JOBS

POLL SAYS MONDALE IS FAVORITE

CHINA SAID TO EASE STAND ON TAIWAN

Group I: Basis of Classification _____

Specific Items: (Use first three or four words of headline)

_____

_____   Subclassification:

_____   1. Basis: _____

_____   Specific Items:

_____   _____

_____   _____

_____

_____   2. Basis: _____

_____   Specific Items:

_____   _____

_____   _____

_____

_____   3. Basis: _____

_____   Specific Items:

_____

_____   _____

_____   _____

Group II: Basis of Classification _____

Specific Items: (Use first three or four words of headline)

_____

_____   Subclassification:

_____   1. Basis: _____

_____   Specific Items:

_____

_____   _____

_____

_____   _____

_____   2. Basis: _____

_____   Specific Items:

_____

_____   _____

_____

_____   _____

_____   3. Basis: _____

_____   Specific Items:

_____

_____   _____

_____

_____   _____

Set A, Exercise 5   The next stage of difficulty is that of classifying pieces of historical information. If you keep in mind that you must be alert to _topical_ themes in research work, you will be able to complete the following exercise. Any research project requires this sort of classification. Classify the following items on a basis that seems sensible to you. There are several points to keep in mind: (1) in classifying things think of _broad_ categories, such as "religious," "social," "ideological," "financial," etc. (though none of these are appropriate as bases of classification for the items below); (2) when you do actual research you should always translate information into your own words (note the example below—Category 1); (3) there should be three items in each of four classifications. The first category has been filled in—note the topical heading and the paraphrasing of each item. All of the information given relates in some way to the Confederate States of America, 1861–1865.

a. The Confederate dream of revolutionizing New Mexico and California ended in March, 1862, when a rebel force was defeated at Pidgin's Ranch, just east of Glorieta Pass in the territory of New Mexico.

b. The Constitution of the Confederacy provided for a cabinet of six members, who were to serve as administrators of their departments and advisors to the president.

c. The Confederacy sent John Slidell as an envoy to France, but he was unable to secure French recognition of the Confederation as an independent government.

d. A stunning loss for the South occurred in mid-1863 when Vicksburg on the Mississippi fell to General Grant, causing him to telegraph Lincoln that "the Father of Waters again flows unvexed to the sea."

e. In 1861 the seceding southern states formed the Confederated States of America, and elected Jefferson Davis as the first president.

f. Though Confederate commissioners were received cordially in London, British dealings with them were minimal because of the strong anti-slavery feelings of the British common people.

g. In the early stages of the Civil War the Southern government had to refuse the enlistments of tens of thousands of young men because there were no firearms for them.

h. The Southern victory at Chancellorsville in 1863, while decisive, was also extremely costly, as one of the South's greatest field commanders, General "Stonewall" Jackson, lost his life there.

i. Estimates of the total number of men in Confederate uniform during the four years of the war run from 700,000 to 900,000.

j   The first Confederate effort at diplomacy failed when U.S. Secretary of State Seward refused to see the southern commissioners sent to establish peaceful relations with the United States government.

k. By the mid-point of the war Southern recruitment of soldiers was bolstered by conscription of able-bodied men between the ages of eighteen and forty-five.

l. Because of the opposition of states' righters, who feared its appellate jurisdiction, the Confederate governmental system had to get along without a supreme court.

Category 1. Basis: <u>Diplomacy/International Relations</u>

1. <u>Envoy Slidell unsuccessful in obtaining French recognition of independence (c)</u>

2. <u>Cordial reception of Confederates in London but little accomplished (f)</u>

3. <u>Refusal of U.S. Government to see peace-seeking Southern diplomats (j)</u>

Category 2. Basis: _____

    1. _____

    2. _____

    3. _____

Category 3. Basis: _____

    1. _____

    2. _____

    3. _____

Category 4. Basis: _____

    1. _____

    2. _____

    3. _____

Set B, Exercise 1   We want you to classify this list of titles in two separate ways: (1) Divide them into two groups using a *geographic* principle and (2) divide the same titles into two, or not more than three, groups using a *chronological* principle.

Parallel Lives of the Noble Greeks and Romans (Plutarch)
Prehistoric Man in the New World (J. D. Jennings)
The Constitutional History of Medieval England (J. E. A. Jolliffe)
Massachusetts People and Politics, 1919–1933 (J. Huthmacher)
Soviet Foreign Policy Since World War II (J. L. Nogee)
The Medieval Papacy (G. Barraclough)
Hitler: A Study in Tyranny (A. Bullock)
Ancient Maya Civilization (N. Hammond)
The Creation of the American Republic (G. S. Wood)
France in Modern Times: 1760 to the Present (G. Wright)
The Spanish Empire in America (C. H. Haring)
Industrial History of the United States (K. Coman)
The Decline and Fall of the Roman Empire (E. Gibbon)
George Washington and the New Nation (J. T. Flexner)
The Explosion of British Society, 1914–1963 (A. Marwick)

Geographic Division:

First Category (Give name):	Second Category (Give name):
_____	_____
Specific Items	Specific Items
_____	_____

_____   _____

_____   _____

_____   _____

_____   _____

_____   _____

Chronological Division:

First Category (Give period):   Second Category (Give period):

_____   _____

Specific Items   Specific Items

_____   _____

_____   _____

_____   _____

_____   _____

_____   _____

Third Category (if used):

_____   _____

Specific Items

_____

_____

_____

_____

_____

Set B, Exercise 2   In the study of history, chronology is a great help to the researcher. If all else fails you can organize your materials in chronological order. However, chronology alone has its limitations as a classification tool. Even writers who are planning to write a strictly chronological historical narrative find they have to organize materials *topically* as well as chronologically. Topical organization involves dividing your materials according to thematic similarity (i.e., "topics").

In this exercise you are asked to classify book titles by listing them under one of the following four *topical* categories. (If you think a given title fits in more than one category, list it as such and be prepared to defend your answer. But remember, you should be trying to find *the best* category for a given title.)

1. **Political**: Relating to government, elections, relations between governmental branches, diplomacy, the process of legislation, etc.

2. **Economic**: Relating to the production, distribution, and sale of goods and services. Also finance, business management, labor-management relations, and the like.
3. **Social**: Relating to popular customs, leisure activities, behavior, social values, problems, life styles, etc.
4. **Ideological/Intellectual**: Relating to the major ideas that influence society, to public opinion and attitudes, to major systems of belief, and so forth.

Titles:

Varieties of Reform Thought (D. Levine)
Climax of Populism: The Election of 1896 (R. F. Durden)
Promised City: New York's Jews 1870–1914 (M. Rischin)
Negro Thought in America, 1880–1915 (A. Meier)
The Presidential Election of 1880 (G. H. Knoles)
From the Depths: The Discovery of Poverty (R. H. Bremner)
Pullman Strike (A. Lindsey)
Race Relations in Virginia, 1870–1902 (C. E. Wynes)
Social Thought in America: The Revolt Against Formalism (M. White)
Boston's Immigrants (O. Handlin)
Families Against the City: Middle Class Homes of Industrial Chicago, 1872–1890 (R. Sennett)
Irish-American Nationalism, 1870–1890 (T. N. Brown)
Catalogues and Counters: History of Sears, Roebuck and Company (B. Emmet & J. E. Jeuck)
Relief and Social Security (L. Meriam)

Political:	Economic:	Social:	Ideological/ Intellectual:
_____	_____	_____	_____
_____	_____	_____	_____
_____	_____	_____	_____
_____	_____	_____	_____
_____	_____	_____	_____

Set B, Exercise 3 The following is a list of headlines taken from the *Omaha World-Herald* (May 6–20, 1984). Using a basis of your own choosing, classify them into two groups. Then divide each of these groups into three subclassifications, providing two or three illustrative headlines. Though you need not fit *every* headline into your classification scheme, try to find themes into which all, or nearly all, of the items can be fitted legitimately. Note the spaces provided.

BOWA LEARNS TO RELAX, GAINS THREE HITS IN CUBS 5–4 WIN

HEAVY SHELLING IN BEIRUT FOLLOWS FIRST PEACE MARCH BY CHILDREN

MONDALE STRONG IN TEXAS: JACKSON GRABS LOUISIANA

CAN PANAMANIAN RETURN MILITARY TO THE BARRACKS?

SCORES DEAD IN INDIA RIOT

CITY COUNCIL SCHEDULED TO DECIDE HOW TO SPEND BUDGET SURPLUS

OMAHA LOSES TO DES MOINES IN BID FOR GREYHOUND OFFICE

BRITANNIA STILL ROAMS THE WORLD

SOVIET CARRIER TOPS EXPECTATIONS

DEFENSE SLOWS MEMPHIS PASSERS AS OAKLAND WINS FOURTH STRAIGHT

SOVIETS REAFFIRM BOYCOTT: ALTERNATE GAMES POSSIBLE

NEBRASKA WESLEYAN SETS $23 MILLION GOAL

SALVADORANS SET FOR CHOICE OF DUARTE OR d'AUBISSON

POPE HOPES HE CAN VISIT SOVIET UNION

O'NEILL: HOUSE LIKELY TO BLOCK MONEY FOR MX

NEBRASKANS TIE FOR FIFTH IN EXCEEDING SPEED LIMIT

REAGAN RE-ELECTION COMMITTEE REACHES CEILING ON FUND RAISING

FREIGHTER BOUND FOR IRAN SINKS AFTER MISSILE ATTACK

SWEATSHOPS MAKING A COMEBACK IN NEW YORK'S GARMENT INDUSTRY

MOSLEMS TO GET MORE POWER IN LEBANON

SCENERY IN NEBRASKA OFFERS RICH REWARDS

ARMY ENLISTMENTS ARE LAGGING: REBOUNDING ECONOMY IS BLAMED

CELTICS EYE SERIES SWEEP AFTER RALLYING PAST BUCKS

MARCOS SOUNDS CONFIDENT ABOUT PHILIPPINE ELECTIONS

TOLL CLIMBS AS SHELLS FLY IN LEBANON

FHA's LIST OF FORECLOSED FARMS MULTIPLIES ACROSS MID-LANDS, U.S.

ARCADIA TEENAGER DIES: TRANSPLANT WAIT TOO LONG

INDY FIELD FASTEST EVER—RUTHERFORD WINS BATTLE TO QUALIFY

SOVIETS ARE WEARING OUT THEIR WELCOME IN AFRICA

ULTRA-LITE AIRCRAFT CRASHES AT MILLARD AIRPORT

Group I: Basis of Classification _____

Specific Items: (Use first three or four words of headline)

_____

_____   Subclassification:

———————————————   1. Basis: ———————————————

———————————————   Specific Items:

———————————————

———————————————   ———————————————

———————————————

———————————————   ———————————————

———————————————   2. Basis: ———————————————

———————————————   Specific Items:

———————————————

———————————————   ———————————————

———————————————

———————————————   ———————————————

———————————————   3. Basis: ———————————————

———————————————   Specific Items:

———————————————

———————————————   ———————————————

———————————————

———————————————   ———————————————

Group II: Basis of Classification ———————————————

Specific Items: (Use first three or four words of headline)

———————————————

———————————————   Subclassification:

———————————————   1. Basis: ———————————————

———————————————   Specific Items:

———————————————

———————————————   ———————————————

———————————————

———————————————   ———————————————

———————————————   2. Basis: ———————————————

———————————————   Specific Items:

———————————————

———————————————   ———————————————

———————————————

———————————————   ———————————————

———————————————   3. Basis: ———————————————

———————————————   Specific Items:

———————————————   ———————————————

_____   _____

_____   _____

Set B, Exercise 4   The next stage of difficulty is that of classifying pieces of historical information. If you keep in mind that you must be alert to *topical* themes in research work, you will be able to complete the following exercise. Any research project requires this sort of classification. Classify the following items on a basis that seems sensible to you. There are several points to keep in mind: (1) in classifying things think of *broad* categories, such as "religious," "social," "ideological," "financial," etc. (though none of these are appropriate as bases of classification for the items below); (2) when you do actual research you should always translate information into your own words (note the example below—Category 1); (3) there should be three items in each of four classifications. The first category has been filled in—note the topical heading and the paraphrasing of each item. All of the information given below relates to Adolf Hitler's Germany and World War II.

a. Though he lacked the qualities of a statesman, Hitler shaped events by the force of his personality. He exuded personal magnetism.

b. In September 1939 the world saw a new form of military power, as the German *blitzkrieg* (lightning war) smashed through Poland in a matter of days.

c. At Munich, in September 1938, the leaders of Germany, France, Italy, and Great Britain "solved" the Czechoslovakian problem with an international agreement that gave the Sudetenland to Germany.

d. By the Nuremberg decree of 1935 German Gentiles were forbidden not only to marry Jews but even to touch them.

e. The Austrian *Anschluss* (union with Germany) in 1938 had been signalled earlier by German-Austrian diplomatic negotiations concerning trade relations.

f. One of the most brilliant achievements of the German *Wehrmacht* (army) was its "end run" around the French Maginot Line, leading to the destruction of the French army as a fighting force.

g. Because he thought in black-and-white terms, Hitler had no difficulty in perceiving those who opposed him as wholly evil.

h. Extensive German demands on Poland in 1939 led to a flurry of diplomatic negotiation between Germany and Russia, culminating in the Nazi-Soviet Pact of that year.

i. Exercising the power given him in the Enabling Act, Hitler decreed that all political parties but his own Nazi party were to be abolished.

j. The German Fuehrer (Hitler) was an opportunist, a man who knew clearly what he wanted and patiently waited for a chance to strike.

k. In 1933 Hitler maneuvered the German Reichstag into passing the Enabling Act, which gave him the power to pass laws without consent of the Reichstag, thus making him a dictator.

l. After a highly successful campaign in North Africa, General Erwin Rommel's *Afrika Korps* was repulsed and thrown back at El Alamein, the first major defeat of a German army in World War II.

Category 1. Basis: Aspects of Hitler's personality

   1. <u>Influenced events by blunt force of personality rather than statesman-ship (a)</u>

   2. <u>Not a subtle thinker—thought in categorical terms (g)</u>

   3. <u>Had clear goals and patiently awaited opportunities (j)</u>

Category 2. Basis: _____

   1. _____

   2. _____

   3. _____

Category 3. Basis: _____

   1. _____

   2. _____

   3. _____

Category 4. Basis: _____

   1. _____

   2. _____

   3. _____

CHAPTER 6

CONTEXT

"Men resemble their times more than they do their fathers."

Arab Proverb

Gathering information can be time consuming and difficult. Far more difficult is the task of interpreting that information, of understanding the interrelationships between confusing and contradictory facts, of communicating your "history" in a meaningful way to a reader. To do all this you must actually "do" history; you must begin to apply the elements of historical-mindedness examined in Chapter 2. There we discussed the importance of sensitivity to how other times and places differ from our own. Now we want to examine this idea more fully. A special problem faced by all historians is how to understand past events in the *context* of values and patterns of thought often far different from those of the present. A distinguishing mark of the good historian is the ability to avoid judging past ages by the standards of the present and to see past societies (to the greatest extent possible) as they saw themselves.

It is extremely difficult, even for the most fair-minded of observers, to understand and evaluate the habits, thoughts, and values of men and women who lived long ago and far away. This difficulty can be understood by anyone who has traveled abroad and confronted a bewildering array of customs, practices, laws, and values that seem strange and even illogical to an outsider. For instance, the reverence toward cows that one finds in India bewilders visitors for whom beef is a major source of nourishment. A siesta during the searingly hot hours of midday is mere common sense to residents of many tropical countries, but to some Americans such behavior smacks of laziness. In Britain drivers stay left, to the constant dismay of tourists who hail from countries where drivers drive on the right. And so it goes. Countless examples of such cultural divergence, some major and some minor, could be added to the list.

To the historian the past is much like a foreign country where things are often done differently. Just as the conscientious traveler today must learn the local customs, values, law, and language to feel at ease in a foreign country so, too, must historians become fully acquainted with the institutions, cultural habits, and beliefs of the society they are studying. Only then can they appreciate the significance and complexity of historical events. In the words of historian Robert Darnton, "other people are other. They do not think the way we do. If we want to understand their way of thinking, we should set out with the idea of capturing otherness."[1] That's why, in the late 1950s, a white writer darkened his skin with dye so that he might experience first hand what it was like to be a Black in America (John Howard Griffin, *Black Like Me*, 1961).

---

[1] Robert Darnton, *The Great Cat Massacre, and Other Episodes in French Cultural History* (New York: Basic Books, 1984), p. 4.

**Context and
Historical
Understanding**
This brings us back to the concept of *context* in the study of history—indeed in the study of any human actions whether past or present. Historical events can *never* be judged in isolation from the wider environment or situation in which they took place. To do so is to risk massive oversimplification or, worse, to misunderstand the events completely. For instance, as children we learned that at the Battle of Bunker Hill during the first year of the American Revolution (June 17, 1775) the commander of the American troops shouted something like: "Don't fire until you see the whites of their [the British troops'] eyes!" Whether this piece of popular patriotism is true or false, it illustrates the danger of taking things out of their proper context. On the surface the order seems to reinforce a rather idealized vision of the colonial rebels as supermen—determined, stalwart, and brave in the face of an attack by disciplined British regular troops. However, a more intimate knowledge of the conventions and technology of eighteenth-century warfare reveals a more mundane explanation for the famous order. Actually, the muskets of the time were so inaccurate that a soldier had no hope of hitting an enemy infantryman unless he could see the "whites of his eyes." Military necessity, not superior military valor, best explains the famous and stirring order. The British commander probably said something similar to his men.

In his book *The Great Cat Massacre, and Other Episodes in French Cultural History*, Robert Darnton supplies one of the most illuminating and convincing lessons on the importance of context in historical studies. The centerpiece of the book is Darnton's intriguing essay, "Workers Revolt: The Great Cat Massacre of the Rue Saint-Severin." The essay deals with a rather grisly and barbaric episode in Paris during the 1730s—the attempt one day of a number of printer's apprentices to kill every cat they could get their hands on. After killing the favorite cat of their employer's wife, "the journeymen drove the other cats across the rooftops, bludgeoning every one within reach and trapping those who tried to escape in strategically placed sacks. They dumped sackloads of half-dead cats in the courtyard. Then the entire workshop gathered round and staged a mock trial. . . . After pronouncing the animals guilty and administering last rites, they strung them up on an improvised gallows."

Grisly and barbaric? Most people today would think so. But there is something decidedly peculiar about the whole thing: the workers who participated in the slaughter thought it was all a hilarious joke. The apprentices, says Darnton, were overcome with laughter and joy as they gathered and dispatched the local cats, and, in the days that followed, they riotously reenacted the comic events of the massacre over and over again. The fact that we have trouble appreciating the humor of the slaughter of animals often considered cuddly pets is an indication that we don't know enough about the era and culture we are studying. As Darnton notes: "Our own inability to get the joke, is an indication of the distance that separates us from the workers of preindustrial Europe."[2]

Darnton has presented an interesting puzzle. Why did those eighteenth-century workers think killing and torturing cats was so hilariously funny?

---

[2] Darnton, *ibid.*, pp. 76–78.

We can find the answer, as Darnton shows, by examining the cultural context in which the event took place. To get the "joke" of the cat massacre we have to enter the thought-world of eighteenth-century popular culture. On one level the frolicsome massacre of cats, as it turns out, represented the venting of worker hostility against an overbearing and unpopular employer. For a number of nights the workers had yowled like cats in order to irritate the master who had been mistreating them. In desperation the master ordered the apprentices to get rid of the offensive "cats." The workers did so with great glee, and in the process killed the house pet of their employer's wife. The master and his wife were outraged, but helpless, in that they themselves had given the order to eliminate the cats.

This helps a little, but it is not enough. The core of Darnton's analysis is his discussion of popular amusements in eighteenth-century Europe and the role cats played in the popular mind. First, the torture of animals of all kinds, but especially cats, was a popular form of entertainment in that era. More important, cats had long been associated in the popular mind with witchcraft, sexuality, fertility, and the like. By first imitating cat cries and then executing the mistress's cat, the apprentices, according to Darnton, were both accusing their master's wife of witchcraft and "assaulting" her in a sexually symbolic way, thus ridiculing the master as having been cuckolded (our term would be "cheated on"). To workers who had grown up in a culture that tortured animals for amusement, who had long suffered insults and mistreatment from an unpopular master, the "great cat massacre" *was* both funny and deeply satisfying.

This bare outline does injustice to the sophistication and intricacy of Professor Darnton's analysis. But the essential point should be clear. To truly "understand" even this relatively minor incident in the history of premodern France, the historian must uncover the rich texture of beliefs, customs, and values within which the event took place. The historian must, in a word, pay close attention to context.

The example above should dramatize the importance of knowing as much as possible about the historical period you are studying in order to interpret the past in a fair-minded manner. The investigator's knowledge, in the words of Jacques Barzun and Henry Graff, "must include an understanding of how men in other eras lived and behaved, what they believed, and how they managed their institutions."[3] Put another way, you should always try to "think" your way into an alien situation and empathize with those who live (or lived) there. To the best of your ability you should imaginatively attempt to see the world through the eyes of those you are trying to study. In the example just discussed, you need not abandon your own values in favor of those of a different place or time; you need not talk yourself into seeing the massacre of helpless animals as a grand joke. You should be able to distance yourself enough from your own values that you can at least *understand* why the printer's apprentices thought killing the local cats was so funny. The exercise of such *imaginative sympathy* is a prerequisite of sound historical thinking.

---

[3] Jacques Barzun and Henry Graff, *The Modern Researcher*, rev. ed. (New York: Harcourt, Brace and World, 1970), p. 116.

All of this is easier said than done. Very often the tendency to judge the past according to one's own values and standards is inherent in the very nature of historical studies. One fact alone makes it impossible for the historian to see events exactly in the same way contemporaries saw them. The historian knows "how things came out," whereas the participants did not. Historians narrate and interpret the past with the enormous advantage of hindsight, and it is much easier to be an armchair quarterback than to play the game itself. The "wisdom" of hindsight makes it tempting for the historian to make grand generalizations about the incompetence, naivete, and shortsightedness of those in the past whose vision was not so clear. Allan Nevins, in *The Gateway to History*, points out the fallacy involved with this sort of history. Historical hindsight, Nevins warns, makes past problems seem much more simple (and more easily solvable) than they actually were, and "the leaders that dealt with them . . . smaller men."[4] Hindsight, in short, makes it very difficult for even the best-intentioned investigators to approach the trials and triumphs of past ages with true imaginative sympathy.

The inherent difficulty of judging another age by its own standards rather than your own is increased when you are trying to understand an individual or event that is repugnant from the standpoint of your own value system. For most people the "great cat massacre" would be such an event. It is difficult to get beyond moral outrage, yet true understanding demands that we do so. The same problem besets historians who write biographies of individuals who elicit little sympathy. One cannot easily work up much genuine affection or sympathy for Adolf Hitler or Genghis Khan. David Harris Willson had this problem when he was working on his biography of King James I of England. The biography, still one of the best treatments of this rather obnoxious king, is a model of impartiality. Willson succeeded in writing a fair and sympathetic treatment of James.[5] However, the author confessed that the work had been difficult to complete, since he really never "liked" James, no matter how hard he tried to do so.

Context and Moral Judgments in History

Above we referred to King James I of England as a "rather obnoxious king." In its most basic sense "obnoxious" means "very unpleasant" or "objectionable." What right do we have to be so moralistic and judgmental? Does not such a label violate the central lesson of this chapter—i.e., thou shalt not judge the past by the standards of the present? Is this not a violation of a basic tenet of historical mindedness? Perhaps, perhaps not.

If, after carefully reading and evaluating the relevant original sources dealing with James' reign, we conclude that many of James' seventeenth-century contemporaries thought James was "obnoxious" (even if they used different words to communicate the same idea), then our epithet "obnoxious" is justified by the evidence. On the other hand, calling James "obnoxious" because *we* find his behavior morally objectionable, is a different matter altogether. In the latter case we could be accused of interpreting events "out of context." Even in King James' case, however, the verdict of

---

[4] Allan Nevins, *The Gateway to History* (Chicago: Quadrangle Books, 1963), p. 257.

[5] D. H. Willson, *King James VI & I* (New York: Oxford University Press, 1967).

CONTEXT AND SUCCESS IN BUSINESS

We have been talking about the importance of the concept of context in the study of history. It should be clear that the principles we have outlined are important not only for the "ivory tower" world of the university classroom. Contextual awareness is equally vital in a wide variety of professional activities. Journalists who ignore the lessons of context do so at their own risk. It is difficult to report and assess the significance of world events if those events are studied independent of cultural and historical context. Likewise government officials would be well advised to consider the "big picture" whenever deliberating on specific policies and proposals. Doctors know it is not enough to ask a mere catalog of symptoms from their patients. It is often vital to know as much as possible about the totality (i.e., context) of a person's life in order to prescribe the best treatment.

A failure to appreciate the importance of context can be expensive, as numerous corporations have discovered. In recent years businesses have made embarrassing and costly marketing errors simply because they were unaware of critical cultural differences in foreign markets. To cite some examples:

—Few people in Southeast Asia responded to Pepsodent's promise to make their teeth whiter. Why? Well, in that area of the world, where many people chew betelnuts, discolored teeth are a status symbol.
—General Foods had trouble marketing Jell-O in England. It turns out that British shoppers buy gelatin in cakes not in powdered form.
—One firm tried advertising refrigerators in the Moslem Middle East by using pictures of the refrigerator full of appetizing food, including a prominent ham. Of course, Moslems do not eat pork.
—Advertising disasters have also resulted from ignorance of the significance of certain colors in various countries. In Japan, for instance, white is the color of death. In Africa green is the color of disease.

As the above examples testify, it is not only the historian who has to cultivate some of the key attributes of historical-mindedness. Abandon the concept of context only at your own peril.

(The examples of business marketing errors were drawn from "Business Blunders: Some Funny but All Costly," *St. Louis Post-Dispatch*, November 13, 1980.)

practicing historians would not be unanimous. In fact there is tremendous disagreement among professional historians about the legitimacy of passing any moral judgments on past events and individuals.

A discussion of the importance of thinking contextually about the past ventures into troubled waters when the issue of moral values surfaces. Many practices today that we, within the context of Western civilization, would view as morally reprehensible, were viewed quite differently in other historical eras (not to mention in other parts of the world even now). Today the institution of slavery is almost universally condemned. Yet in many places, in many historical periods, human slavery was part of the natural order of things. In the ancient world slavery was a prominent feature of Greek and Roman life. In the European Middle Ages serfs lived lives not far removed from formal slavery. As late as the nineteenth century slavery was an integral part of the culture of the American South. In cases such as this, what position should the conscientious historian take? Should these past cultures be condemned as "immoral" because they countenanced slavery? Should the historian become a moral "relativist" and judge those societies in terms of their own standards of right and wrong? Or should the historian avoid making moral judgments altogether?

Herbert Butterfield, the eminent British historian, believed that moral judgments were irrelevant to historical understanding. If readers did not recognize the immorality or morality of past deeds, the historian's moralistic pronouncements would certainly not change their mind. Further, moral judgments would do nothing to help researcher or reader understand the past in any meaningful way. Says Butterfield: "Moral judgments on human beings are by their nature irrelevant to the enquiry and alien to the intellectual realm of scientific history. . . . These moral judgments must be recognised to be an actual hindrance to enquiry and reconstruction. . . ."[6]

Butterfield and those like him are, historiographically speaking, "amoralists." That is, they believe that moral judgments do not serve any useful purpose in a historical narrative. Ranked opposite Butterfield are those who believe historians have a right and duty to inject moral pronouncements into their history. Their case also has merit. Some within this group believe that certain moral and ethical norms are universal and transcend time and space. It is appropriate, then, to point the finger at evil and condemn it. Such is Goldwin Smith, who writes: "A sound historical morality will sanction strong measures in evil times; selfish ambition, treachery, murder, perjury, it will never sanction in the worst of times, for these are the things that make times evil—Justice has been justice, mercy has been mercy, honour has been honour, good faith has been good faith, truthfulness has been truthfulness from the beginning."[7] Or, to put it in other terms, if we rank "understanding" above moral values, we sacrifice too much.

Others in this group are less absolutist in their thinking. They believe it is legitimate and important for historians to provide moral critiques of the past. But they also believe (along with Butterfield) that the historian should not play the role of the judge, condemning the guilty and absolving the innocent. This position, held by American historian John Higham, is more complex than that of the absolutists. Higham believes that what he calls

---

[6] Quoted in Hans Meyerhoff, ed., *The Philosophy of History in Our Time* (New York: Doubleday, 1959), p. 230.

[7] Meyerhoff, *ibid.*, p. 225.

"moral history" can be an important spur to historical understanding. "Moral history" can help us appreciate the nature and importance of moral imperatives in different times and places. And it can help us understand how certain values—honor, courage, concepts of "character"—changed over time. It can also help us "ponder the moral responsibility of the agents of decision [leaders]" by helping us understand the real alternatives available to leaders at key moments in history. In Higham's words, "The historian is not called to establish a hierarchy of values, but rather to explore a spectrum of human potentialities and achievements."[8] Higham's position, then, is somewhat "relativistic." The historian can and should venture into the realm of moral judgments, but those judgments must take into account the broad context of the time and place being studied.

The debate goes on. Wherever your sympathies lie on this issue, keep in mind that there is a problem here with no easy solution. The historian's job is to understand and interpret the past, and this is most difficult if basic moral values are in conflict. Perhaps the best advice is this: Be aware of the dilemma, so that in your own studies and researches you can act out of conscious choice rather than ignorance.

In this chapter we have explored an issue that is considerably more sophisticated than anything discussed earlier. We want this book to be a means of developing certain skills, but it is also important to examine some of the complex aspects of historical-mindedness. The exercises that follow are intended to advance your sensitivity to times and places different from your own.

EXERCISES

Set A, Exercise 1: Cromwell in Ireland

The following excerpts are intended to help you appreciate the importance of trying to understand past events within the proper historical context. The passages (drawn from secondary sources) are all concerned with a notorious episode in the life of Oliver Cromwell (1599–1658), the English revolutionary leader who led the anti-royalist Parliamentary forces during the English Civil War (1642–49). By 1649 Parliament had won the civil war, had executed the king, Charles I, and Cromwell had become the effective ruler of England. In the same year Cromwell led an army to Ireland to snuff out an anti-English rebellion that had been raging since 1641. It is Cromwell's behavior in Ireland that is the primary concern of the passages that follow. When in Ireland, Cromwell's soldiers massacred the inhabitants of two towns, Wexford and Drogheda. The following passages attempt to examine the event by putting it in a broader historical context. The aim is not to justify a military atrocity, but to help you *understand* the event as thoroughly as possible.

After reading the initial passage, read the subsequent passages carefully in order to see what new pieces of evidence each presents. Note how a wider appreciation of the situation in 1649, the mind-set of Cromwell, the

[8] John Higham, *Writing American History* (Bloomington: Indiana University Press, 1970), pp. 150–56.

worldview of the seventeenth century, and the relevant historical background all help us to understand better the complex dynamics of a seemingly straightforward occurrence. Then answer the questions that follow.

The Event:

> Cromwell stayed in Ireland for a little over nine months—from August 1649 to May 1650. His siege of Drogheda lasted ten days (September 2–11), and its successful conclusion was followed by four days of general massacre directed by Cromwell himself, during which period some four thousand people were murdered. When on October 1, Wexford too was stormed, the same vengeance was exacted, and two thousand people more—men, women, and children, priests, nuns, and laymen— were put to death. . . . Having given this grim warning, Cromwell refrained from further atrocities in Ireland. . . . Nevertheless, on account of Drogheda and Wexford, Cromwell left behind him in Ireland a name for cruelty such as the passage of three hundred years has scarcely erased from memory.

Supplementary Information:

A.   What then is the explanation of Cromwell's cruel and compulsive behavior in Ireland? From childhood he had been raised in an atmosphere of paranoiac hatred for Catholicism. When he was only six, a group of desperate English Catholics had tried to blow kings, Lords, and Commons sky-high; after the Gunpowder Plot of 1605, a fear and loathing of Catholicism that was to last for many years swept England and formed the background of Cromwell's childhood education. . . . Finally, in Cromwell's adult years came the reports of the unspeakable atrocities committed by Irish Catholics in 1641—reports that, as we have seen, were grossly overstated but that seemed to establish irrefutably the unchanging nature of the evil that was Catholicism.

B.   The rules of war of the time, with regard to sieges, were clear. If a commander refused to accede to a summons to surrender, and the town was subsequently won by storm, then he put at risk the lives not only of all his men, but of all those who could be held to be combatants. The significant moment was when the walls were breached by the opposing side: thereafter quarter could not be demanded. . . . Nor was the civilian population of the town necessarily protected from the rash consequences of the commander's refusal to surrender. . . . Grotius in *De Jure Belli ac Pacis*, a work first printed in 1625, that attempted to prescribe some limits to the vengefulness of war as a result of the appalling slaughters of the Thirty Years' War [1618–48], still postulated that it was lawful to kill prisoners of war, and furthermore, that "the slaughter of women and children is allowed to have impunity, as comprehended in the right of war and 137th Psalm."

C.   Cromwell's Irish policy was not personal but national. When he crossed to Ireland in 1649 the Irish revolt against English rule . . . had dragged on for eight years. So long as it continued, Ireland offered a backdoor to foreign intervention against the regicide republic [Cromwell's Parliamentary party had beheaded King Charles I in January 1649], now isolated in monarchical Europe. . . . The government of the English republic decided that Ireland must be subdued quickly. Hence the massacres of Drogheda and Wexford, for which Cromwell is remembered in Ireland to this day.

D.   In England [Cromwell] was prepared in fact to tolerate Catholics as well as Episcopalians: Roman Catholic historians agree that their coreligionists were better off during the Protectorate [the period of Cromwell's rule] than they had ever been under James or Charles I. But in Ireland it was different. . . . Again we must refer, by way of explanation though not justification, to the *political* associations of Irish Catholicism. . . . It was a *political* religion in a sense in which Catholicism in England had ceased to be political.

E.   It is necessary to set this story in perspective because it has so often been used to picture Cromwell as a monster of cruelty, differing from other generals and statesmen in English history, and secondly because it is frequently assigned as a main reason for the poisoning of Anglo-Irish relations in modern times. In fact, Cromwell's Irish policy—wrongheaded as it may have been—was identical with that of Queen Elizabeth I, King James I, Strafford, and Pym. All of them sponsored the colonization of Ireland by Protestant settlers. To the Puritans Ireland was a nearer alternative to Massachusetts or Virginia and the natives as capable of absorption or extrusion as the Indians.

F.   Cromwell resolved to put the garrison to the sword primarily for military reasons: "Truly I believe this bitterness will save much effusion of blood," he wrote. . . . To Sir Winston [Churchill] the atom bomb [in 1945] was a "miracle of deliverance"; to Cromwell the slaughter of the Drogheda garrison was "a marvelous great mercy." . . .
    It was a grave and deliberate act of policy after full warning had been given (as at Hiroshima and Nagasaki); and Cromwell explained it and defended it as such.

Sources   "The Event" & A. Giovanni Costigan, *A History of Modern Ireland* (New York: Pegasus, 1970), pp. 76–77, 79.
    B. Antonia Fraser, *Cromwell* (New York: Knopf, 1973), pp. 335–36.
    C. Christopher Hill, "Political Animal," *New York Review of Books*, June 9, 1977, p. 40.
    D. C. Hill, *God's Englishman* (New York: Harper & Row, 1972), pp. 121–22.
    E. Maurice Ashley, *The Greatness of Oliver Cromwell* (New York: Collier Books, 1966), pp. 233–34.
    F. *Ibid.*, pp. 232–33.

Questions   1. For *each* passage (A through F) note the specific additional pieces of information that enable you to put the massacres of Wexford and Drogheda into a broader historical context:

            Passage A: _____

            Passage B: _____

Passage C: _____

Passage D: _____

Passage E: _____

Passage F: _____

2. The quoted passages help put Cromwell's expedition into historical perspective by supplying: (1) information on Cromwell the individual (*personal* values and beliefs); (2) commentary on the *immediate* political situation (i.e., 1649); (3) insights into the broad cultural, religious, and moral values of seventeenth-century society (the "worldview"); and (4) relevant historical background information (developments in England and Ireland *before 1649*) that had an impact on events.

Indicate by letter (A–F) the specific passage or passages that contain important information related to each of the general categories just listed.

a.   Cromwell the individual: _____

b.   Immediate political situation: _____

c.   Societal values/worldview: _____

d.   Historical background (pre-1649 in England): _____

Discussion   1. Generally, the quoted passages allow you to make a more balanced appraisal of Cromwell's Irish campaign because they suggest what a modern-day court of law would call "mitigating circumstances." The purpose is not to condemn or exonerate Cromwell's behavior, but to allow you to *view Cromwell's actions as his fellow countrymen in the seventeenth century might have viewed them.* In what ways do you think the seventeenth-century assessment would differ from a twentieth-century judgment? Why?

2. Passage F compares Cromwell's justification for the massacres in Ireland with the American and British justification for dropping the atomic bomb on Japan in 1945. In both cases it was argued that one act of violence would save lives in the long run by shortening the war. How valid or useful is this parallel? Why?

3. Which passage or passages added most to your understanding of the events in question? Least? Why?

Set A, Exercise 2:   Write a brief paragraph-length account of Cromwell's expedition. Be sure
Essay   to include all the background information that you see as essential for a clear understanding of the events in question. You might find it profitable to compare your paragraph with those of your colleagues in class.

Set B, Exercise 1:   This exercise is intended to help you appreciate the importance of trying
The Great Witch   to understand past events within the proper historical context. The "event"
Craze   in this case is the witch craze of the sixteenth and seventeenth centuries.

The 1500s and 1600s were centuries of great intellectual progress in the Western world. "Renaissance" and "Scientific Revolution" are two of the labels often applied to these centuries. Paradoxically, or seemingly so, these were also the centuries of the greatest anti-witch hysteria in western history.

Witchcraft is difficult to define. Generally a witch is thought of as a person who has the power to do good or evil (primarily evil) by manipulating supernatural forces. In late medieval Europe the concept was added that a witch was a person who had formed a pact with the devil in order to harm people and undermine the true Christian faith. However defined, witchcraft, in that age of "enlightenment" and scientific advance, was seen as a threat to the very existence of society.

In many parts of Europe witches were hunted with evangelistic fervor. Neighbors denounced neighbors, authorities tortured suspected witches to wring confessions of evil-doing, and witch trials and witch executions were commonplace. Literally thousands of men and women, mostly women, were consumed in the bonfires lit by anti-witch zealots. The most grisly witch persecutions took place on the European continent.

England escaped the worst excesses of the anti-witch hysteria, but accusations and criminal persecutions of witches were still quite common. The American colonies, though far from the European mainstream, were not immune. The 1692 witch trials in Salem, Massachusetts, were the most famous American example of the witch delusions of the time.

To a secular, rationalist, and skeptical age such as our own, the sixteenth and seventeenth century witch mania seems incomprehensible. How could the contemporaries of Copernicus, Locke, Newton, and Kepler fall for such a base superstition? How could they believe in black magic, pacts with the devil, witches riding brooms to secret rendezvous? How could they torture and execute tens of thousands of innocent people on the pretext that they were witches?

We want you to begin answering those questions by reading the passages below. Of course, a complete answer is impossible given the brevity of the sample passages. But you can start by appreciating the importance of understanding the total environment in which the witch craze took place as a precondition to understanding the witch hysteria itself. The passages below can help you understand the historical *context* out of which the anti-witch crusade emerged.

Read the passages below (they are drawn from secondary sources). In the spaces provided at the end of the exercise, note the *new pieces of information* each passage provides to help you better understand the great witch craze of the sixteenth and seventeenth centuries.

Supplementary Information: A.   We should remember also that the seventeenth century firmly believed in a dualistic universe: in a material or visible world, and a spiritual or invisible world as well. Heaven was still a concrete reality, as were the Angels who inhabited it; so was Hell and its Devils. . . . Like other learned men of his time, [English philosopher John] Locke not only believed in a world of spirits, but that spirits can appear in this material world: "that Spirits can assume to themselves bodies of different bulk, figure, and conformation of parts." To be sure, Locke warned that "universal certainty" concerning the world of spirits was beyond us; we could know it, he thought, only as it impinges on our senses. But that, of course, is precisely what was thought to happen in witchcraft.

B.   In a society technologically more backward than ours the immediate attraction of the belief in witchcraft is not difficult to understand. It served as a means of accounting for the otherwise inexplicable misfortunes of daily life. Unexpected disasters—the sudden death of a child, the loss of a cow, the failure of some routine household task—all could, in default of any more obvious explanation, be attributed to the influence of some malevolent neighbour. There was virtually no type of private misfortune which could not thus be ascribed to witchcraft, and sometimes the list of injuries might be extremely miscellaneous. . . . But a supernatural explanation was particularly seductive in the field of medicine, where human impotence in the face of a variety of hazards was only too obvious.

C.   When we read the confessions of sixteenth- and seventeenth-century witches, we are often revolted by the cruelty and stupidity which have elicited them and sometimes, undoubtedly supplied their form. But equally we are obliged to admit their fundamental "subjective reality." For every victim whose story is evidently created or improved by torture, there are two or three who genuinely believe in its truth. . . .

That external suggestion alone does not account for witches' confessions is clear when we descend to detail. Again and again, when we read the case histories, we find witches freely confessing to esoteric details without any evidence of torture, and it was this spontaneity, rather than the confessions themselves, which convinced rational men that the details were true.

D.   Recent studies of witchcraft have concentrated on how witchcraft accusations are related to the whole social structure rather than individual tensions. Instead of seeing witchcraft as the result of the conflict between the individual and society, the phenomenon is analysed in terms of the relationship between various groups in society.

[I]t is not surprising to discover a high correlation between Salem Village factionalism and the way the Village divided in 1692 over the witchcraft outbreak. . . . Almost every indicator by which the two Village factions may be distinguished, in fact, also neatly separates the supporters and opponents of the witchcraft trials.

E.   Toward the end of the Middle Ages and the beginning of the Renaissance both church and state began to take witchcraft more seriously. The crucial century was the fifteenth. . . . At the end of this century, in 1490, *Malleus Maleficarum (The Hammer of Witches)* was published. The authors were James Sprenger and Henry Kramer, two German Dominicans. . . . *Malleus* gave a thorough definition of witchcraft, with rules on how to investigate, try, and judge cases of witchcraft. It remained an important work for more than two hundred years. . . .

F.   To appreciate the light in which the witch appeared to her neighbors it is necessary to recall the importance which the inhabitants of sixteenth- and seventeenth-century England attached to social harmony, and the variety of means they employed to check all signs of dispute or nonconformity. . . . Indeed if the records of Tudor and Stuart village life leave any single impression, it is that of the tyranny of local opinion and the lack of tolerance displayed towards nonconformity or social deviation.

Rural society lacked much of the modern concept of privacy and private life. . . . [The witch] was the extreme example of the malignant or nonconforming person against whom the local community had always taken punitive action in the interests of social harmony.

Sources
A. Chadwick Hansen, *Witchcraft at Salem* (New York: Mentor, 1969), pp. 28–29.

B. Keith Thomas, *Religion and the Decline of Magic* (New York: Scribner's, 1971), pp. 535–36.

C. H. R. Trevor-Roper, *The European Witch-Craze of the Sixteenth and Seventeenth Centuries and Other Essays* (New York: Harper and Row, 1969), pp. 123–24.

D. A. D. J. Macfarlane, *Witchcraft in Tudor and Stuart England* (New York: Harper and Row, 1970), p. 246; and Paul Boyer and Stephen Nissenbaum, *Salem Possessed* (Cambridge, Mass: Harvard Univ. Press, 1974), p. 185.

E. Hansen, *Witchcraft at Salem*, p. 27.

F. Thomas, *Religion and Decline of Magic*, pp. 526–30.

Questions
1. For each passage (A through F) note the specific additional pieces of information that enable you to put the witch craze into a broader historical context.

   Passage A: _____

   Passage B: _____

   Passage C: _____

   Passage D: _____

   Passage E: _____

   Passage F: _____

2. Which passage or passages added most to your understanding of the witch persecutions of that time? Why?

3. Which passage or passages added least to your understanding of the witch craze? Why?

Set B, Exercise 2: Essay
Write a brief paragraph summarizing the historical circumstances and beliefs that are *most useful* in helping you understand the witch craze of the sixteenth and seventeenth centuries.

CHAPTER 7

QUESTIONS AND THE HISTORIAN'S FRAME OF REFERENCE

"It is better to know some of the questions than all of the answers."

James Thurber

James Thurber's wry remark that knowing questions is more important than knowing answers is closer to the truth than he may have realized. In many endeavors and walks of life the ability to ask the right question at the right time often separates success from failure. How many times is it the quality of the questions that separates the good journalist from the mediocre one or the excellent physician from one who is merely adequate? The same applies to history.

Fortunately for all of us, the ability to question effectively is not inborn; it is a skill that can be learned. With patience and a method of attack, even the knottiest historical problem can yield to curiosity and probing. Whenever faced with complexity—and even the most limited historical event can be devilishly complex—it is best to begin by breaking the "whole" into some manageable "pieces." Historians' use of periodization (see Chapter 5) is a good example of this process. Historians, as we have seen, chop the totality of the past into convenient segments so that they can study manageable units of time. Tennis coaches are doing the same thing when they have their students concentrate exclusively on learning the serve, volley, or groundstroke. It is easier to master the game of tennis in segments rather than try to assimilate it in its entirety.

The Importance of Questions

When applied to the study of events, this process is called "analysis." Analysis, according to one dictionary, means "a separating or breaking up of any whole into its parts so as to find out their nature, proportion, function, relationship, etc." Applied to historical events this means you should begin by looking at separate "pieces" of an event in isolation as a step toward understanding the event in its totality. How do you do this? *You ask questions—appropriate questions—that will lead you through an event step by step.*

Teachers want students to know the events of the past, of course, but more than that they want them to develop the habit of asking certain broad questions in order to *understand* those events. In other words students need to develop "a sort of wisdom about how things tend to happen." We will even say that this habit of wider vision is one of the crucial intellectual skills to be gained through the study of history.

Before going any further, we want to emphasize that the beginning point of historical inquiry is rarely just the "change" that occurred at a given time. Because the word "change" implies passing from one stage or condition to another, it is obvious that any self-respecting historian has to know what existed before the "change" took place. More concretely, the historian must understand the established ways of the society in question: common beliefs and attitudes, fixed elements of the social structure, long-existing economic arrangements, relatively permanent governmental patterns, and the like. Without a knowledge of such basic continuities, any concept of change is meaningless.

We can illustrate this point with two examples. To begin, let's ask this question: How significant to you is it that the inimitable Chicago Cubs won the 1984 National League East divisional championship if you don't also know that 1) the Cubs hadn't won a baseball title for thirty-nine years; 2) they had an unsurpassed record of collapsing under pressure in tight title races; and 3) they generally were regarded as one of the longest-standing jokes in sports? Or, on quite another plane, does the Japanese bombing of Pearl Harbor in 1941 (which brought the United States into World War II) make sense without also knowing that 1) Japan and the U.S. had serious long-standing conflicts of interest in East Asia; 2) Japan had been trying to solve the problem of its limited resources for years; and 3) the military played a central role in Japanese policy making?

To reiterate the point: Change in history has no meaning when considered by itself. It takes on meaning only when it is seen in relation to other conditions and events existing in a given time and place. In a way this is a reprise of the message of the last chapter: it is important to understand the *context* in which an event takes place. However, we are saying something more as well: change is a modification of an existing situation, but much of that existing situation continues as it was and *sets limits to the extent of change*.

In this chapter, and in the exercises at the end, remember that whatever question the historian asks concerning an event or situation, he or she is looking for two things: 1) dynamic forces that upset the status quo and 2) elements in the status quo that were strongly resistant to change and that made whatever change that occurred less far-reaching than it otherwise would have been.

What sorts of things does a historian seek to know in order to understand the how and why of a historical event? A list of specific questions that historians might ask would be endless, but certain broad categories of questions are more or less standard. When attempting to understand a specific segment of the past, historians usually like to ask, at minimum: How did ideas, both emergent and traditional, affect the situation? What was the role played by organized groups? by important individuals? by economic and technological factors? How influential were long-standing legal, customary, and diplomatic practices or situations? Before we examine these questions, a few important qualifications are in order.

1. These questions are "starter" questions. They are aimed at making sure that you "touch all the bases"—i.e., follow a systematic search pattern. You will find some of the questions irrelevant when you apply them to a particular historical situation. Others will yield results, often in the form of promising conjectures that must be checked against the evidence—a process that leads to more pointed and precisely phrased questions. In any event, the lists of questions below are meant to be suggestive, not definitive.

2. The starter questions are primarily "macro" in character, which means that they lead to a grasp of major factors (ideas, economic forces, etc.) that have operated to produce the event, often over a long period of time. For example, isolationism, long a characteristic of American public opinion, contributed significantly to American rejection of the League of Nations in the early 1920s. Sensitivity to such "macro" forces will enable you to perceive the basic continuities in historical development and to appreciate better the importance of the constants ever at work in any society.

3. While it is true that the historian must ask the standard questions while studying a given historical event, it is also true that he or she usually, as a matter of personal inclination, winds up emphasizing only one or two of the standard questions when presenting the story. Survey textbook writers often try to cover all the bases, usually to the numbing frustration of their readers. Most historians choose just one or two main themes, which results in the varieties of history (economic, political, intellectual, etc.) that exist.

Ideas in History

The adage that "men do not possess ideas, rather they are possessed by them" has considerable truth, especially if "ideas" are taken to include ideals, attitudes, and values. Often ideas are below the surface, not mentioned in a direct way, but present nevertheless as assumptions. In his public addresses, for example, President John F. Kennedy never specifically cited Keynesian economic ideas, but he used them to revitalize the economy in 1962. The American electorate's unspoken but instinctive distaste for radicalism was a decisive factor in Senator George McGovern's crushing loss in the presidential election of 1972.

At least as often ideas are "out front" in the movement of events. When English power in North America was at its height, in the seventeenth and eighteenth centuries, her statesmen publicly espoused and followed the principles of mercantilism. The American radicals in 1776 just as candidly borrowed the main ideas of John Locke in their Declaration of Independence. Other examples include the impact of *Uncle Tom's Cabin* (written by Harriet Beecher Stowe), which changed northern perceptions of slavery in the pre–Civil War period; the seapower ideas of Alfred T. Mahan, which brought an enormous naval buildup in late-nineteenth-century Germany; and the anti-Semitism of the German people, which Hitler so successfully manipulated in the 1930s. In any case the historian must remember to look for *both* emergent ideas of compelling power *and* traditional ideas with their enduring hold on people's loyalties.

Various questions that one might ask in exploring the role of ideas in shaping a given historical situation are:

—Had any particular idea become newly fashionable?
—Had certain familiar and almost axiomatic truths begun to be questioned?
—What prestigious old ideas continued to hold the loyalty of major individuals and groups that were involved in the situation?

—Is there any evidence of manipulation of opinion by appeals to traditional ideas?

—Does it appear that some individuals and groups were in a sense "imprisoned" by certain ideas?

—Did any individual's conception of the situation or of his or her role in it have importance?

—Was there a distinctive "public mood" that appears to have aided any groups or individuals?

—Did the "intellectuals" have a marked influence at any particular point?

Again, these questions are merely suggestive of the angles of inquiry that may be pursued. Also, it should be obvious that few of them permit spontaneous answers. Rather, they point in the direction of further reading and research.

Economic and Technological Factors

"Economic factors" is a broad umbrella indeed. Fundamentally, "economics" refers to the processes by which a society and its members make a living. That immediately involves us in such matters as market demand, trade patterns, accessibility to raw materials, the interest of economic classes and subgroups, productivity, employment levels, and the like. However, this is not the place for a minicourse in such matters. Moreover, in order to do their job, historians do not usually need to venture very far into the economic thicket.

The following sorts of questions can be helpful in sorting out the economic factors that affected a historical situation.

—Were the markets for the nation's or region's major products and services improving or declining?

—Were existing trade patterns within and without the nation or region being disrupted by new developments?

—Did entrenched economic interests feel endangered by new government policies? by competitive pressures? by other economic groups?

—Were serious clashes occurring among different economic classes within the population?

—Were declining industries and unemployment creating social problems?

—Was the nation or region in a discernible stage of the economic cycle (depression, recovery, boom, recession)?

All of the foregoing are large-scale questions which, while useful in framing the overall picture, are not sufficiently focused to define the more localized economic forces and motivations in a historical situation. One must ask "small-scale" questions as well, perhaps something like:

—What were the economic stakes involved in a particular strike that occurred, i.e., for the workers—fringe benefits, wage levels, etc., and for the employer—the competitive situation in the market?

—To what extent did an office-seeker's financial resources affect the outcome of an election?

—Was any key figure in any way motivated by greed, e.g., leading him or her to cut corners on a building project or to manipulate the contractor awarding process?

We will have more to say later in this chapter about such small-scale or "micro" questions. You'll note that some of the above questions, particularly several of the large-scale questions, do require a certain amount of economic literacy but not at a level much beyond that obtained by reading newspapers and weekly news magazines.

Related to economic factors are technological developments that influence a society's production processes and its life style. Such developments can bring sharp changes in a society's direction, as happened in America in 1793. Before that date slavery was commonly regarded in the South as a crumbling system. Southerners lacked a profitable cash crop to support its expenses. Then, while visiting at a South Carolina plantation, young Eli Whitney put together a simple but ingenious device called a "cotton gin." It made what was then called "green-seed cotton" a viable crop—and at exactly the time when English mills were voraciously consuming every fibre of cotton that could be produced. Thus, for the South, cotton became "map-maker, trouble-maker, history-maker."

Rarely are technological developments in the foreground of historical situations. Rather, they become integrated with a society's economy, creating new products that displace others, enhancing one region's economic potential at the expense of another's, shifting balances in international trade. Still, though technology is in a sense submerged, it is an area that calls for occasional scrutiny because of its impact on the economy and popular culture.

Organized Groups There are few historical situations that can be understood without careful consideration of the role that group interests have played in shaping the course of events. We use "interests" here in a broad sense and include in it all of the following: organized political parties, such as Republican, Democratic, Populist, Tory, Socialist, Communist, and others; shades of political opinion within parties—liberal, centrist, conservative; pressure groups of all kinds (religious, economic, environmental, political, educational, etc.); lobbying organizations; little cabals like "kitchen cabinets" or "the gang in the back room"; government bureaucracies; legislative bodies; commissions; and many, many others.

The variety of organizations and groups listed above suggests a frightening complexity to human affairs. Fortunately, in most historical situations only a few such groups play a significant role at a given time. The key to the whole business is for us to keep ever in mind David Potter's dictum that historians deal with human beings less as individuals than as groups—religious groups, cultural groups, ideological groups, interest groups, occupational groups, or social groups.[1] What this means in practice is that the historian must be acutely conscious of groups, and in research and

---

[1] David M. Potter, "The Historian's Use of Nationalism and Vice Versa," *American Historical Review*, 67 (July, 1962): 924.

reading see them as the focal points both of change and resistance to change. Put another way, human affairs should be viewed as an arena in which groups with differing interests band together or oppose one another to achieve their goals.

Some questions worth considering when addressing any historical situation are:

—What organized groups played an important role in the situation you are investigating?

—How well organized and how disciplined were each of the various groups that were involved in the situation? How committed was each group on the issues involved in *this* situation?

—Where did any given group stand in the "pecking order" of political, economic, and social prestige?

—How much political clout did each group have? How much access to the power centers? What methods did they utilize to achieve their ends?

Individuals in History

This is not the place to engage in the debate over whether "the individual makes the times" or "the times make the individual"—the "superman or any man" argument. Suffice to say that since human beings do act, their personalities, characters, and motives are of inevitable importance in influencing events. Henry VIII (1509–1547), for example, was a spendthrift, and his extravagant ways made England a difficult place in which to live, thus preparing the way for "the great historic going forth of the English people" to America and elsewhere. Woodrow Wilson (president, 1913–1921) was a man of such lofty moral principles that he found it impossible to compromise with more mundane souls over the issue of his "morally right" League of Nations. Did he thus help set the stage for World War II? Lyndon Johnson (president, 1963–1969) was devious enough perhaps to have engaged in questionable election practices in his native Texas, but he also was compassionate enough to have made an extensive civil rights program a reality in the mid-1960s. The point of these examples is to show that individuals—with their quirks, principles, virtues, and vices—do affect the course of events.

Concerning the man or woman who was at or near the center of a historical situation, these are some of the questions you might want to ask:

—What aspects of his or her personality were dominant?

—To what and to whom were key individuals loyal?

—Did temperamental factors enter into his or her choice of action?

—How was the individual reflected in his or her policies?

—What qualities of leadership did the individual conspicuously display or lack?

—What were his or her relations with other major figures, and how much did their support (or nonsupport) influence matters?

We cannot list all possible questions here, but we can indicate the kinds of questions you might ask concerning individual actors in the historical drama.

Long-standing Legal, Customary, and Diplomatic Conditions

In a sense this category overlaps each of those preceding it, but it deserves to be treated independently. To understand fully any historical event we must not only look at the influence of groups, ideas, individuals, etc., we must consider the basic "rules of the game" that serve as a permanent backdrop to all human dramas. This is an admittedly foggy category, but it refers to all those habitual and relatively consistent patterns of behavior which most of us take for granted in our day-to-day lives. These patterned responses, sometimes based on formal law and sometimes on custom or social convention, do affect the course of events and must be taken into account by the historian. The laws, institutions, traditions, diplomatic ties, and social customs of a people live beyond the events of the moment or even the lives of individuals. These things do change, of course, but (periods of revolution excepted) not quickly. Most historical situations are, to a greater or lesser degree, influenced by the weight of legal and behavioral tradition. As William Faulkner said in *Absalom, Absalom!* "the past is never dead, it's not even past." Two examples might make this clearer.

The historian who is trying to write the history of a given presidential election, say the Reagan vs. Carter election of 1980, will certainly ask the first four "macro" questions: what was the role played by key individuals and groups, and by economic and ideological factors? To answer those questions our imaginary historian will also have to know, at minimum, something about the laws that govern the nominating process and the election and the traditional voting behavior of various ethnic, religious, regional, and professional groups. Our intrepid historian will also have to know something about the intangible and unwritten "rules" that set limits as to how candidates can and cannot behave. For example, there is no law that says a male candidate must wear a suit and tie while campaigning, but they all do. (When was the last time you saw a presidential candidate make a speech wearing levis and a sweater?)

Sometimes habitual behavior patterns become so entrenched that they frustrate the best attempts of individuals and groups to initiate change. Such behavioral inertia is a characteristic of many large bureaucracies. For instance, beginning in the early 1920s Soviet leaders had serious problems in directing the large-scale collectivization of Russian industry and agriculture. Soviet leader V. I. Lenin complained five years after the Revolution that though he had in place a "vast army of governmental employees," he lacked any real control over them, and that "down below . . . the bureaucrats function in such a way as to counteract our measures."[2] More than thirty years later, Soviet Premier Nikita Khrushchev similarly lamented bureaucratic obstructionism: "It is very difficult indeed to carry through specialization and cooperation in production where there are so many ministries and departments, because the departmental interests of the numerous ministries and central boards raise obstacles in the way."[3]

Use of these five categories will give assurance that you asked the im-

---

[2] Merle Fainsod, "The Pervasiveness of Soviet Controls," in Michael Dalby and Michael Werthman, *Bureaucracy in Historical Perspective* (Glenview: Scott Foresman, and Co., 1971), p. 121.

[3] E. Strauss, "Varieties of Bureaucratic Control," in *Ibid.*, p. 86.

portant questions. Still, we hasten to add that there are situations where other categories enter into the picture, and you must be ready to identify them and pursue them if necessary. For example, in many historical situations demographic (i.e., population), environmental, or geographic factors play a central role. It is impossible to understand English foreign policy, for example, unless one takes into account the fact that England is an island. The greatest catastrophe in European history, the Black Death epidemic of the fourteenth century, is inexplicable without close study of the environmental situation. Geographic and environmental factors also have a direct impact on a region's economy.

One of the difficulties in explaining historical events is that each of them is more or less unique. Lurking in the background surrounding each event are the various "macro" factors already discussed, but they are present in varying proportions in each case, some strong, some weak, some nonexistent. Yet, while these factors have a major background importance, in many historical situations specific unforeseen events decisively affect the situation. These "micro" factors divert attention away from the larger forces, bringing a shift from a wide-angled view to a close-in focus on some very specific events.

As examples, consider the following: 1) The assassination of the Austro-Hungarian crown prince at Sarajevo in 1914 provoked his government into a harsh line against Serbia, thus setting into motion a chain of countermeasures that soon brought the onset of World War I. 2) The news that Democratic candidate Grover Cleveland had fathered a bastard child changed the tone of the presidential election of 1884. 3) On D-Day, June 6, 1944, when Allied forces assaulted the Normandy beaches, Germany's most skillful field commander, General Erwin Rommel, was back in Germany visiting his family. His absence from the scene of operations almost surely contributed to the Allied success in establishing a beachhead on that vital day. 4) Media emphasis on the Iranian hostage crisis contributed in a major way to Jimmy Carter's defeat in the presidential election of 1980.

Other particular and unpredictable events can change the course of history: the delivery of an effective speech; a sudden illness; a badly handled press conference; the murder of the French politician Marat in 1793; the Boston Tea Party; the sinking of the battleship Maine in 1898; the breaking of the German code during World War II. Such events can change a historical situation and push the "macro" forces into the background, though not eliminate them entirely. Chance events are like "wild cards" in a poker hand, decisively changing its value and thus affecting the outcome of the game.

Engaging in historical inquiry is like peeling an onion. It must be done from the outside, with each layer separately removed (each of the "starter" questions separately asked). As we get closer to the onion's center we sometimes get to layers we can't at first name—in history these are known as "special" or "chance" factors. Since those special factors are so close to the heart of the onion (the historical occurrence), they must be carefully studied, even though, strictly speaking, they may not be classifiable under one of the major headings given in this chapter.

For all of the "macro" influences we have given you a set of starter questions you might ask. Unfortunately the same cannot be done for the "micro" side. Far too many variables exist in human affairs to list all the potentially useful questions you might ask. All we can do is emphasize that "macro" questions will carry you a long way toward understanding any historical situation, but that the deepest understanding often requires special attention to developments that are unique to the event you are studying.

Questions and the Historian's Frame of Reference

Earlier in this chapter we said that historians often choose to explore in depth only one or two of the possible subcategories of history. They may ask exclusively economic questions or emphasize the life and influence of a single individual. If all the questions we have discussed are important, how can this narrowing of focus be justified?

Sometimes the concentration on one or two questions is warranted by the character of the event or events under investigation. It is certainly understandable why a historian of the early years of the industrial revolution might ask predominantly economic questions or why a commentator on an election would concentrate on politics.

Something more is at work here, however. Questions are not determined only by the nature of the events being studied, but by the *frame of reference* of the investigators themselves. Historians (obviously) choose subjects and ask questions that *interest* them. They are not impersonal automatons programmed to investigate every relevant aspect of a topic, whether of interest to them or not. Such choices reflect the values and attitudes of the historian—the "frame of reference."

"Frame of reference" refers to a person's assumptions about the world: ideas about the relation of cause and effect, economic theories and political loyalties, values and biases, views of human nature, etc. In their totality these and other attitudes represent an individual's "working model" of how things tend to happen. These elements are always in the background of a person's mind and come forward whenever various intellectual inquiry is undertaken.

In practice a frame of reference inclines you to ask certain questions or to make certain tentative hypotheses. For example, many nineteenth-century capitalists, seeing slum poverty, would have interpreted the squalor as evidence of lack of character among the poor. A radical socialist in the same era would have interpeted the slum poverty as yet another instance of capitalist oppression. Each interpreted reality according to his or her own frame of reference or value system.

Consider, for a moment two brief news stories based on the same (imaginary) basketball game.

> New Litchfield (AP)—Walt Morner scored 22 points and Greg Mitchell added 21 as New Litchfield held off a frantic second-half comeback attempt to edge Sargasso University 72–70 in a game here Wednesday night.
>
> After falling behind 17–5, the eventual victors went on a 16–2 tear to grab a 21–19 lead with 12:17 left in the first half. But Sargasso fought back to tie at 32–32 at the buzzer. In the second half Sargasso lost one player to fouls and another to an ankle injury, allowing New Litchfield to hang on for the win.

Or, another version:

> New Litchfield (AP)—Coaching isn't everything in the game of basketball, but its importance was again highlighted Wednesday night as New Litchfield edged Sargasso University 72–70. Cougar coach Shorty Howard employed a 2–3 zone that closed down Sargasso's vaunted inside game. At the other end of the floor the Cougars employed the familiar Howard style of waiting for defensive mistakes to give them close-in shots. Clearly, the Cougar's coach won this particular battle of wits.

Obviously there are similarities between the two sport stories—both give essential facts such as place, time, score, teams involved, and important individuals. But the difference between them is striking: the first account attributes the victory to factors related to the availability of key players; the second focuses almost exclusively on the contribution of New Litchfield's coach.

The stories show how important an author's frame of reference is when explaining a past event. Both writers saw the same game, but *explained* the outcome in a very different way. Both perhaps asked some of the same questions of the event: What role did the referees play? Did the crowd affect the outcome? Which players made significant contributions? Who did the best job of coaching? In the end, each writer chose to emphasize one set of factors over the others. Since both watched and analyzed the same game, we can assume that the differences arose out of something they did *not* have in common: their individual frames of reference. It was the same game, to be sure, but they "saw" it differently.

Put another way, each story indirectly reflects a large number of unstated assumptions. For example, in the second story, the writer's central thesis— the game was a coaching victory—is plausible, but debatable, being based on certain assumptions and inferences. The writer assumes that 1) basketball teams follow their coach's orders, 2) the referees were impartial, 3) the losing coach had developed an intelligent strategy, 4) the players on the losing team played up to par, 5) the crowd was not a vital factor, and 6) coaching strategy is an important factor. Any real student of basketball knows that the writer could be wrong in at least some of these assumptions. Another sports writer might headline the story with something like "Sargasso Five Snores Through Yet Another Loss." All this is said *not* to discredit the "coach thesis," but only to recognize it for what it is: a perception based on that writer's frame of reference, or to put it another way, a construction based on facts but held together by the historian's assumptions—the frame of reference.

Our message here is to avoid making judgments simply because they are compatible with your values. You should realize, however, that no work of history can be entirely free from the influence of the author's values and beliefs. That historians choose to specialize in the study of different times and places, and ask distinctly different questions of the pasts they study, is evidence of this fact.

Finally, once you become aware that all writing reflects, to a greater or lesser degree, the writer's frame of reference, you can learn to avoid being imprisoned by your own. In fact, we would argue that education often aims at the progressive enlargement and refinement of one's frame of reference. Certainly such is the case with the discipline of history. Training in historical thinking is specifically directed toward enlarging your working model of how human societies typically function and hence refining your ability to "ask the right question."

EXERCISES

Set A, Exercise 1: Questions

The following exercise is intended to deepen your awareness of the variety of factors that can enter into a historical situation. The excerpt below ranges across many of the categories we have discussed, showing that the historian who wrote it asked many of the questions we have emphasized in this chapter. Your task is *not* to try to identify "causes," but only to note the factors that somehow helped shape the situation, at least in this historian's view. Read the passage and then respond to the questions that follow. (As you read be alert for evidence of the influence of ideas, economic factors, group action, important individuals, and entrenched behavior patterns—legal, customary, diplomatic.)

This excerpt (from Robert Kelley, *The Shaping of the American Past*, © 1975, pp. 665–666) deals with President Woodrow Wilson's policy towards Mexico in 1913–1914. Reprinted by permission of Prentice-Hall, Inc., Englewood Cliffs, New Jersey.

Much graver events were underway in Mexico. A dictator named Porfirio Diaz had ruled the country since the 1870s. As iron-fisted executive who kept relative peace and good order, he welcomed American investment. By 1910 American railroad and mining engineers had flooded into the country to build transportation lines and open up natural resources. American cattlemen and agriculturalists had huge land holdings, and United States businessmen carried on much of Mexico's trade. Such men supported Diaz, for he created the conditions in which more than a billion American dollars was invested in Mexico by 1910, and some 40,000 American citizens could live there in safety and profit. In 1911, however, a liberal revolution led by Francisco Madero took over the country, calling for genuine representative government, widespread social reforms, and a curbing of foreign investment. American businessmen were hostile to Madero, and the American ambassador, Henry Lane Wilson, shared their sentiments. With his aid, one of the victorious generals in the rebellion, Victoriano Huerta, was able to overthrow Madero, who was then promptly murdered, apparently at Huerta's instigation.

This was the situation when Woodrow Wilson took office. Huerta had seized power only weeks before Wilson's inauguration. The contrast between the two regimes could hardly be more dramatic. Wilson was immediately besieged with advice from businessmen and bankers, including his own ambassador in Mexico City, that he extend diplomatic recognition to Huerta. This, after all, was standard practice. Nations did not then sit in judgment on each other, at least in the daily conduct of foreign relations. If a new government had de facto power—was in reality the effective government of a country—then it would be recognized: ambassadors would be exchanged; consuls established in various cities to ease trade relations; and all commercial interactions regularized.

But Wilson broke with this immemorial practice. He was deeply offended by the bloody-handed Huerta and hardly allowed the man's name to be uttered in the White House. The Mexican regime, in Wilson's words, was a "government of butchers," and he would have nothing to do with it that even remotely implied moral acceptance. The State Department was staffed with people of the old diplomacy, and they were shocked at Wilson's new approach. They could understand the use of high-handed diplomacy in order to open markets and protect American property, but the same tactics adopted to reform the government of another nation seemed inconceivable. Wilson relied, therefore, on nondiplomats to carry out his policies. William Jennings Bryan was his secretary of state, and that doughty reformer knew practically nothing of foreign affairs and certainly little of Mexico. Then Wilson chose another nondiplomat, John Lind, a former governor of Minnesota, to do nothing less than persuade Huerta to stand aside, allow free elections, and declare that he was not a candidate for the presidency. This proposal was, of course, indignantly rejected.

So far as historians are aware, most of the Mexican people despised Huerta, but they too reacted angrily at Wilson's efforts to change their government. Whatever their problems, they wished to settle them among themselves, without the indignity of intervention by a moralistic, preaching *Norteamericano* (the term uniformly preferred in Latin America for citizens of the United States, *American* carrying the implication that only those living north of the Rio Grande can be so named). Whatever the "Colossus of the North" does in Latin America is necessarily regarded with distrust, just as Scots distrust their larger neighbor, England, and Danes react against everything German.

Questions   Indicate in the spaces provided in what way any of the following were involved in the situation. In each instance note the appropriate paragraph number(s). If you feel a given element was not present, write "none."

1. Ideas:

New Ideas: _____

_____

Entrenched Ideas: _____

_____

2. Economic Factors:

Economic Goals Sought: _____

_____

Established Trade Patterns: _____

_____

Concerns of Entrenched Economic Interests: _____

_____

3. Organized Groups:

Groups Actively Pursuing Interests: _____

_____

Activity by Established Bureaucracy: _____

_____

4. Individuals:

Individuals Playing Major Role: _____

_____

Evidence of Individual's Distinctive Conception of Role:

_____

_____

Evidence of Personality Traits Influencing Situation:

_____

_____

_____

5. "Rules of the Game:" (i.e., long-standing legal, customary, diplomatic practices and situations)

_____

_____

_____

Set A, Exercise 2: The Historian's Frame of Reference

In the final segment of this chapter we discussed how a frame of reference can shape a historian's explanation of an event. Remember, frame of reference influences the questions historians ask as well as the elements of a historical situation they choose to emphasize in their writings.

Each of the passages below tries to explain the governmental corruption during President Ulysses S. Grant's administrations of 1869–1877. And each explanation emphasizes the importance of one (possibly two) of the following variables at the expense of the others: ideas, economic or business factors, Grant's individual personality traits, the "rules of the game" (in this case primarily political "rules"). Read each passage, then in the spaces provided classify the author's frame of reference according to whether he emphasizes 1) ideological factors, 2) economic/business factors, 3) elements of the political system (rules of the game), or 4) individual traits as most responsible for the corruption under Grant. Briefly explain your choice(s). In some cases more than one orientation might be present.

1. No President before 1869 had been so unqualified for office as was
    Ulysses S. Grant—a man who had no experience in politics, no capacity
    for absorbing such experience, no sensitivity for statescraft, and little
    judgment about men. Grant had impeccable personal integrity. He had
    as a soldier displayed the qualities of leadership and fortitude that won
    him deserved glory. He had, as his enemies in battle had learned, in-
    comparable courage. But as a public servant Grant was a fool and a
    failure. He appointed an undistinguished Cabinet, of which several
    members were knaves who duped him shamelessly. He found most mat-
    ters of public policy utterly bewildering. He did not himself generate
    the gross and greedy spirit of the time, but a stronger and wiser man
    would have yielded less readily than Grant to its rapacious temper.
    Truly pathetic in his inadequacies, he was also singularly obtuse about
    his choice of friends. He accepted expensive gifts from favor-hunters;
    he received personal loans from Jay Cooke, whose Northern Pacific
    Railroad was seeking federal subsidies; he welcomed the company of
    Jim Fisk, a conscienceless gambler in stocks. (John M. Blum, et al., *The
    National Experience* [1977])

Orientation: _____

Basis: _____

2. One of the many ironies in the reconstruction story is that some of the
    radical Republicans took the first steps toward destroying the political
    alliances on which the Republican political position in the South de-
    pended. During the first Grant administration a new set of leaders won
    a dominant position in the presidential circle. These were men who
    were most responsive to the economic pressures created by the cyclonic
    growth of American capitalism after the Civil War. They helped to make
    Congress, the state legislatures, and state political machines the willing
    collaborators of railroad, oil, textile, and steel interests that wanted gov-
    ernment favors. The older crusading radicals found this new Republican
    leadership appalling, particularly as evidence of corruption began to
    come to light. "Like all parties that have an undisturbed power for a
    long time," wrote Senator James Grimes of Iowa, "(the Republican
    Party) has become corrupt, and I believe it is today the most corrupt
    and debauched political party that has ever existed." (Edwin C. Roz-
    wenc, *The Making of American Society* [1973])

Orientation: _____

Basis: _____

3. But even the most determined presidential effort could not have imme-
    diately tamed the spoils system. The sheer numbers, combined with the
    cost of maintaining party machinery, led to the development of a system
    which obliged party workers to pay fees for appointments, or incum-
    bent officeholders were taxed an annual assessment on their salaries. Of-
    ficeholders, well aware that their tenure was impermanent, unsurpris-
    ingly took it for granted that they were to milk the post for all it was
    worth. The result was inescapably a pervasive corruption. Efforts to
    control the system, as more than one president swiftly discovered, ran
    afoul of the congressional presumption that spoils were its peculiar pre-

rogative—a presumption which if defied was promptly sustained by congressional refusals to support executive proposals. (J. P. Shenton, et al., *U.S. History Since 1865* [1975])

Orientation: _____

Basis: _____

4.   Profiteering, dishonesty, and political corruption neither began nor ended with Ulysses S. Grant; scandal had been disturbingly constant in American political life. But during the Grant era no one seemed to mind. For a time Americans shrugged their shoulders at corruption, apparently figuring that the self-made politician compromised himself no more than the self-made industrialist, who made a fortune and became a folk hero. Even when the politician and the industrialist joined forces, the popular reaction seemed more often envy than disgust. (Henry F. Bedford, et al., *The Americans: A Brief History* [1976])

Orientation: _____

Basis: _____

5.   Men like Blaine and Conkling remained the party's most influential national spokesmen throughout the period. They largely shaped national legislation during the era. Since they were Republicans, they believed in an effective and energetic national economic policy. In general, the purpose of this policy was to encourage industrial expansion. For this they were often criticized by Democratic politicans who retained their party's traditional faith. This Democratic faith rested on the belief that government should not meddle actively in the economic lives of Americans.

    But the Republican Party, founded in an era when the national government had to expand its powers to preserve the Union, saw nothing wrong with continuing this trend at the war's end. To encourage economic development, party leaders aided business in every possible way. In accomplishing this purpose, they forged an informal alliance between the national government and the great majority of businessmen—bankers, industrialists, and merchants in foreign trade. While this alliance did further economic growth, it had other less fortunate consequences as well. It gave the era a reputation for corruption unparalleled in American history until then. (Allen Weinstein, et al. *Freedom and Crisis* [1974])

Orientation: _____

Basis: _____

6.   During Grant's two terms as President, the word "politician" became synonymous with double-talking and self-serving. The corruption in Washington, and elsewhere in the country, was the result of a lowering in the moral tone of the nation during and after the Civil War. Immense fortunes in industry had been made during the war. Wealth was worshipped, and material display became a passion. Few politicians could resist the bribes for favors which businessmen dispensed freely. Grant was not responsible for this general moral laxity, but by his in-

fatuation with business success and his negligence in office he allowed it to flourish. The early idealism of the Republican Party was smothered in this atmosphere of materialism. In fact, both major parties became agencies for obtaining and dispensing the spoils of office. (Rebecca Brooks Gruver, *An American History* [1976])

Orientation: _____

Basis: _____

Sources
1. John M. Blum, Bruce Catton, et. al., *The National Experience* (New York: Harcourt Brace Jovanovich, 1977), p. 369.
2. Edwin C. Rozwenc, *The Making of American Society*, Vol. II (Boston: Allyn and Bacon, 1973), p. 596.
3. J. P. Shenton and Alan M. Meckler, *U.S. History Since 1865* (Homewood, Ill.: Learning Systems Co., 1975), p. 16.
4. Henry F. Bedford and Trevor Colbourn, *The Americans: A Brief History*, 2nd ed., (New York: Harcourt Brace Jovanovich, 1976), p. 288.
5. Allen Weinstein and R. Jackson Wilson, *Freedom and Crisis* (New York: Random House, 1974), p. 532.
6. Rebecca Gruver, *An American History* (Reading, Mass.: Addison-Wesley, 1978), p. 600.

Set B, Exercise 1: Questions

The following exercise is intended to deepen your awareness of the variety of factors that can enter into a historical situation. The excerpt below ranges across many of the categories we have discussed, showing that the historian who wrote it asked many of the questions we have emphasized in this chapter. Your task is *not* to try to identify "causes," but only to note the factors that somehow helped shape the situation, at least in this historian's view. Read the passage and then respond to the questions that follow. (As you read be alert for evidence of the influence of ideas, economic factors, group action, important individuals, and entrenched behavior patterns—legal, customary, diplomatic.)

This excerpt (from Robert Kelley, *The Shaping of the American Past*, © 1975, pp. 624–626) deals with President Theodore Roosevelt's labor policies during the 1902–1907 period. Reprinted by permission of Prentice-Hall, Inc., Englewood Cliffs, New Jersey.

[President Theodore] Roosevelt had a complicated relationship with the labor movement. Fundamentally, he was on the side of the employer, who was, after all, the man on the top. But as a compassionate person, the president had long been disturbed by the conditions in which workers, especially women and children, labored. Furthermore, he looked on big unions as he did on big business—as a natural and valuable evolutionary growth that brought order and efficiency to the system. Workers had economic interests: they should be allowed to organize to achieve them.

In 1902 Roosevelt intervened spectacularly in a crucial labor-management dispute. The coal miners in Pennsylvania's anthracite region, under the leadership of the United Mine Workers and its chieftain, John Mitchell, a careful and cautious tactician, went on strike. The miners' hours were long, a rising cost of living pressed them cruelly, and their work was extremely dangerous. But the owners, primarily controllers of the six railroads that crossed the region, arrogantly refused even to talk to the workers.

As the months passed, Roosevelt fumed. Always frightened of the possibility of social revolution, he regarded the coal operators as the kind of businessmen who, by their selfishness, would destroy the country. Panic buying pushed the cost of coal sky-high; in the fall of 1902 schools began closing for lack of fuel. Finally, in October, the president, who lacked any legal powers whatever to intervene in the strike, succeeded in bringing both the operators and the union men to the White House for a conference. The operators protested against being made to "deal with outlaws" and elaborately pretended that John Mitchell was not even present. When the president asked them to arbitrate, they absolutely refused. Thoroughly angered after the conference concluded, Roosevelt decided to send thousands of federal troops to take over the mines, dispossess the operators, and produce coal. Conservative senators, getting wind of the plan, immediately brought heavy pressure on the operators to relent. The president's threatened plan, they believed, would be a long step toward socialism. A public commission of investigation was agreed to, production began again, and eventually the miners were given an approximate ten-percent increase in pay. Organized labor looked in gratitude to the president, for he was the first chief executive ever to have taken their side. . . .

Even so, labor regarded "marvelous Teddy" warily. Sometimes they gave him warm and enthusiastic support as their first friend in the White House; but they never felt wholly comfortable with him, for his attitudes were still those of an upper-class patrician. Besides, he was a Republican, and in these tumultuous years of constant labor-management disputes, it seemed to workers that the employer was always a Republican. Roosevelt might warm their hearts, but when it came to elections they often turned to the Democrats. Whatever Roosevelt did, the core of the labor movement was still composed of ethnic minorities, and most of them found the Republicans still too much the party of nativism and Anglo-Saxon Protestantism for them to support it.

In the middle of his second term, a curious thing happened to Theodore Roosevelt. The man who deplored radicals now became one himself. Why? Partly because he noted the rising tide of progressivism throughout the country. Moreover, he was highly praised by progressives, while being violently attacked by conservative Republicans. His reforms, limited as they were, had aroused hysterical criticism. A president aiding labor, meddling with business, talking constantly of reform? To many Americans, the spectacle was a monstrous, frightening departure from everything formerly known. Senator Joseph B. Foraker, a Republican from Ohio, led a bitter attack on Roosevelt as a president leading the nation to socialism.

Ever the man of pride, Roosevelt exploded. He issued a string of spectacular statements attacking great fortunes as "needless and useless" and his Wall Street opponents as sordid plutocrats. When a severe financial panic struck the country in 1907, and Roosevelt's attacks on corporate greed were bitterly blamed for it, the president refused to give in. He accused "certain malefactors of great wealth" of making the panic worse "in order to discredit the policy of the government." No matter, he cried—his massive arms waving, his face contorted—he would continue his struggle aginst "speculation, corruption, and fraud."

The president fired off a surprisingly radical message to Congress in December 1907 calling for inheritance and income taxes, national regulation of corporations, limitation on labor injunctions, compulsory investigation of large disputes, expansion of the eight-hour workday, and workmen's compensation. Shortly afterward came another message calling for federal regulation of the stock markets, where, he said, the most flagrant and unconscionable gambling was going on. It was "predatory wealth . . . the wealth accumulated on a giant scale by all forms of iniquity, ranging from the oppression of wage workers to unfair and unwholesome methods of crushing out competition, and to defrauding the public by stock jobbing and the manipulation of securities," that blocked his program.

The Republicans sat stonily in Congress while these radical words were read, but the delighted Bryan Democrats sent up volleys of applause. The *New York Times* said that Roosevelt's "delusions . . . would ordinarily be commended to the attention of a psychiatrist," but most of the country cheered. Progressive Republican newspapers joined Democratic organs in praising Roosevelt's message as one of the "really memorable state papers in the history of the nation."

Nothing concrete came of it, for conservatives still controlled Congress. But the irrepressible Roosevelt had opened the way for the future. By the time he left the White House, the country had finally been thoroughly aroused to the cause of progressive reform, and in his last radical utterances he laid out the agenda for that reform.

Questions Indicate in the spaces provided in what way any of the following were involved in the situation. In each instance note the appropriate paragraph number(s). If you feel a given factor was not present, write "none."

1. Ideas:

New Ideas: _____

_____

Entrenched Ideas: _____

_____

Threatening Ideas: _____

_____

Impact of Public Opinion: _____

_____

2. Economic Factors:

Economic Goals Sought: _____

_____

Actions of Entrenched Economic Interests: _____

_____

Class Conflicts: _____

_____

3. Organized Groups:

Groups Actively Pursuing Interests: _____

_____

Consumer Interests Involved: _____

_____

Strongly Entrenched Group: _____

_____

Group Gaining in Prestige: _____

_____

4. Individuals:

Individuals Playing Major Role: _____

_____

Evidence of Individual's Distinctive Conception of Role:

_____

_____

Evidence of Personality Traits Influencing Situation:

_____

_____

5. "Rules of the Game:" (i.e., long-standing legal, customary, diplomatic practices and situations)

_____

_____

_____

Set B, Exercise 2: The Historian's Frame of Reference

In the final segment of this chapter we discussed how a frame of reference can shape a historian's explanation of an event. Remember, frame of reference influences the questions historians ask as well as the elements of a historical situation they choose to emphasize in their writings.

Each of the passages below tries to explain why the Versailles Treaty (1919), which ended World War I and provided for the establishment of a League of Nations, failed ratification in the United States Senate. Each explanation emphasizes the importance of one (possibly two) of the following variables at the expense of the others: ideas/ideology, the political interests of organized groups, individual personality characteristics. Read each passage, then in the spaces provided classify the author's frame of reference according to whether he emphasizes the importance of 1) ideological factors, 2) group political activity, or 3) individual personality traits. Briefly explain your choice(s). In some cases more than one orientation might be present.

1.   The leading opponent of the League of Nations in the Senate was Henry Cabot Lodge, a prominent Republican who was a lifelong friend of Theodore Roosevelt's. It has often been said that Lodge defeated the treaty. That is assuming a great deal. Mr. Lodge was not a big enough man to defeat anything that had a popular following. . . . The anonymous authors of *The Mirrors of Washington* wrote of him that he "always creates the impression that it is a condescension on his part to God to have allowed Him to create a world which is not exclusively possessed by the Cabots and the Lodges and their connections."

No; the League Covenant was defeated by the American people. Wilson realized that public opinion was opposed to his cherished measure. He thought the people were not informed clearly as to its purport, and he went on a long speaking tour for the purpose of instructing them.

He was already a sick man, and the cold reception that he encountered broke his heart. At Pueblo, Colorado, on September 26, 1919, he had a paralytic stroke from which he never recovered.

On March 19, 1920, the treaty was voted down in the Senate [for the final time]. (W. E. Woodward, *A New American History* [1937])

Orientation: _____

Basis: _____

2.   It [the League of Nations] was a useful proposal, but Wilson viewed it in terms of a mission so grand and all-encompassing, so noble in purpose, that no alteration was possible. Minor compromises would have secured ratification in the United States Senate of both the Peace Treaty and the League, and would not have weakened the League's chance to prove itself in the arena of world affairs. But Wilson was unable to compromise. In his mind the method had become totally identified with the goal; the League was world peace. . . .

Wilson's tragedy was that faced with one of the great decisions of his life, he failed to recognize that there is more than one road to Rome. He became a prophet, not a leader. It is a dangerous matter to take on one's shoulders the burden of saving mankind, and to assume that you alone have the key to salvation. . . .

[When] the Treaty came up for consideration in the Senate, he refused to give way, and without concessions from him the Treaty died. So did he, unrelenting, in 1924. (G. D. Lillibridge, *Images of American Society*, Vol. II [1976])

Orientation: _____

Basis: _____

3.   At first, the Treaty's chances looked good. Wilson's prestige was still great, and the idea of a League of Nations had long attracted American support. Yet the Treaty aroused many kinds of opposition. Among its enemies were the disappointed minorities of German, Italian, and Irish descent, isolationists who feared that the League would involve America

in European affairs, liberals who objected to the compromises of democratic principle, and, vaguer but crucially important, many Americans already reacting against wartime enthusiasm and sacrifice. . . .

In the long struggle, opposition to the Treaty was marshalled by Henry Cabot Lodge, an enemy of Wilson and a master tactician. In order to attract the crucial Reservationists, Lodge proposed not the rejection of the Treaty but its passage with a number of changes. These were carefully calculated to sound plausible, but to be unacceptable to Wilson. Lodge knew his opponent. Wilson forbade Democrats to accept the reservations, thus making impossible a two-thirds majority. (Charles Sellers and Henry May, *A Synopsis of American History* [1969])

Orientation: _____

Basis: _____

4.   The failure of Wilson's larger aims was an American, as well as a personal, tragedy. The characteristically American ideal of a world order transcending the anarchy of power had no chance without the participation of the United States. But Wilson's stubborn righteousness of purpose prevented American support for his peace settlement at the moment when crusading idealism was evaporating in a feverish search for peacetime normality. The American people had been exposed too briefly and too superficially to the threat against their continental security to assume the continuing duties which their austere President had assigned to them. Instead they withdrew into isolation. . . .

The man primarily responsible for scotching American membership of the League was Senator Henry Cabot Lodge. Lodge . . . represented those conservative nationalists who believed American interests best served, not by a moral crusade for a universal "collective security" but by the protection of American strategic interests, narrowly interpreted. In the mood of the 1920s conservative nationalism swung back from Roosevelt's interventionism to an isolationist phase from which it only reemerged after the attack on Pearl Harbor. (Frank Thistlethwaite, *The Great Experiment* [1955])

Orientation: _____

Basis: _____

5.   Wilson mistook his countrymen's flaming enthusiasm in World War I for an eagerness to accept international responsibility. He was not aware of the speed with which they were becoming indifferent to foreign affairs. The old American illusion about war—"The game's over, we've won, let's go home!"—had taken hold. . . . so Senator Henry Cabot Lodge of Massachusetts, the suave and powerful "scholar in politics," had no difficulty in martialing opposition to the League, this "evil thing with a holy name."

Lodge hated Wilson with an implacable hatred. Even though he personally favored a world organization, he wanted none bearing the Wilsonian stamp. So Lodge moved to block the treaty by hobbling it with reservations and hamstringing it with debate. . . .

When defeat of the League appeared imminent, he [Wilson] rejected advice to compromise with a fierce, "Let Lodge compromise! Better a thousand times to go down fighting than to dip your colors to dishonorable compromise."

This, from the same man who at the peace conference had made a religion of compromise. In the end the League did go down. On November 19, 1919, it was defeated in the Senate, and an attempt to rescue it the following year was also defeated. (Robert Leckie, *The Wars of America* [1968])

Orientation: _____

Basis: _____

6.   By 1919 Wilson's declining health . . . made him increasingly irrational, irritable, and temperamental. He handled the Senate particularly badly. Though he was aware that their two-thirds approval was vital for any treaty, he ignored them and did not consult with the powerful Foreign Relations Committee, perhaps because it was headed by a man he detested, Henry Cabot Lodge of Massachusetts. . . .

The treaty was delayed by the Senate, which added reservations about America's Monroe Doctrine rights in the Western Hemisphere, tariffs, immigration policy, and armaments. The 14 "Lodge Reservations" were on the whole reasonable. They may have been unnecessary if Wilson had troubled to consult with the Senate beforehand. Lodge was not a blind isolationist who wished to wreck the League. . . .

In fairness, President Wilson felt he had already compromised a great deal at Versailles. He ignored several political pointers, such as growing opposition to the League from particular American ethnic groups, not only German and Irish, but Italian-Americans, upset over the disposition of Fiume. The president was sick and out of touch with political realities. . . . Self-deluded, he told Senate Democrats to vote *against* the treaty in two votes of November 1919 and March 1920. They obeyed. (Peter d'A. Jones, *The U.S.A.* [1976])

Orientation: _____

Basis: _____

Sources   1. W. E. Woodward, *A New American History* (New York: Literary Guild, 1937), pp. 798–99.
2. G. D. Lillibridge, *Images of American Society*, Vol. II (Boston: Houghton Mifflin, 1976), p. 195.
3. Charles Sellers and Henry May, *A Synopsis of American History* (Chicago: Rand McNally, 1969), p. 317.
4. Frank Thistlethwaite, *The Great Experiment* (Cambridge: Cambridge Univ. Press, 1955), pp. 292–93.
5. Robert Leckie, *The Wars of America* (New York: Harper and Row, 1968), pp. 665–66.
6. Peter d'A. Jones, *The U.S.A.*, Vol. II (Homewood, Ill.: Dorsey Press, 1976), pp. 549–50.

CHAPTER 8

EVIDENCE

"The documents are liars."
　　　　　　　T. E. Lawrence

*"The central methodological problem for the
historian . . . is to know how to interrogate witnesses,
how to test evidence, how to assess the reliability
and the relevance of testimony."*
　　　　　　　　　　　　Robin Winks

The famous soldier-scholar, Lawrence of Arabia, once wrote a friend: "The documents are liars. No man ever yet tried to write down the entire truth of any action in which he has been engaged."[1] Lawrence exaggerated, but he certainly had a point. Not all documents are "liars," but neither do they always contain the whole truth. Whatever the imperfections, historical records and artifacts are the basic raw materials for even the simplest historical reconstruction. In this chapter we will consider the types of sources the historian uses to learn about the past and to write history. We will also examine some of the critical techniques used by the historian to evaluate and interpret the raw data of the past. We will, in short, consider how to examine evidence.

Surviving records are the only link to those countless past events that really happened but are irrevocably beyond our reach. The link provided by those records is as fragile as a gossamer web shimmering in the summer breeze. As we saw in Chapter 1, every surviving record is a number of times removed from the events it purports to discuss. Like the product of a multi-layered filtration system, historical records represent but a tiny fraction of the past that produced them (see Figure 1, p. 5). From the very large reservoir of human actions that constituted a given historical situation, only a small part was observed by those in a position to do so—the filter of *limited observation*. Of all the richness of detail that was observed by witnesses, only a relatively small part was remembered—the filter of *limited memory*. Of all that was remembered by witnesses, only a small portion was ever committed to writing—the filter of *limited recording*. And, of all that was recorded, only a miniscule fraction has survived to our own day—the filter of *limited survivability*. What remains of that huge reservoir that symbolizes the human past is the evidence upon which historians attempt to reconstruct the "truth" of human experience on this planet.

Surviving evidence (when compared to the totality of the past) is lamentably sketchy, scattered, and incomplete. Even this fact is not the least of the problem in unlocking the secrets of the past. Before any body of

---

[1] Jacques Barzun and Henry Graff, *The Modern Researcher*, rev. ed. (New York: Harcourt, Brace and World, 1970), p. 50.

evidence can be used constructively, it must be thoroughly sorted and sifted by the historian. Evidence is found in tangled bundles, with relevant and irrelevant information mixed like kernels of grain and their husks. Only a small part of the evidence will be relevant to the specific questions a historian may be investigating, and it is the historian who must separate the wheat from the chaff.

The Sources: Primary and Secondary

The problem of weighing evidence is never an easy one, but the difficulty can be eased by an appreciation of the various types of sources historians rely upon in their work. There are two basic categories of sources used by students of history, whether beginners or seasoned professionals.

Primary sources (also called original sources) are those materials that were written or created during the period under investigation. Primary sources are those documents or artifacts produced by the eyewitnesses of, or participants in, the events the historian is attempting to reconstruct. Primary sources, in short, are the records that make the study of history possible: letters, reports, diaries, government records, parish registers, newspapers, business ledgers, works of art, buildings, and a host of others. These are the sources the historian uses to create an account or interpretation of the past (our definition of history in this book).

Secondary sources are the accounts written by historians. Secondary sources are works of reconstruction and interpretation based on the primary sources. Secondary sources transform the raw data contained in primary sources into coherent accounts of past events. They also attempt to explain *how and why* events happened as they did—that is, provide an *interpretation* of evidence which, by itself, is mute. Most simply, secondary sources are the books, articles, and essays through which we learn most of the history we know.[2]

The distinction between primary and secondary sources is not always as clear as the above definition implies. For instance, a newspaper is definitely a primary source for the period in which it was published, but a newspaper also has many of the characteristics of a secondary source. Rarely, for example, is a journalist an eyewitness to the events written about. Consequently, the journalist (a historian of sorts) constructs a narrative based on primary sources—documents and eyewitness testimony. Another "hybrid" source is the personal memoir written by the retired politician, military officer, or movie star. Such a memoir (or autobiography) is certainly a primary source in that the author is writing an account of events he or she participated in or observed. However, memoirs display many of the char-

---

[2] Textbooks and similar works represent a special category of "tertiary" sources. Most general survey texts are not based on research into primary sources so much as they reflect the findings of a wide variety of secondary sources—that is, other history books. An author who attempted to cover the history of Western Civilization from 1500 to the present could not in a lifetime read all the primary sources necessary to discuss such a long and complex period. Such an author must, therefore, rely on the researches of other scholars (i.e., on secondary sources). Thus textbooks are a step or two further removed from the original sources than are most secondary works.

acteristics of secondary sources. Memoir writers often use public and private records, diaries, tape recordings, and letters—a variety of primary sources—to jog their memory or to give substance to their version of events. To the extent they must rely on such documents, their accounts will be "secondary" in nature.

To confuse the matter further, many sources can be categorized either as primary or secondary *depending on the subject being studied*. For instance, Henry Kissinger, National Security Advisor and then Secretary of State under President Richard Nixon, wrote (before entering government service) a study of European diplomacy during and after the Congress of Vienna (1815). This book, *A World Restored*, is a *secondary source* for someone studying the diplomatic history of Europe between 1812 and 1822. But it is a *primary source* for anyone who desires to understand Henry Kissinger's ideas on international relations. Thus, if the Congress of Vienna is the subject, Kissinger's book is a secondary source: if Henry Kissinger himself is the subject, it is a primary source.

Finally, a note of caution: Many primary sources have been published in book form. In spite of the resemblance in form to secondary sources, these materials remain primary. Remember, the basic question to ask is *when the materials originated*, not when they were published or reprinted. The Constitution of the United States and the Declaration of Independence printed in a textbook are still primary sources for the revolutionary period of American history, even though the textbook itself is not.

Using Primary Sources[3]

Without primary sources history as a discipline could not exist. Yet primary sources are notoriously fickle, and coaxing the truth from them can be a frustrating task. For some eras there are too few primary sources (the Medieval period in Europe is a good example); for others (e.g., our own century) there are far too many for any one individual to master. The sources can be seductive or coldly aloof. They can mislead, lie, or lure you into a false sense of security. They can be written in the obscure languages of the ancients or the incomprehensible jargon of the modern bureaucrat. They can lead the researcher into blind alleys, false turns, and dead ends. For all the frustrations, however, unlocking the secrets of the records of the past can be an immensely satisfying task. The historian is a detective; the primary sources are the clues.

The variety of potential primary source materials is immense. Clearly, the largest category of primary sources is made up of many types of *written material*—i.e., literary or documentary evidence. In fact, even though human beings have been a recognizable species for tens of thousands of years, historians have typically limited themselves to the study of societies for which we have written records. (The study of preliterate, or "prehistoric" cultures and societies is the domain of cultural anthropologists and archeologists.) Not all primary sources, however, are in written form. Remember our definition: A primary source is one that came into existence during the period that the historian is studying. From this perspective, just about anything that survives is fair game for the historical detective—buildings,

---

[3] Techniques for reading and analyzing secondary sources were discussed in Chapter 4.

tools, works of art, weapons, coins, and, more recently, films, tapes, and records.

Peruse the list below and see if you can identify those items that could be used by the historian as a primary source.

Inscriptions	Works of art
Buildings	Baptismal and burial records
Coins	Newspapers
Royal Charters	Magazines
Tapes of TV shows	Mystery novels
Laws	Autobiographies/Memoirs
Government publications	Legislative debates
Diplomatic dispatches	Maps
Court records	Poetry
Police reports	Films
Advertisements	Your parents
Minutes of organizations	Photographs
Private letters	Folk songs
Diaries	Language
Business records	Furniture
Railroad schedules	Telephone books

A brief glance should convince you that *every* item on the list is a potential primary source. And the list is far from complete, for *anything* that survives (including your aunt Matilda) is a primary source. At first it might seem strange to categorize folk songs as primary sources. But songs, poems, and stories that pass from generation to generation (even if never written down) still originated sometime in the past. In spite of changes in form and content over the years, they can still tell the historian something about that past time. Alex Haley, author of the 1977 best seller *Roots*, learned a good deal about the history of his family from such orally transmitted stories.

Even though objects and artifacts of all kinds are potential primary sources, *written evidence* is still the traditional lifeblood of most historical scholarship. If, however, you look only at the categories of documentary evidence in our list of sources, you will realize quickly that not all types of written evidence are equally "primary." That is, some types of primary evidence are less useful and less trustworthy than others. Newspaper accounts, as mentioned before, are frequently not written by eyewitnesses or participants but by journalists (really contemporary historians) who piece together stories from many sources. Such stories are further removed from the events they describe than other forms of written evidence. Accuracy, moreover, can be further compromised by deadline pressures. In the same category are memoirs and autobiographies. Much like secondary sources, they are typically written years after the events they describe, and they are subject to distortions resulting from the failing memory, personal interpretation of events, or vanity of the author.

Ideally, you should learn something about the strengths and weaknesses of each type of primary source. In practice, it is sufficient to master the important distinction between the "intentional record" and "unwitting testimony." Historian Arthur Marwick states, "Essentially the special expertise of the historian lies in examining and assessing the 'unwitting testimony' of the past."[4]

The researcher, according to Marwick, must become skilled at discovering things in the evidence that the original writers never intended—i.e., the "unwitting testimony." The researcher must ask of *all* evidence: "What is said here that is not *directly* said?" For instance, Renaissance merchants kept business records in order to keep track of their financial situation—their debtors and creditors. This was the original intent of the records. However, the historian doesn't really care if some Florentine wool merchant was solvent or not, but rather what can be learned from such records that the fifteenth-century merchants never intended to convey. The historian, in fact, can learn a great deal. These early ledgers might be used to study the evolution of modern banking and business techniques, to study the ups and downs of the Florentine economy, or to examine the ways in which certain segments of the population earned a living.

Another example: In their book *Salem Possessed* (Cambridge, Mass., 1974), historians Paul Boyer and Stephen Nissenbaum used (among other things) detailed town plans and income records of Salem Town and Salem Village (now Danvers), Massachusetts, to show how the Salem witch trials, in part, grew out of social, economic, and geographic divisions within the community. Boyer and Nissenbaum saw in these relatively sterile and uninteresting records things that the original record keepers had no intention of revealing. They milked unwitting testimony from documents created for dramatically different purposes.

Indeed, some of the most valuable insights into the human past are derived from such unwitting testimony—just as we can often learn more from a candid photo than a posed portrait (an "intentional" record). In Arthur Marwick's words, "a primary source is most valuable when the purpose for which it was compiled is at the furthest remove from the purpose of the historian."[5] The historian must be prepared to ask questions of the evidence that those who created the source never intended to answer. In a very real sense the good historian is a person who is adept at "reading between the lines."

The distinction between intentional record and unwitting testimony is even more important when dealing with actual narratives of one sort or another—letters, pamphlets, news stories, diaries, political speeches, memoirs, government press releases, and the like. In all of these cases the writer or writers are providing a specific *version* of events, and the historian has to be careful not to accept any such version uncritically. Much can be learned from these materials, but it is the information that the author never intended to provide (the unwitting testimony) that is often the most useful for the historian. For example, a political speech might or might not reveal what the candidate *really* believes concerning the issues of the day. It is a much better guide, at least in many cases, to what the candidate thinks will win the most votes. That is, the speech can (unwittingly) be a reliable guide

[4] See Arthur Marwick, *The Nature of History* (New York: Knopf, 1971), pp. 177–78.

[5] Marwick, *Ibid.*, p. 177.

to the popular fears, aspirations, and preoccupations of the voters the candidate is trying to woo.

Primary Sources and Critical Method

The most challenging task of the historian-detective is to draw "testimony" from the records of the past. Here the historian has two aims, neither of them simple: (1) to determine if a source is *authentic* and (2) establish the *meaning and believability* of the contents. The first is accomplished through external criticism; the second through internal criticism.

External criticism, in the words of one historian, "authenticates evidence and establishes texts in the most accurate possible form."[6] This is clearly work for professionals and beyond the scope of this book. Suffice it to say that many historical records lack precise dates or correct attribution (i.e., who wrote them). Many texts, after years of copying and recopying, are inaccurate, and forgeries are not uncommon. Highly specialized techniques are required to authenticate documents and artifacts: carbon dating, linguistic analysis, chemical analysis, and the like. Extensive knowledge of the period in question is also a prerequisite. Beginners rarely have either the background knowledge or the specialized skills for such criticism so that we need not dwell on this aspect of critical method. For present purposes assume that the documents in the exercises and the sources you might be using in a class are authentic.

Once the authenticity of a document has been established, the historian faces the far more important challenge of reading and interpreting the contents. This is called *internal criticism*, and the techniques involved are much less mysterious.

The most valuable attribute the historical researcher can have is a sense of healthy skepticism, which American novelist Edgar Saltus calls "history's bedfellow." We have a tendency to believe anything if it is written down. That tendency becomes almost irresistible if the document in question is very old and perhaps written in an ornate script. We have to remind ourselves constantly, however, that no age has a monopoly on lying or shading the truth.

Documents do not reveal their secrets easily. You must learn to question the evidence like an attorney in a courtroom—from different angles, from different perspectives, relentlessly, suspiciously. Even an account written by an individual of unimpeachable honesty can be marred by error and half-truth. It is the historian's job to separate the true from the false. What sort of questions should you ask of the evidence? Below is a partial list of some of the most important.[7]

1. **What exactly does the document mean?** Often the *literal* meaning differs from the *real* meaning. Diplomatic communications, for example, are notorious for veiling harsh international disagreements in extremely polite language. Diplomats are trained to phrase messages in such a restrained fashion that even an impending war can be made to

---

[6] R. J. Schafer, ed., *A Guide to Historical Method* (Homewood, Ill.: Dorsey Press, 1969), p. 100.

[7] These questions are based on those printed in Shafer, *Ibid.*, pp. 137–38.

sound no more threatening than a neighborly disagreement over the backyard fence. Because of this, the historian must become familiar with the conventions of diplomatic correspondence in order to understand the real meaning of the dispatches. Another problem facing the historian is that words change meaning from one age to the next. A nineteenth-century reference to a "gay" person means something quite different from a similar reference in the 1980s. Or, remember the earlier exercise question that asked you to find the eighteenth-century meaning of the word "enthusiasm." The advice given in Chapter 6 is appropriate here: Make sure you know as much as possible about the social and political context of the period you are studying.

2. **How well situated was the author to observe or record the events in question?** Here there are a number of subsidiary questions. What was the author's physical location? Was he or she a direct eyewitness or did the information come from someone else? What was the author's *social ability* to observe? That is, might the person's social or economic position in the society have influenced how the event was seen? A police officer would tend to see a student-police confrontation differently than would a student radical. A person on welfare might be far more able to understand the impulse behind a hunger march than a member of the jet set. Finally, did the witness have *specialized knowledge* that could affect the nature and credibility of the testimony? A lawyer's report of a murder trial might be far more insightful than that of a sensation-seeker in the audience.

3. **When, how, and to whom was the report made?** Obviously, the longer the time between the event and the report, the greater the chance that memory will play tricks on the writer. This is one reason why personal memoirs can be treacherous sources for the historian. In addition, the intended purpose of the report should be discovered. An army officer reporting to a superior may tell what the commander wants to hear rather than the less-than-satisfying truth. The number of casualties inflicted by American soliders on the enemy during the Vietnam War (1961–1975) was constantly exaggerated as field commanders turned in unrealistically high "body counts" to please their superiors at headquarters.

4. **Is there bias, either in the report, or in yourself, that must be accounted for?** Personal bias can be the enemy of truth on two levels. The author of the document in question might have had personal beliefs or convictions that might have intruded into the account. To discover if this is so, you should find out as much about the writer as possible. A student using Arthur Schlesinger, Jr.'s *A Thousand Days* (1965) as a source to study the Kennedy presidency (1961–1963) should know that Schlesinger was a staunch supporter and enthusiastic admirer of John Kennedy. In the same way your own values can often blind you to much that the sources reveal. A person who habitually regards all official government statements as lies or half-truths, or, conversely, a person

who views government pronouncements as akin to divine writ, is in a poor position to evaluate political documents objectively.

5. **What specialized information is needed to interpret the source?** Many times you will have to look up names, places, dates, and technical terms to get the full meaning of a statement.

6. **Do the reported actions seem probable according to the dictates of informed common sense?** Here the significant words are "probable" and "informed common sense." For most questions in history, especially the important ones, we can never get absolutely conclusive answers.

   The test of the believability of a given piece of testimony is the inherent *probability* of its being true. The issue is not whether a version of events is possible (just about anything is at least possible), but whether, given all the evidence, it is probable.

   In determining this the historian's most useful interpretive tool is simple common sense, seasoned with appropriate relevant information. In the end, the credibility of testimony must be judged in the light of our understanding of how people behave. But there are pitfalls. Our "common sense" may deceive us unless we also have all the special knowledge necessary to make it work. Reports of eighteenth-century armies marching great distances in short periods of time violate our "common sense" notion of what infantrymen can accomplish. Yet such reports are too numerous to have been fabricated. Clearly, we must supplement our native cleverness with solid information.

7. **Is there corroborating testimony?** No document can stand alone. Even if we ask all of the preceding questions we can not be certain that the testimony we read is true. We must seek other witnesses—what lawyers call corroborating testimony—to reinforce and substantiate the first account. Just as corroboration is necessary in the courtroom, it is essential to good history.

   This list of questions to ask of evidence is meant to be no more than a rudimentary guide. In the end there is no critical or imaginative skill that cannot be applied to the internal evaluation of evidence. Nor can you know too much. The more you know about the period in question, human behavior, and the workings of the natural world, the better off you will be.

"Legitimate Inference" and Historical Method

One further point needs to be made. As stated above, no one source can ever provide undisputed "truth." Even when corroborating testimony is found, the collective evidence cannot provide definitive and direct answers to many historical questions. The larger the historical question, the more this is true. Even with a relative wealth of evidence for certain periods and subject areas, there are questions that we may never be able to answer definitively. When precisely did President Franklin Roosevelt decide that the United States should enter World War II? To what extent is it fair to blame Roosevelt for the massive increase in Russian influence in Eastern

Europe that resulted from that war? Did President Harry Truman, Roosevelt's successor, really have to drop the atomic bomb on Japan in order to bring World War II to a speedy end? These are just a few of the questions historians have debated, and will continue to debate, concerning the World War II period. There is a mountain of evidence that deals with World War II, and still it yields no direct answers to such questions. Why is this so?

Documentary evidence, of course, can provide some "facts" that most historians will accept. But moving from the facts contained in the records (the evidence) to explanatory generalizations that constitute the heart of written history requires the application of what Robin Winks calls "legitimate inference."[8] The interpretation of historical evidence is based on *inferences*, but inferences (logical conclusions or deductions) can never be established with the certainty of, say, a simple scientific proposition.

There is nothing mysterious about the process of inference. We make countless inferences daily in our personal lives. Your refrigerator is empty on Sunday; you infer that someone forgot to do the Saturday grocery shopping. (A logical assumption, but not necessarily true. Your visiting cousin from Toledo might have decided to set a new record for marathon eating on Saturday night.) A fire bomb is thrown through your window; you infer that someone is angry with you. (Perhaps true. But maybe the bomber got the address wrong.) The point is, even though inference is a perfectly acceptable mental tool for making sense of the world, the conclusions it leads to are often not subject to absolute proof. What all of this means, in practice, is that any historical account is inevitably a compound in which "the certain, the probable, and the speculative will co-exist."

EXERCISES

Set A, Exercise 1: Primary Sources

As noted on pages 138–139, historians make a distinction between primary and secondary sources. Below are sources you might consult if you were preparing a paper on President Harry S. Truman's decision to drop the atomic bomb on Japan at the end of World War II. Truman had to make the decision shortly after he unexpectedly became president in April 1945. The first atomic bomb was exploded on July 16, 1945, and less than three weeks later, on August 6, another bomb was dropped on the Japanese city of Hiroshima. In the spaces provided indicate whether the sources should be classified "primary" (P) or "secondary" (S). If you think a source shares both primary and secondary characteristics, write "PS."

_____ 1. Harry S. Truman, *Memoirs*, Vol. I, *Year of Decisions [1945]* (1955).
_____ 2. Margaret Truman, *Harry S. Truman* (1973).
_____ 3. Herbert Feis, *The Atomic Bomb and the End of World War II* (1966; orig. 1961).
_____ 4. Leslie R. Groves, *Now It Can Be Told* (1964). [Groves was the commanding general of the bomb project.]

---

[8] Robin Winks, ed., *The Historian As Detective* (New York: Harper Colophon, 1970), p. xv.

_____   5. U.S. Atomic Energy Committee, *In the Matter of J. Robert Oppenheimer: Transcript of Hearing Before Personnel Security Board* (1954). [Oppenheimer was one of the scientists who built the bomb.]

_____   6. Louis Morton, "The Decision to Use the Atomic Bomb," *Foreign Affairs* (January, 1957).

_____   7. *Presidential Papers: Harry S. Truman*, 1945, I.

_____   8. *New York Times*, 1945.

_____   9. Joseph M. Siracusa, ed. *The American Diplomatic Revolution: A Documentary History of the Cold War, 1941–47* (1977).

_____   10. Henry L. Stimson, "The Decision to Use the Atomic Bomb," *Harper's Magazine* (February, 1947). [Stimson was Secretary of War and Chairman of the Interim Committee on the Atomic Bomb.]

_____   11. Alice Kimball Smith, "The Decision to Use the Atomic Bomb, 1944–45," *Bulletin of the Atomic Scientists* (October, 1958).

If you wrote "PS" by any of the items, briefly give your reason for each such classification.

_____

_____

_____

_____

Set A, Exercise 2: Types of Primary Sources

As we have seen, there are many types of primary sources. Each type has its characteristic potentials and problems. For instance, records of congressional debates provide invaluable insights into the deliberative processes of the U.S. House of Representatives and the Senate. Yet congresspeople are allowed to insert into the *Congressional Record* speeches that were never delivered or edited copies of speeches that were delivered. The *Congressional Record*, obviously, is not an altogether accurate source for what goes on in Congress. Even if the words were recorded with absolute accuracy, we can never be sure if the sentiments expressed in the formal debates reflect the true beliefs of the speaker or whether they were intended primarily to impress the constituents back home. None of this implies that you should avoid the *Congressional Record* as a source. It means, simply, you should always be aware that you can be led astray if you read a source uncritically.

This exercise requires that you use your imagination (actually your critical intelligence) since we have not discussed the possible benefits and hazards inherent in each type of primary source. Even if you feel you are venturing into unfamiliar territory, write down what you think might be *the potential weaknesses of each type of evidence listed below*. We are accepting as a given here that each type of source can be extremely valuable depending, of course, on the topic under investigation. For this exercise we are asking that you consider the potential traps that might await the unwary researcher who attempts to use a particular piece of evidence. In what ways might each of the following sources *mislead* the researcher? What characteristics must the investigator be aware of in order to use each type of evidence most effectively? We have answered the first item to give you a start.

1. Memoirs/Autobiographies

SAMPLE ANSWER: *The primary problems with memoirs and autobiographies are 1) potential bias on the part of the author (i.e., the author is writing about his or her own life); and 2) potential memory lapses on the part of the author. (Note, these are "potential" problems. Bias or inaccuracy come to light only after you do a good deal of research to corroborate what a memoir writer says.)*

2. Newspapers

COMMENTS: _____

_____

_____

_____

_____

_____

3. Diplomatic Correspondence Between Nations

COMMENTS: _____

_____

_____

_____

_____

_____

4. Political Speeches

COMMENTS: _____

_____

_____

_____

_____

_____

5. Wartime Military Communications Between Subordinates and Commanders

COMMENTS: _____

_____

_____

_____

_____

_____

6. Public Opinion Polls

COMMENTS: _____

_____

_____

_____

_____

_____

7. Government Publications

COMMENTS: _____

_____

_____

_____

_____

_____

Set A, Exercise 3: Reading Evidence

The first task in dealing with primary sources is to make sure you understand the *literal* meaning of the document. This is often not as simple as you might think. Styles of expression change from era to era and vary from individual to individual. Often, even today, you will confront material written in a style that seems foreign and confusing.[9] Before you can begin to interpret the meaning of a document, you have to know precisely what the writer meant to say.

It is also important to be able to "translate" the material into your own words so that you are sure you understand it and can communicate it to a contemporary reader. Even if no translation is necessary, when you take notes you should *paraphrase* the material. That is, you should summarize the major ideas in your own words. A brief summary is much more useful than a note that takes up almost as much space as the original material. Writing in your own words is a good protection against the arch academic crime of plagiarism (passing off someone else's words as your own).

This is an exercise in reading, "translating," and paraphrasing evidence. Below is an excerpt from Edmund Burke's *Speech to the Electors of Bristol* (1774). Burke (1729–1797) was a English politician and political philosopher known for his spirited defense of the American colonists during the

_____

[9] The United States and Britain, for example, have been described as two cultures separated by a common language. In a British mystery novel one finds the sentence: "Pushing her pram onto the zebra, a nearsighted nanny stepped off the curb." Translation into American English: "Pushing her baby carriage onto the crosswalk, a nearsighted children's nurse stepped off the curb."

1770s and his equally passionate condemnation of the French Revolution in the 1790s. In this speech Burke, a member of the English Parliament, explains to his constituents his conception of the responsibilities of an elected representative. In two to four sentences summarize *in your own words* Burke's position concerning the role of a Member of Parliament.

Certainly, gentlemen, it ought to be the happiness and glory of a representative to live in the strictest union, the closest correspondence, and the most unreserved communication with his constituents. Their wishes ought to have great weight with him; their opinions high respect; their business unremitted attention. . . . but his unbiassed opinion, his mature judgment, his enlightened conscience, he ought not to sacrifice to you, or to any set of men living. These he does not derive from your pleasure; no, nor from the Law and the constitution. They are a trust from Providence, for the abuse of which he is deeply answerable. Your representative owes you, not his industry alone, but his judgment; and he betrays, instead of serving you, if he sacrifices it to your opinion. . . .

To deliver an opinion is the right of all men; that of constituents is a weighty and respectable opinion, which a representative ought always to rejoice to hear; and which he ought always most seriously to consider. But *authoritative* instructions, *mandates* issued, which the member [of Parliament] is bound blindly and implicitly to obey, to vote, or to argue for, though contrary to the clearest conviction of his judgment and conscience—these are things utterly unknown to the laws of this land, and which arise from a fundamental mistake of the whole order and tenor of our constitution.

Parliament is not a *congress* of ambassadors from different and hostile interests . . . but parliament is a *deliberative* assembly of *one* nation, with *one* interest, that of the whole; where not local purposes, not local prejudices, ought to guide, but the general good, resulting from the general reason of the whole. You choose a member indeed; but when you have chosen him, he is not member of Bristol, but he is a member of *parliament*.

Your Summary (2–4 sentences) of Burke's Argument:

_____

_____

_____

_____

_____

_____

_____

_____

_____

_____

_____

Set A, Exercise 4: Inference

Inference, as we noted, is a major tool in the interpretation of evidence. Because the questions that interest historians are often quite different from the objectives of those who created various pieces of primary evidence, historians constantly have to make logical deductions that may not be provable in any absolute sense. For instance, in the automobile trip log of Mr. Smith, a travelling salesman, you read that on July 19 he was in Seattle, Washington, and on July 20 in Portland, Oregon (a trip of about 180 miles).

On the basis of the evidence (the trip log) it seems probable that Mr. Smith drove from Seattle to Portland on July 19 or July 20, although *nowhere in the log does it say so specifically*. Our conclusion is an *inference*. We don't know for sure, on the basis of this piece of evidence alone, when he made the trip nor by what road. But the record suggests the fact *that he did make the trip and that he made it by car*. Note: There is always the possibility, unless we find corroborating evidence that Mr. Smith was indeed in Seattle on the 19th and Portland on the 20th, that the log entry was a fabrication created for any number of reasons. There is also the possibility that for this particular trip Mr. Smith left his car in Seattle and took a plane. Our inference is a logical one, and it is supported by the evidence; but without corroborating testimony we can never be absolutely sure that we are correct. It might be worth recalling here that the test of an inference is the *probability*, given the existing evidence, that it is true.

Below are a number of short statements followed by some inferences. Read the statements and then examine the possible inferences one might draw. Indicate for each inference whether it is a VALID inference (V), an INVALID OR FALSE inference (F), or an inference for which we have INSUFFICIENT DATA (ID) to determine its validity or invalidity. If you label an inference "F" (False/Invalid), indicate your reasons on the lines provided at the end of each unit. Note: A "False" inference (F) is one that can be *disproved* using the passage in question. ID (Insufficient Data) should be used for inferences that can be neither proved nor disproved using the information in a given passage.

For the purposes of this exercise assume that the statements reflect the best judgment of the speaker or writer. Also assume that for any statement of fact there exists corroborating evidence. The first unit is already completed as an example.

A. Statement of Dr. Victor C. Vaughan comparing his medical experiences during the Spanish-American War with those during World War I (1914–1918; U.S. participation, 1917–1918). Quoted in Paul Starr, *The Social Transformation of American Medicine* (1982).

> I served in the war with Spain in 1898, and I went time and time again to a division officer and made certain requests or offered certain advice. As a rule, I was snubbed and told by action, if not by words, that I was only a medical officer, and that I had no right to make any suggestions, and it was impudent of me to do so.
>
> The commanding general at Chickamauga [a Spanish-American War army camp], when we had an increasing number of cases of typhoid fever, would every day ostentatiously ride up to a well which had been condemned and drink of this water to show his contempt. But in the

late war [World War I] I had a different experience. I never went to a line officer with a recommendation but that he said, 'Doctor, it will be done. . . .'

Possible Inferences (V=Valid; F=Invalid/False; ID=Insufficient Data):

<u>V</u>   1. Doctors were not treated with much respect in the military during the Spanish-American War.

<u>V</u>   2. There was a change in the attitude of the military towards medical doctors between 1898 and 1918.

<u>ID</u>   3. Dr. Vaughan was a good physician.

<u>F</u>   4. The commanding general at Chickamauga camp believed that the well water caused typhoid.

<u>ID</u>   5. Typhoid was not as serious a problem in World War I as it was in the Spanish American War.

COMMENTS: *Remember, you are to assume that corroborating evidence exists for statements of fact made in each excerpt. Statements 1 and 2 are, then, valid inferences. We labelled statements 3 and 5 "ID" (Insufficient Data) because, though perhaps true, neither inference is addressed at all in the excerpt. Statement 4 is invalid since the general's behavior (drinking the well water) suggests he believed no such thing.*

B. A soldier's account of his experiences in the Vietnam War. From Philip Caputo, *A Rumor of War* (1978).

To keep the troops from becoming complacent, the company gunnery sergeant, a broad-chested cheerful man named Marquand, would send them to their positions with prophecies of impending attacks. 'They're gonna hit us tonight. I gar-untee you. We're gonna get hit.' But nothing happened. Our role in the alleged counteroffensive was limited to making detailed reports of whatever firing we heard forward of our respective platoon sectors. I am not sure who did what with that information, but I think it helped the battalion intelligence officer plot what is known in the jargon as a 'sitmap'—a map showing the dispositions of friendly and enemy forces.

Possible Inferences:

_____   1. Boredom was a problem for soldiers in Vietnam.

_____   2. The information collected for the "sitmap" was used for planning future military operations.

_____   3. Caputo thought the counteroffensive accomplished little of value.

_____   4. Sergeant Marquand was well liked by his troops.

_____   5. This unit saw a lot of action during this period.

Reasons for "F" Labels:

_____

_____

C. Henry Mayhew's account of "Shilling Day" (i.e., bargain admission day) at London's Great Exhibition of 1851. The Great Exhibition was the first "world's fair." From E. Royston Pike, *Golden Times: Human Documents of the Victorian Age* (1972).

> And inside the Great Exhibition the scene is equally different from that of the first week or two. The nave is no longer filled with elegant and inert loungers—lolling on seats, and evidently come there to be seen rather than to see. Those who are now to be found there, have come to look at the Exhibition, and not to make an exhibition of themselves. There is no air of display about them—no social falsity—all is plain unvarnished truth. . . . The shilling folk may be an 'inferior' class of visitors, but at least, they know something about the works of industry, and what they do not know, they have come to learn. . . .
>
> For many days before the 'shilling people' were admitted to the building, the great topic of conversation was the probable behavior of the people. Would they come sober? Will they destroy things? . . . But they have surpassed in decorum the hopes of their wellwishers.

Possible Inferences:

_____   1. Victorian Britain was a society marked by significant class divisions.
_____   2. At the time this passage was written there was a widespread fear of class conflict in Britain.
_____   3. The people who first attended the Exhibition were members of the upper class and they were not especially interested in the exhibits.
_____   4. At least some members of the upper class thought better of members of "inferior" classes after their good behavior on shilling day.
_____   5. Mayhew's statement is evidence that the gap between classes was becoming narrower in the 1850s.
_____   6. There was no vandalism at all during the entire run of the Great Exhibition.

Reasons for "F" labels:

_____

_____

D. Excerpt from Albert Speer's memoirs. During the 1930s and 1940s Speer was Adolf Hitler's architect and, later, armaments minister. From Albert Speer, *Inside the Third Reich*, (1970).

> The twenties in Berlin were the inspiring backdrop to my student years. Many theatrical performances made a deep impression upon me—among others Max Reinhardt's staging of *A Midsummer Night's Dream*, Elisabeth Bergner in Shaw's *Saint Joan*, Pallenberg in Piscator's version of *Schweik*. But Charell's lavishly mounted revues also fascinated me. On the other hand, I took no pleasure in Cecil B. DeMille's bombastic pomp—never suspecting that ten years later I myself would be going his movie architecture one better. As a student I thought his films examples of 'American tastelessness.'

Possible Inferences:

—— 1. The cultural scene in 1920s Berlin was cosmopolitan and varied.
—— 2. Speer liked to go to the theater.
—— 3. Speer's architecture, in the subsequent years, was probably grandiose and monumental, like C. B. DeMille's films.
—— 4. Speer disliked all American films.
—— 5. Speer was born in Berlin.

Reasons for "F" labels:

_____

_____

E. Some of the provisions of the English Bill of Rights (1689).

1. That the pretended power of suspending laws . . . by regal authority, without consent of Parliament, is illegal.

4. That levying money for or to the use of the Crown by pretense of prerogative, without grant of Parliament . . . is illegal.

5. That it is the right of the subjects to petition the King, and all commitments and prosecutions for such petitioning are illegal.

6. That the raising or keeping a standing army within the kingdom in time of peace, unless it be with consent of Parliament, is against law.

7. That the subjects which are Protestants may have arms for their defense suitable to their conditions, and as allowed by law.

9. That freedom of speech, and debates or proceedings in Parliament, ought not to be impeached or questioned in any court or place out of Parliament.

10. That excessive bail ought not to be required, nor excessive fines imposed, nor cruel and unusual punishments inflicted.

13. And that for redress of all grievances, and for the amending, strengthening, and preserving of the laws, Parliament ought to be held frequently.

Possible Inferences:

For this unit try to draw some VALID inferences (at least three to four) of your own. What sort of (tentative) conclusions might you draw from the document above? What do the listed provisions tell you about the ideas and events that preceded Parliament's passage of the Bill of Rights? For example, what do they tell you about the relationship of King to Parliament? Catholics to Protestants? the role of law in society?

Sample inference: Before 1689 at least some kings prosecuted and

jailed "petitioners" to the crown. (See item 5.)

_____

_____

_____

_____

_____

Set A, Exercise 5: Analysis of Evidence

The Kent State Incident, May 4, 1970

One of the most tragic and controversial events during the Vietnam era in the United States was the violent confrontation between the Ohio National Guard and a large group of students at Kent State University on May 4, 1970. On that day four students were killed and nine wounded. What exactly happened at Kent State, and why, will never be known with absolute certainty. In spite of reams of testimony, Kent State remains a highly controversial subject.

The late 1960s were a time of increasing unrest on America's college campuses. The Vietnam War spurred student protests all over the country, and radical student political groups (like the SDS—Students for a Democratic Society) proliferated on many campuses. Student outrage over the U.S. failure to get out of Vietnam peaked when President Richard Nixon announced, on April 30, 1970, that he ordered U.S. troops into Cambodia, thus apparently expanding the war.

The next four days were marked by escalating student unrest on the campus of Kent State University and in the town of Kent itself. On Friday, May 1, there were disorders in the city; on Saturday a group of students burned the campus ROTC building, and the authorities requested troops from the National Guard; on Sunday the first confrontations between the Guard and the students took place; on Monday, the fateful day, the accumulated tensions climaxed with the killings that shocked and aroused the nation.

How could such a thing happen? This question led to newspaper investigations, grand jury proceedings, civil suits, the creation of a government commission on student unrest, and many books and articles. It is not our purpose to answer that question. By examining some of the eyewitness testimony, we can get a better idea of how the historian "questions" evidence. The evidence below relates to one very specific question that many investigators tried to answer after the shootings: was the National Guard endangered by the student mob on May 4? Was the Guard justified in firing at the students in self-defense?

In this exercise your task is NOT to determine whether or not the National Guard was threatened by the students. Instead you should try to note any facts about each source that may help you assess its believability. Make pertinent observations concerning the authorship, circumstances of composition, content, and potential credibility of each piece of testimony. To do so you should ask of each piece of evidence the following questions:

1. Are there any problems in understanding the literal meaning of the document? That is, are there words you have to look up? phrases you don't understand? Etc.
2. Who made the report and under what circumstances?
3. When was the report made?
4. How well placed was the witness to observe and record the event?
5. Is bias present? (ideological, class, personal?)
6. Might your own biases influence your interpretation of the evidence?

7. Is specialized information necessary to understand the document? If so, what information is required?

For a discussion of these questions, review pages 142–144.

The Evidence

1. Statement of General Robert Canterbury, Assistant Adjutant General of the Ohio National Guard, to the President's Commission on Campus Unrest, August 25, 1970. (From *The Report of the President's Commission on Campus Unrest*, 1970, pp. 269–70.)

> As the troop formation reached the area of the Pagoda near Taylor Hall, the mob located on the right flank in front of Taylor Hall and in the Prentice Hall parking lot charged our right flank, throwing rocks, yelling obscenities and threats, 'Kill the pigs,' 'Stick the pigs.' The attitude of the crowd at this point was menacing and vicious.
>
> The troops were being hit by rocks. I saw Major Jones hit in the stomach by a large brick, a guardsman to the right and rear of my position was hit by a large rock and fell to the ground. During this movement, practically all of the guardsmen were hit by missiles of various kinds. Guardsmen on the right flank were in serious danger of bodily harm and death as the mob continued to charge. I felt that, in view of the extreme danger to the troops at this point, that they were justified in firing.

ANALYSIS: Sample Answer

There is no problem with the literal meaning, save we need to know what the "Pagoda" is. Actually it is not a building but a piece of modern "sculpture" (See question #1 above). The report is made by a military man who should be a credible witness in such a circumstance (#2), but as commander of the Guard contingent there is the possibility he is biased and trying to protect the reputation of his troops (#5). Canterbury was in position to witness the events (we don't know precisely where), but this piece of testimony comes more than three months after the event (#4, #3). The authors of this book have to be aware of their own potential biases: one is an ex-military man who might tend to give the benefit of the doubt to General Canterbury; the other, a student during the late 1960s who participated in antiwar protests, might be prone to sympathize with the students (#6). All in all, if corroboration is found, the testimony seems credible enough. We should find out more about the background and views of General Canterbury, however.

2. Reflections of a Kent State student, Yvonne Mitchell, who, according to the *New York Times*, was an "average student, not greatly involved in anything, but concerned." (*The New York Times*, May 11, 1970)

> Question from Reporter: Did you think the Guard was seeking a confrontation?

Yvonne Mitchell: There's one thing that should be said here. It was noontime. And lunchtime. And a change of classes. There were people who were just curious. And there were some kids who were really just trying to go to class. And the last thing in anyone's mind was that anyone would be getting shot. That's the sad part. There weren't just kids messing with the National Guard, or radical kids, or conservative kids. There was just, like I say, an integration of everybody. I heard so many times people say, 'Well, if you're straight, if you're not starting anything, they won't bother you.' Well, I'm here to tell you, they didn't care who you were. If you were in the way, you just got run down.

Analysis: _____

_____

_____

_____

_____

_____

_____

_____

3. Testimony of Claudia Van Tyne, a 20-year-old junior at Kent State at the time of the shootings. (From *The Middle of the Country: The Events of May 4th As Seen By Students and Faculty at Kent State University*, ed. by Bill Warren, [June, 1970], pp. 119–21.)

For what occurred on Kent State University's campus I can only give one term—murder. . . . The area was filled with students in the middle, many spectators on the outskirts and the pigs were lined-up waiting. I don't like the expression "pig" but it is the only word I shall ever use again to refer to law officials. . . . The pigs then informed us that we must disperse over their bull horn. In our response, we informed them that they, not us, should get off *our* campus and we began to chant 'Power To The People—Off The Pigs' etc., etc. They then began making their advance and everyone walked, telling others not to run but to walk, up the hill. We were all choking and sputtering because the tear gas (pepper pellets) had already been shot. . . . The pigs advanced, came up the hill and marched down into the old football practice field behind Taylor Hall (architecture building) where they gassed us again. Many of us picked up the cannisters and tossed them back. Finding themselves out of tear gas, the pigs retreated followed by jeers and a few rocks. I was next to the architecture building, about twenty feet away from them, when suddenly they turned and fired. I was stunned to say the least. We all were. No one expected it. . . .

Analysis: _____

_____

_____

_____

4. Report of the special grand jury that investigated the Kent State tragedy. The grand jury was composed of fifteen middle-aged local residents. The grand jury began meeting on September 14. (*The New York Times*, October 17, 1970)

> Those orders [to disperse], given by a Kent State University policeman, caused a violent reaction and the gathering quickly degenerated into a riotous mob. . . .
>
> Those who acted as participants and agitators are guilty of deliberate criminal conduct. Those who were present as cheerleaders and onlookers, while not liable for criminal acts, must morally assume a part of the responsibility for what occurred. . . .
>
> It should be made clear that we do not condone all of the activities of the National Guard on the Kent State University campus on May 4, 1970. We find, however, that those members of the National Guard who were present on the hill adjacent to Taylor Hall on May 4, 1970, fired their weapons in the honest and sincere belief and under circumstances which would have logically caused them to believe that they would suffer serious bodily injury had they not done so. They are not, therefore, subject to criminal prosecution under the laws of this state for any death or injury resulting therefrom.
>
> It should be added, that . . . the verbal abuse directed at the guardsmen by the students during the period in question represented a level of obscenity and vulgarity which we have never before witnessed!

ANALYSIS: _____

_____

_____

_____

_____

_____

_____

_____

5. Testimony of unnamed Guardsman—a 23-year-old, married machinist. (Reported in a Special Report by the Akron *Beacon Journal*, May 24, 1970. Quoted in I. F. Stone, *The Killings at Kent State* [1970], p. 125.)

> Q.—Did you shoot to save your life?
> A.—No. I didn't feel that. Because, like it was an automatic thing. Everybody shot, so I shot. I didn't think about it. I just fired. . . .

Q.—Did you feel threatened?
A.—No. I didn't think they'd try to take our rifles, not while we could use the bayonets and butts. . . . The guys have been saying that we got to get together and stick to the same story, that it was our lives or them, a matter of survival. I told them I would tell the truth and couldn't get in trouble that way.

ANALYSIS: _____

_____

_____

_____

_____

_____

_____

_____

_____

6. Testimony of Richard Schreiber, Assistant Professor of Journalism. Shreiber had been in the army and was a life member of the National Rifle Association. (From James Michener, *Kent State: What Happened and Why* [1971], p. 359).

I went out on the south porch of Taylor with my binoculars and saw something which has caused a lot of discussion. While the Guard was pinned against the fence, the students kept throwing rocks, but they were rather far away and most of the rocks were falling short. I happened to have this one Guard in my glasses and I saw him raise his revolver and bang away. I've fired many hundreds of rounds with a .45 and I know a shot when I see one. There can be no question but that he fired the first round of the day. But the damnedest thing happened. Even while he was firing, some student ran up with a gas grenade and threw it at him. Where could he have possibly got it? Didn't look like the ones the Guards had been using. One of the Guardsmen, foolishly I thought, picked up the grenade and threw it back. It seemed like horseplay, so I turned away.

ANALYSIS: _____

_____

_____

_____

_____

_____

_____

For Discussion
1. Which pieces of evidence do you find most convincing? Which do you find least convincing? Why?
2. On which "facts" does there seem to be general agreement?
3. What are the central points of disagreement?

Essay
Based on the evidence above, write a paragraph-length account of the incident at Kent State. Use as a first sentence: "In trying to unravel what happened at Kent State on May 4, 1970, we must determine whether or not the National Guard faced a serious danger from the student crowd." In your paragraph try to state clearly what can be established beyond doubt (assume the excerpts above are all the sources you have available to you), what is *probable* given the above evidence, and what cannot be established with certainty.

Set A, Exercise 6: Using Statistics

There are an increasing number of historians who base their research on statistical and quantifiable evidence. It is not the aim of this book to provide a lesson in the use and misuse of statistical evidence. Yet it is an inescapable fact that statistical evidence continues to play a greater and greater role in historical writing. Students of history would do well to develop their ability to read and interpret graphs, tables, charts, opinion-poll data, and the like.

The exercise below does no more than scratch the surface in this area, but it will provide a taste of the sort of reasoning and analysis that the use of statistical evidence requires. Note, however, that the tables reproduced below do not represent primary sources in the purest sense. The historian who drew up the charts, John Demos, has culled the information from many original documents and has done the counting for you. Moreover, the organization of the information reflects the questions that Demos wished to investigate.[10] Nevertheless, the charts do represent raw data which does not "speak for itself." It must be interpreted by the historian.

The tables printed below categorize by age, sex, and marital status those people who, during the infamous Salem witchcraft trials in 1692, were either accused of being witches or who accused others of witchcraft. On the basis of the evidence presented, what general conclusions can be made concerning the "types" of people most likely to be accused of witchcraft (group I) compared with the "types" of people who accused others of witchcraft (group II)?

I. Persons accused of being witches:

Age	Male	Female	Total
Under 20	6	18	24
21–30	3	7	10
31–40	3	8	11
41–50	6	18	24
51–60	5	23	28
61–70	4	8	12
Over 70	3	6	9
Total	30	88	118

Marital Status	Male	Female	Total
Single	8	29	37
Married	15	61	76
Widowed	1	20	21
Total	24	110	134

[10] John Demos, "Witchcraft in Seventeenth-Century New England," *American Historical Review* (June 1970): 1311–26. Statistical tables reprinted by permission of the author.

II. Persons who accused others of witchcraft:

Age	Male	Female	Total		Marital Status	Male	Female	Total
Under 11	0	1	1		Single	5	23	28
11–15	1	7	8		Married	0	6	6
16–20	1	13	14		Widowed	0	0	0
21–25	0	1	1		Total	5	29	34
26–30	0	1	1					
Over 30	0	4	4					
Total	2	27	29					

1. General characteristics of persons in group I:

_____

_____

_____

_____

2. General characteristics of persons in group II:

_____

_____

_____

_____

Set B, Exercise 1: Inference

Below are a number of short statements followed by some inferences. Read the statements and then examine the possible inferences one might draw. Indicate for each inference whether it is a VALID inference (V), an INVALID OR FALSE inference (F), or an inference for which we have INSUFFICIENT DATA (ID) to determine its validity or invalidity. If you label an inference "F" (False/Invalid), indicate your reasons on the lines provided at the end of each unit. Note: A False inference (F) is one that can be *disproved* by using the passage in question. ID (Insufficient Data) should be used for inferences that can be neither proved nor disproved using the information in a given passage.

For the purposes of this exercise assume that the statements reflect the best judgment of the speaker or writer. Also assume that for any statement of fact there exists corroborating evidence.

A. President Lyndon Johnson (1963–1968) to the National Security Council on the Vietnam War in 1965. (*The People's Almanac #2*, 1978).

> Hell, Vietnam is just like the Alamo. Hell, it's just like if you were down at that gate, and you were surrounded, and you damn well needed somebody. Well, by God, I'm going to go—and I thank the Lord that I've got men who want to go with me from [Secretary of Defense, Robert] McNamara right down to the littlest private who's carrying a gun.

Possible Inferences:

_____ 1. President Johnson did not hesitate to use expletives in conversation.

_____ 2. Johnson had misgivings about the possible success of intervention in Vietnam. He compares Vietnam to the Alamo, and the Alamo fell.

_____ 3. The entire U.S. defense establishment agreed with Johnson.

_____ 4. Johnson knew at least some Texas history.

_____ 5. Johnson enjoyed watching cowboy movies.

Reasons for "F" labels:

_____

_____

B. General Dwight Eisenhower's reflections on his World War II experiences. (Dwight Eisenhower, *Crusade in Europe*, 1948)

> Except during World War I, the U.S. public has habitually looked upon Europe's quarrels as belonging to Europe alone. For this reason every American soldier coming to Britain was almost certain to consider himself a privileged crusader, sent there to help Britain out of a hole. He would expect to be treated as such. On the other hand, the British public looked upon itself as one of saviors of democracy, particularly because, for an entire year, it had stood alone as the unbreakable opponent of Nazism and the European Axis. Failure to understand this attitude would of course have unfortunate results.

Possible Inferences:

_____ 1. Eisenhower feared U.S. and British troops would not get along.

_____ 2. Eisenhower feared that arrogance in American troops would create conflicts with the British public.

_____ 3. Eisenhower saw no reason why Americans and Britons could not get along well.

_____ 4. Eisenhower had studied American history at some time in his life.

_____ 5. There were many conflicts between British troops and American troops during the latter stages of World War II.

Reasons for "F" labels:

_____

_____

C. Letter from warehouse worker in England to the *Nottingham Daily Guardian* in 1863. (E. R. Pike, *Golden Times*, 1972)

> Sir,—I have been a lace warehouse girl about 13 years, and should know a little about the regulations of warehouses. Is there not an Act which compels the masters of factories to let children leave their employment at six o'clock at night? If there is, can any one tell me why this Act is not applied to lace warehouses, which are heated with steam, for children and young women are kept there at work from 8 in the

morning till 7, 8, and 9 o'clock at night, for about 3s 6d to 8s per week, which, in my opinion, is worse than slavery in South America, for I do not think they work above 12 hours a day; and if they do, they are better off than a portion of the warehouse girls of Nottingham, who have to work in cellars not fit for pigstyes, much more for human beings.

Possible Inferences:

_____ 1. Some members of the working class who worked very long hours learned how to read and write.

_____ 2. Child labor was still common in the England of the 1860s.

_____ 3. The government had taken no action to correct ill-treatment of workers.

_____ 4. Apparently there had already been an attempt to limit the length of the working day for some workers in some industries.

_____ 5. Only women and children worked in lace warehouses.

Reasons for "F" labels:

_____

_____

D. A scholar's statistical summary of the role of women in medicine in the nineteenth century. (Paul Starr, *The Social Transformation of American Medicine*, 1982)

By 1893–94, women represented 10 percent or more of the students at 19 coeducational medical schools. Between 1880 and 1900, the percentage of doctors who were women increased nationally from 2.8 to 5.6 percent. In some cities the proportion of women was considerably higher: 18.2 percent of doctors in Boston, 19.3 percent in Minneapolis, 13.8 percent in San Francisco. With more than 7,000 women physicians at the turn of the century, the United States was far ahead of England, which had just 258, and France, which had only 95.

Possible Inferences:

_____ 1. In the U.S. a higher percentage of women studied medicine than in western Europe, during the twenty years after 1880.

_____ 2. Women had an easier time becoming doctors in the United States because women's rights were more widely recognized in America than in Europe.

_____ 3. American women were smarter than European women.

_____ 4. A lower percentage of American women is studying medicine in the United States today than in 1900.

_____ 5. More women could study medicine in the U.S. (as opposed to Europe) because there were more medical schools in the U.S.

Reasons for "F" labels:

_____

_____

E. Below are listed some of the "Dooms" (i.e., laws) of England's King Alfred (871–899). Alfred was king during the Anglo-Saxon era (ca. 500s–1066), a period for which there are few surviving sources. Historians have to infer a great deal from a limited supply of documents. Using the list of laws below, try to draw some VALID conclusions (at least three to four) about the nature of law and society in ninth-century England. (*Documents in English History*, edited by B. Blakely and J. Collins, 1975)

> Then I, King Alfred, collected these together and ordered to be written many of them which our forefathers observed, those which I liked; . . . But those which I found anywhere, which seemed to me most just . . . I collected herein, and omitted the others. [The numbering that follows does not conform to the original.]

1. If anyone with a band of men kills an innocent man of a two-hundred wergild [a monetary worth of 200], he who admits the slaying is to pay the wergild and the fine, and each man who was in that expedition is to pay 30 shillings as compensation for being in the band. [There follow similar provisions for the killing of a man worth 600 and worth 1200.]
2. If anyone binds an innocent *ceorl* [peasant], he is to pay him six shillings compensation.
3. If in insult he disfigures him by cutting his hair, he is to pay him 10 shillings compensation.
4. If he cuts off his beard, he is to pay 20 shillings compensation.
5. If anyone fights in a meeting in the presence of the king's ealdorman, he is to pay wergild and fine, as is fitting, and before that, 120 shillings to the ealdorman [a royal official] as a fine.
6. If he disturbs a public meeting by drawing a weapon, [he is to pay] 120 shillings to the ealdorman as a fine.
7. If anyone fights in the house of a *ceorl*, he is to pay six shillings compensation to the *ceorl*.
8. Moreover we command: that the man who knows his opponents to be dwelling at home is not to fight before he asks justice for himself.
9. If he [the attacker] has not sufficient power to besiege him in his house, he is to ride to the ealdorman and ask for support; if he will not give him support, he is to ride to the king, before having recourse to fighting.
10. Moreover we declare that a man may fight on behalf of his lord, if the lord is being attacked, without incurring a vendetta. Similarly the lord may fight on behalf of his man.
11. In the same way, a man may fight on behalf of his born kinsman, if he is being wrongfully attacked, except against his lord; that we do not allow.
12. And a man may fight without incurring a vendetta if he finds another man with his wedded wife, within closed doors or under the same blanket, or with his legitimate daughter or his legitimate sister, or with his mother who was given as a lawful wife to his father.

Possible Valid Inferences:

_____

_____

_____

_____

_____

_____

_____

Set B, Exercise 2: Analysis of Evidence

Lexington Green, April 19, 1775

The first shots of the American Revolution were fired at Lexington, Massachusetts, on April 19, 1775. British troops on their way to destroy colonial military stores in nearby Concord were confronted by colonial militiamen at Lexington Green. Shots rang out and military hostilities began.

Since neither the British nor the American colonists wished to appear the aggressor, both sides denied firing the first shot. Below are four brief accounts of the event. Your task is _not_ to determine who fired the first shot, but to examine the reports with the critical eye of the historian. Again, what points about each account should be noted by the historian wishing to weigh the probable validity of each? Make pertinent observations concerning the authorship, circumstances of composition, content, and potential believability of each piece of evidence. Use the seven questions on pages 154–155 as a basis for your analysis.

1. Robert Douglass swore to the following deposition on May 3, 1827:[11]

> In about fifteen minutes after we entered the tavern, a person came to the door and said the British were within half a mile. I then heard an officer (who I afterwards learned was Captain Parker) call his drummer and order him to beat to arms. I paraded with the Lexington company between the meeting-house and the tavern, and then marched to the common near the road that leads to Bedford; there we were ordered to load our guns. Some of the company observed, 'There are so few of us, it would be folly to stand here.' Captain Parker replied, 'The first man who offers to run shall be shot down.' The Lexington company began to break off on the left wing, and soon all dispersed. I think no American was killed or wounded by the first fire of the British, unless Captain Parker might have been. No one of Captain Parker's company fired on the British, to my knowledge, that morning, and I think I should have known it, had they fired. I knew but two men of the Lexington company, and I never heard any person say that the Americans fired on the British that morning at Lexington.

---

[11] Excerpts 1 and 2 taken from Peter S. Bennett, ed., _What Happened on Lexington Green_ (Reading, Mass.: Addison-Wesley, 1970), pp. 13–14. Excerpts 3 and 4 are from Allen French, _General Gage's Informers_ (Ann Arbor: University of Michigan Press, 1932), pp. 53–54, 55.

After the British marched toward Concord, I saw eight men who had been killed, among whom were Captain Parker and a Mr. Porter of Woburn.

ANALYSIS: _____

_____

_____

_____

_____

_____

_____

_____

2. The official deposition of the commander of the colonial militia, John Parker:

Lexington, April 25, 1775

I, John Parker, of lawful age, and commander of the Militia in Lexington, do testify and declare, that on the nineteenth instant, in the morning, about one of the clock, being informed that there were a number of Regular Officers riding up and down the road, stopping and insulting people as they passed the road, and also was informed that a number of Regular Troops were on their march from Boston, in order to take the Province Stores at Concord, ordered our Militia to meet on the common in said Lexington, to consult what to do, and concluded not to be discovered, nor meddle or make with said Regular Troops (if they should approach) unless they should insult us; and upon their sudden approach, I immediately ordered our Militia to disperse and not to fire. Immediately said Troops made their appearance, and rushed furiously, fired upon and killed eight of our party, without receiving any provocation therefor from us.

John Parker.

ANALYSIS: _____

_____

_____

_____

_____

_____

_____

3. British commander Major John Pitcairn's official report to General Gage:

> I gave directions to the Troops to move forward, but on no account to Fire, or even attempt it without orders; when I arrived at the end of the Villiage, I observed drawn up upon a Green near 200 of the Rebels; when I came within about One Hundred Yards of them, they began to File off towards some stone Walls on our Right Flank—The Light Infantry observing this, ran after them—I instantly called to the Soldiers not to fire, but to surround and disarm them, and after several repetitions of those positive Orders to the men, not to Fire &c—some of the Rebels who had jumped over the Wall, Fired Four or Five Shott at the Soldiers, which wounded a man of the Tenth, and my Horse was Wounded in two places, from some quarter or other, and at the same time several Shott were fired from a Meeting House on our Left—upon this, without any order or Regularity, the Light Infantry began a scattered Fire, and continued in that situation for some little time, contrary to the repeated orders both of me and the officers that were present— It will be needless to mention what happened after, as I suppose Col. Smith hath given a particular account of it. I am sir

> Boston Camp   Your most humble Servant,
> 26th April, 1775   John Pitcairn.

ANALYSIS: _____

_____

_____

_____

_____

_____

_____

_____

4. Personal account by British ensign Jeremy Lister written in 1832:

> However to the best of my recollection about 4 oClock in the Morning being the 19th of April the 5 front [companies] was ordered to Load which we did, about half an hour after we found that precaution had been necessary, for we had then to [fire] . . . and then was the first Blood drawn in this American Rebellion. It was at Lexington when we saw one of their [Companies] drawn up in regular order Major Pitcairn of the Marines second in Command call'd to them to disperce, but their not seeming willing he desired us to mind our space which we did when they gave us a fire they run of[f] to get behind a wall. we had one man wounded of our [Company] in the Leg his Name was Johnson also Major Pitcairns Horse was shot in the Flank we return'd their Salute, and before we proceeded on our March from Lexington I believe we Kill'd and Wounded either 7 or 8 men.

ANALYSIS: _____

_____

_____

_____

_____

_____

_____

_____

For Discussion
1. Which pieces of evidence do you find most convincing? Which do you find least convincing? Why?
2. On which "facts" does there seem to be general agreement?
3. What are the central points of disagreement?

Essay   Based on the evidence above, write a paragraph-length account of the confrontation on Lexington Green. Use as a first sentence: "Historians have long disputed whether the colonial militia or the British regulars fired the first shot of the American Revolution." In your paragraph try to state clearly what can be established beyond doubt (assume the four excerpts above are all the sources you have available to you), what is *probable* given the above evidence, and what cannot be established with certainty.

CHAPTER 9

INTERPRETATION

"The writing of history reflects the interests, predilections, and even prejudices of a given generation."
John Hope Franklin

Nearly all of us have had the experience of riding through a strange city, getting glimpses of this and that—busy intersections, distinctive buildings, storefront displays, fast food places, residential streets, garish billboards—in all, a melange of assorted sights, sounds, and smells. Later on when asked for impressions of that city, we need time to sort out our memories because of the variety of detail. The historian has just about the same problem. The historian spends hours viewing some foreign scene (some segment of the past), and must sort through a wealth of detail before offering an "impression." The historian must decide what things best characterized that scene, how much of this and that to include, how much detail to give, how much weight to assign each item, and what to exclude.

Actually, "impression" is not quite the right word. In history the more exact word, and the one more commonly used, is "interpretation." The prime purpose of this chapter is to give you a clear idea of this vital term, for interpretation is the most basic and final product of historical study. Its clear-cut presence makes any student paper an intellectual achievement; its absence reduces a paper to an empty recital of facts.

Interpretation is, in its most fundamental sense, *generalization*. It is that mental act in which one rises above the details of a given experience and makes a statement that characterizes the entire experience according to its principal elements. Such a simple statement as "I had a great time last night" can illustrate the essential nature of generalization. What the speaker has done—in an instant—is recall elements of the evening (including the attractiveness of the person one was with, the drinks, the warmth, and friendliness of the other company, the quality of the music, the level of conversation, etc.), and, finding that they reflect a pattern, summarize the whole experience: "a great time." The speaker can, if asked, supply corroborating detail to support the generalization offered.

So it is with history, though the raw materials you work with are historical sources rather than personal experience. A generalization (interpretation) about George Washington's military role in the American Revolution might read: "Washington's military genius manifested itself repeatedly in his avoidance of defeat rather than in a string of victories." Many of us might be inclined to accept that statement. But we should not do so until we are supplied with corroborating details such as Washington's refusal to commit his full army to a frontal battle at Boston, his dilatory campaign around New York, his withdrawal at Monmouth, his patience at Philadelphia, etc. In other words, just as a listener expects to have some detail about the "great time" last night, so, too, does a reader expect a historian to provide detailed support for generalizations.

Types of Generalization

Indeed it is possible to say that "all learning of history is learning about generalizations—how to form them, how to understand and remember them."[1] For our present purpose, a generalization can be treated as belonging at one of three levels: limited, intermediate, and broad. By "limited" generalization we mean such narrow statements as, "The Democratic party achieved a landslide victory in the elections of 1936." A limited generalization, indeed, and a rather unsophisticated one. Still, it must be supported with facts such as the following: President Franklin Roosevelt re-elected; Democrats retain control of House and Senate; Democratic governorships increased.

At the other extreme are broad, overarching generalizations, such as, "Christianity shaped the values and institutions of modern Europe," or "the prime motive force in history has been the economic mode of production prevailing during any epoch," or, yet again, "the primary factor in shaping the American character was the two-hundred year frontier experience of its people." Such far-reaching statements are exceedingly difficult to validate. They require massive accumulation of specific supporting information and even then remain quite speculative. Generalizations of such magnitude, though often necessary and occasionally very thought-provoking, are best left to professional historians or even philosophers.

Most worthwhile historical interpretations are generalizations at the *intermediate* level. They provide truths of a manageable size, modest units of knowledge that can be supported by citing the particulars on which the generalization is based. For example, a carefully written student essay on Franklin Roosevelt's first term in office (1933–1937) might set forth the generalization: "The emergence of radical political movements in the mid-thirties brought a leftward shift in New Deal policy." The writer could then make such a statement plausible by examining some specific "radical political movements": Huey Long's "Share Our Wealth" crusade, Francis Townsend's over-sixty scheme, Father Charles Coughlin's attack on Roosevelt's monetary policy, followed by a discussion of the new direction signified by the Wagner Labor Act and the Social Security Act.

Intermediate generalizations and their supporting elements are the "meat-and-potatoes" of historical discourse: they compel assent; they advance understanding; they deepen knowledge; they give a signal that the writer knows the subject. How much better is such a student generalization than a vague and almost meaningless statement like "Roosevelt had trouble in the late years of his first administration," a thesis that seems suspended in midair, suggesting little connection to events and developments of the times.

Intermediate generalizations, in addition to being supportable, should also add to the readers' (or listeners') *understanding*. They should provide an explanation of how and why something happened as it did; a generalization should explain the causes behind the event. To do so, one need not kill a mosquito with a sledgehammer, that is, bring into play all possible remote, proximate, underlying, or indirect "causes." Such an approach only diminishes the intermediate generalization and makes it insupportable. The example given in the previous paragraph does a creditable job of

---

[1] Robert V. Daniel, *Studying History* (Englewood Cliffs: Prentice-Hall, Inc., 1966), p. 37.

explaining. So does the following generalization concerning the Allied invasion of Hitler's "Fortress Europa" in 1944: "The indecisiveness of the German high command fatally weakened shoreline defenses" (provided of course, that the supporting points for such a statement are presented and developed).

Of course, history books (and good student papers) are more complex than the foregoing remarks indicate. Characteristically, they generalize at the upper levels of the intermediate stage and use as supporting elements lesser intermediate generalizations. We can illustrate this point by going back to the earlier example of the student who wrote a good paper about Roosevelt's administration. The student gave as one of the supporting elements "Francis Townsend's over-sixty scheme." That item might have been developed in the following way:

> Meanwhile a third figure loomed on the Western horizon—a lean, bespectacled oldster named Dr. Francis Townsend. A former city health officer, almost destitute himself, Townsend had absorbed some of the economic panaceas floating around California. He was brooding over the plight of himself and his generation when—so the story went—he looked out his bathroom window one morning and saw three old women rummaging in a garbage pail for scraps to eat. From that moment the old man's crusade was on. He came up with a plan that—to old people at least—was spinetingling in its sweep and simplicity. Everyone sixty and over would get a monthly pension of two hundred dollars provided—and what a wonderful proviso it was—that he spent his money within thirty days.[2]

This point gets us back to a central idea stated earlier that all history is learning about generalizations and how they relate to each other. This theme could be enlarged to say that getting one's generalizations in proper relationship to each other is a major purpose of education and also the beginning of wisdom.

Developing Interpretations

The reader might ask "Where are we at this stage?"—a good question. To summarize briefly, a few chapters ago we began with the axiom that in order to understand any historical development you must learn its *context*—the cultural and intellectual setting in which it took place (Chapter 6). You do this, in part, by asking the *questions* described in Chapter 7. Some of the questions are large scale, and some small scale, but all of them are answerable only on the basis of *evidence* (Chapter 8). As we explained in the last chapter, sifting through evidence is not an easy task. Now comes the difficult but rewarding step of trying to *interpret* the evidence you have found. In essence, you will be trying to discover the answers to a series of historical questions—what happened? how did it happen? why did it happen? etc.

We cannot emphasize enough that interpretation is a *process* not a singular episode. Usually you begin an investigation with some preliminary and ten-

---

[2] James MacGregor Burns, *Roosevelt: The Lion and the Fox* (New York: Harcourt Brace Jovanovich, 1956), p. 212.

tative conjectures about why things happened the way they did. These initial conjectures may have to be modified or cast aside as you dig deeper into the evidence, and new ideas may be "tried on for size." In essence, you are creating a *preliminary hypothesis* that will allow you to begin your research with a sense of direction and purpose. At each stage of your project, you will have to refine your interpretation as new evidence comes to light and as your understanding of the material becomes more sophisticated. In the end, your final interpretation, or thesis, must be constructed so that it does justice to *all* the evidence you have discovered.

In this section, we've described a special kind of intellectual experience, and we'd like to pause and reflect on it a bit. In essence, the historian first lifts an event from its temporal surroundings, and second examines those surroundings for elements that bear a crucial relationship to the event under scrutiny. In a way it is like unravelling a snarled skein of yarn. Perhaps the real source of the difficulty is that the historian is attempting to turn the world, complex and multi-layered, into language, which is linear and can deal with only one idea or relationship at a time. The process is one of mental reconstruction. Eventually the hours of reading, mental shuffling, and reorganizing pay off: there emerges a *synthesis*, a mental image that combines elements experienced separately. Some would use the term "pattern," others "insight," instead of synthesis. Whatever word is used, the exact processes of the mental experience described here remain a mystery to psychologists. Sometimes the synthesis builds slowly, often laboriously, occasionally with a sudden flash. Whichever the case, undue haste in trying to "make it come" can be counterproductive. Understanding relationships seems to have a slow-paced chronology, a point brilliantly made by novelist Eudora Welty in a recent work.

> Connections slowly emerge. Like distant landmarks you are approaching, cause and effect begin to align themselves, draw closer together. Experiences too indefinite of outline in themselves to be recognized for themselves connect and are identified as a larger shape. And suddenly a light is thrown back, as when your train makes a curve, showing that there has been a mountain of meaning rising behind you on the way you've come, is rising there still, proven now through retrospect.[3]

Thus, after studious and extended consideration of the historical situation in which an event is contained, the historian sees (or begins to see) that event as part of a larger whole. The event is like a piece of jigsaw puzzle, which suddenly makes sense when seen in the context of other pieces. For example, Adolf Hitler's confidence that his invasion of Poland in 1939 would not be seriously challenged makes sense when seen in the context of his experience of the repeated British and French pacifism of the preceding years. Basically, the historian comes to see an event as part of a whole composed of numerous individual acts, of certain prevailing conditions, and certain action-producing pressures.

---

[3] Eudora Welty, *One Writer's Beginning* (Cambridge: Harvard University Press, 1984), p. 90.

It is important to reiterate that an interpretation does not jump out of an assembled body of factual data nor does the historian passively await a moment of inspiration. In contrast, interpretations are aggressively sought, a point clearly made by British historian G. J. Renier: "It cannot be stated with sufficient emphasis that the historian's principles of serialization [interpretation] are introduced into history by him, not deduced from it. . . ." What this means in practice is that the historian approaches a historical situation with certain expectations about how human affairs work and uses these expectations in his or her analysis of it. Expectations originate in how experience has taught the historian to read the world—what moves human beings, typical tendencies of motivation, relations between economic and political power, the relations between geography and economic development—generally all manner of regularities that experience has reinforced. What this means of course is that those with wide experience in human affairs have something of a head start in historical interpretation. However wide the experience, the rules of the game require that one's ideas should be applied in any given situation not as a formula but as a tool that may (or may not) prove useful in explaining the event under consideration.

Variations in Interpretation

All that we have said leads us to a crucial question—what can one say about the validity of interpretations? It is best to avoid a counsel of perfection on this matter. For one thing, all historical generalizations are *probabilistic* rather than certain. That is, if generalizations are rooted solidly in evidence, they are *probably* valid. Scientists may say with certitude that all physical objects must descend according to a mathematically predictable rate of acceleration. Historians are in no such position, because their evidence is never complete and they can never be sure that the evidence they do have is representative. The historian is more or less in the situation of a person driving down a street, who, seeing five black cats, is tempted to conclude that all cats on that street are black. Perhaps it is so, but there are likely a number of cats on the block that haven't been seen. As a rule most generalizations—in day-to-day life, in the social sciences, and in history—have a "rickety" quality. They are usable as temporary and usually effective ways of organizing information, but rarely can they be regarded as absolute truth. For exactly this reason, some historians prefer to use the term "construct" to describe a historical generalization. A "construct" is a mental representation that organizes data into a thought unit that is both manageable and convincing while maintaining a certain tentative quality.

Thus, the issue of validity must be viewed within the context of the limited, or probabilistic, character of historical generalization. However, there is another, equally important side to the matter. *Any historical occurrence may be interpreted in a variety of ways.* Because historians approach the past with different interests and goals, they may differ greatly in how they "locate" an event in the broad context of the period they are studying. Thus an event may plausibly be seen as the end event of an economic sequence, or of a political sequence, or of an ideological sequence, or of a combination of such factors. For example, the election of Franklin D. Roosevelt in 1932 can legitimately be regarded as part of the public's reaction to economic distress, as the product of a series of political failures by Republicans, as part of an ideological shift by the American people, or (in a more sophisticated way) as a combination of all these. Behind each of these interpretations (patterns) is a particular frame of reference and point of view. As we have seen, when historians start from different places, they inevitably must travel different roads to the same destination. Nowhere is this basic feature of history better expressed than in Patrick Gardiner's *The Nature of Historical Explanation:*

> There are no absolute Real Causes waiting to be discovered by historians with sufficiently powerful magnifying-glasses. What do exist are historians writing upon different levels and at different distance, historians writing with different aims and different interests, historians writing in different contexts and from different points of view.[4]

Thus, readers of history should not only get used to but come to expect major differences in the way several historians interpret one single event. Such difference is well illustrated in the discussion of the Social Security Act of 1935 in the following passages, each of them written by historians highly respected within the profession. Please note the marginal comments.

William E. Leuchtenburg, *Franklin D. Roosevelt and the New Deal* (New York: Harper & Row, 1963), pp. 129–30.

As seen by Leuchtenburg, the Social Security Act was part of the pattern of "doing something for everybody" that FDR had adopted early in his administration. This passage is preceded by descriptions of various relief agencies, such as the WPA and the NYA. But these agencies, and others like them, missed a good many Americans; hence, the Social Security Act.

By predepression standards, Roosevelt's works program marked a bold departure. By any standard, it was an impressive achievement. Yet it never came close to meeting Roosevelt's goal of giving jobs to all who could work. Of the some ten million jobless, the WPA cared for not much more than three million. Workers received not "jobs" but a disguised dole; their security wage amounted to as little as $19 a month in the rural South. The President split up the billions among so many different agencies—the Department of Agriculture got $800 million of it—that Hopkins had only $1.4 billion to spend for WPA. By turning the unemployables back to the states, he denied to the least fortunate—the aged, the crippled, the sick—a part in the federal program, and placed them at the mercy of state governments, badly equipped to handle them and often indifferent to their plight.

Roosevelt's social security program was intended to meet some of the objections to his relief operations.

Oscar Theodore Barck, Jr. and Nelson Manfred Blake, *Since 1900*, 4th ed. (New York: Macmillan, 1965), p. 479.

Emphasizing ideological factors, the authors of this passage see the depression experience as having eroded traditional American individualistic ideas. The change in national ideology was manifested early in the 1930s by the AFL resolutions and by a plank in the

Another foundation stone of the Second New Deal was the Social Security Act of August, 1935. Behind its passage lay a reversal in prevailing American opinion. Old-age pensions, unemployment insurance, and provisions for sickness and accident benefits under government administration had been commonplace in Europe before World War I. But most Americans persisted in the belief that saving against old age and misfortune was an individual problem. The depression provided a cruel disillusionment. Thrifty citizens saw their life savings swept away by bank failures, while the average individual's inability to guarantee his own security in a complex economic system was demonstrated in

---

[4] Patrick Gardiner, *The Nature of Historical Explanation* (London: Oxford University Press, 1963), p. 109.

Democratic National Platform. Here the Social Security Act is seen as part of that same pattern of ideological change.

This is a most interesting passage that not only presents a pattern clearly different from the preceding two but also reflects an evident authors' bias. Note the editorial in line 5—"This move was long overdue." Note also the usage of such emotion-charged words as "quackery," "hating," "demagogues," and "Nazi Germany." The authors reflect a liberal, perhaps class-conscious point of view. As to the pattern they present, they see the Social Security Act as politically necessary because of the popularity of extremist proposals, including those of Huey Long, Francis Townsend, and Father Coughlin. The Social Security Act was part and parcel of the "turn to the left" of the Roosevelt administration in 1935.

many other ways as well. By 1932 there was a widespread demand for government action. The AFL passed resolutions asking unemployment insurance with compulsory payments by employers and the state—reversing its earlier hostility to the proposal—and the Democratic National Platform included a plank advocating both unemployment and old-age insurance under state laws.

But building a social security system exclusively on state legislation offered many difficulties. . . . Some Federal program to coordinate action on a national basis seemed to be required. . . . In January, 1935, the President transmitted to Congress . . . recommendations for joint Federal-state action.

Henry J. Carman, Harold C. Syrett, and Bernard W. Wishy, *A History of the American People*, Vol. II (Philadelphia Book Co., 1967), p. 634.

For the first two years of its existence, the New Deal did little to provide long-range protection against the risks of a private economy for working people. But in 1935, it set up a social security program for the care of dependent children, the aged, the handicapped, and the temporarily unemployed. This move was long overdue. . . .

Throughout the 1930s, but especially during the first years under the New Deal, the bitterness and frustration built up by the depression provided fertile grounds for demagogic movements and quackery of various sorts. . . .

Some of the panaceas hawked for the illnesses of depression were harmless, but others were dangerous because of both their simplification of complex issues and their openly antidemocratic bias. . . . Senator Huey Long, dictator of Louisiana and self-styled "Kingfish," had promised to make "every man a king"; Dr. F. G. Townsend had assured his aged followers that his plan would give them $200 a month; and demagogues like Father Coughlin and Gerald L. K. Smith had outlined programs that were startlingly similar to those of Nazi Germany and Fascist Italy. The popularity of these and similar proposals among the poor, as well as humanitarian considerations, convinced Roosevelt that the national government could no longer put off the adoption of social-security legislation.

Nothing is more typical than *difference* in historical interpretation, an axiom which returns us to the question of validity with which we began this section. Simply because interpretations reflect individual points of view and must always be considered tentative does not mean that any and every interpretation is acceptable. Evaluation of interpretations remains an important intellectual task. Judging the soundness of a historical interpretation can be a complex and time-consuming endeavor, but that sober reality should not keep you from trying. From a practical, day-to-day standpoint, historians ask two things when evaluating an interpretation.

1. **Does the author adequately support the interpretation with evidence?**
   What we as readers want is a generalization clearly tied to the reality

being described. We want the particular segment of the past about which the author is writing to "make sense" when we have finished our reading. We expect the author to have taken a reasonably wide look at the evidence and sought out the points essential to support the generalization. We want the author to avoid providing information extraneous to the interpretation presented. We are willing to recognize that no one can cover everything and that the author is obligated only to cover the material relevant to the interpretation being developed. In short, we want an "intermediate generalization" that is manageable within the limits of a book, article, or research paper.

2. **Does the author avoid being overwhelmed by personal intellectual preoccupations or theories?** All of us are aware that we have certain biases, be they political, national, racial, class, religious, or moral. We know that our viewpoint can be decisively shaped by them, leading to a refusal to look honestly at evidence that does not fit our point of view. Perhaps it is true that history is "neither made nor written without love or hate," but we must distance ourselves from our personal attitudes as much as possible and recognize their inherent dangers. This process is a matter of intellectual honesty as much as anything else. Just as an advertiser can distort the qualities of a product, so too can a historian distort the reality of the past. In fact, the world's libraries have many books full of misrepresentations founded on misplaced nationalism, political ideology, or similar preoccupations.

Broad Generalizations and Grand Theories

Not only can bias get in the way; so, too, can extremely broad generalizations, if relied on excessively. They can blind us to significant details which do not happen to fit the generalization. One such generalization, for example, is the "frontier thesis" of Frederick Jackson Turner. Turner argued that the major character traits of Americans emerged out of the demands made by the frontier environment on generations of pioneers over a 250-year period. A generalization like this provides an insightful way of organizing the specifics of the American past but, relied on exclusively, misses many other dimensions of the American experience. Another example of a broad, appealing (and dangerously misleading) generalization is the "melting pot" thesis of American immigration. A popular concept of generations of scholars and journalists, the "melting pot" thesis held (and still holds) that America's many immigrant peoples will gradually be assimilated into mainstream American culture, just as different metals melted together form a new and uniform alloy. This thesis, however, has so little validity that its exclusive application may cause us to miss the many examples of racial and ethnic groups that have *not* been assimilated into the dominant American culture. In too many cases excessive generalization distorts rather than clarifies reality.

Beyond such generalizations, and on a different plane, are a group of "grand theories" of human development that frequently appear in historical writing. Such large-scale conceptualizations attempt to put all of human experience within their explaining power. Two common types of grand theory exist: progressive and cyclical. Progressive theorists see humanity as

INTERPRETATION: ANOTHER OF HISTORY'S TRANSFERABLE SKILLS

The Delaney Corporation was a well-established firm in the vinyl and leather products field, specializing in the manufacture of eyeglass cases.* However, in 1979, it found itself in difficulties. Unable to find a solution to their problems, the company's board decided to call in a consulting firm for assistance. The consulting firm was hired to undertake a thorough review of Delaney Corporation's situation.

The completed report was lengthy, but the salient facts were these:

—For years the Delaney Corp. had sold to two different kinds of customer: specialty retailers who sold (among other things) high-fashion glass cases, and opticians who gave to their customers free cases when they purchased eyeglasses.
—The company had no product research and development section, nor did it do any market research.
—In the preceding five years major changes in eyeglass fashion and in case design had occurred. Also, there had been changes in the ways cases were carried by users.
—In the same period the sale and use of contact lenses had increased sharply.
—The sales force of Delaney Corp. consisted of four individuals, each of whom dealt with five or six wholesalers.

After lengthy discussion and analysis of Widmer's report, the consulting firm drew up the following summary of the Delaney Corporation's situation:

The Delaney Corporation seems to be living in the past, using marketing strategies poorly suited to today's business environment. Its salesmen are not directly in contact with either of the two types of customer for their product, and thus cannot provide feedback to product design. Because the salesmen are so far removed from their customers, they cannot provide them the assistance and marketing counsel that other firms offer. Moreover, the organization gives its salesmen little or no current information about market patterns, despite the fact that these patterns have changed substantially in recent years. All of this leads to a mode of operation almost guaranteed to bring continued decline, and, most likely, eventual bankruptcy.

Our recommendations for structure and policy changes are given in the following numbered sections. . . .

We have simplified the foregoing case study, of course, but its meaning is clear: the "interpretation" of data is as vital in day-to-day business affairs as it is in the study of history.

*This case study is fictional, but based on a number of actual cases.

on a ladder, climbing gradually though erratically to the top rung, which represents a perfected human society or even a material paradise. Marxism belongs in this category (humanity is progressing toward the "classless society"); so too is Christianity "progressive" in this sense (human history will come to an end at the time of the final judgment). Opposed to the progressivists are cyclic philosophers, who see the human race as on a wheel, going through repeated "cycles" of growth, maturity, and dissolution. The word "philosopher" above was intentionally chosen. Both progressive and cyclic theories are so large scale that they cannot be proven through the historical record. They are "metahistorical" speculations (i.e., speculations "beyond history") and as such are the province of the philosopher not the historian. Because such theories have had an important impact on the writing of history, those who read history should be alert to their presence.

Interpretation is the centerpiece of the historian's work. In this chapter we have discussed the meaning of interpretation; the levels of limited, intermediate, and broad generalization; the importance of hypothetical generalizations; the chronology of development of an interpretation; and finally, the validity of interpretation. The next chapters will examine the culminating step of the historian's labor, putting it all on paper.

EXERCISES

Set A, Exercise 1[5] Interpretation may be regarded as the pinnacle of the historian's work. All the steps of library research, classification, questioning, and analysis of evidence lead to it. The steps of writing or talking about the past depend upon and lead away from it. Interpretation is the *essence* of history as a discipline. It is therefore essential that you have some experience in doing this crucial stage of the historian's work.

Earlier in this chapter we described interpretation as being *a supportable generalization that in some way makes some segment of the past understandable.* Before starting the exercises let's examine this matter more concretely.

Suppose you were given the following five factual statements about Latin America in the period 1915–1930:

—trade was greatly increased during this period
—substantial capital investment by the United States promoted the growth of local industries
—an urban middle-class arose that challenged landholder control of local governments
—lower classes became more politically active, especially in demanding social legislation
—a spirit of cooperation with the United States began to emerge

---

[5] Credit for the overall theme of this exercise is to be given to Barry K. Beyer, "Using Writing to Learn in History," *The History Teacher*, XIII (February, 1980), 170.

What does all of this mean? What are we to make of it? After examining these statements (and thinking about them), one student clarified the issues as follows:

> For most of Latin America the period 1915–1930 was one of sharp change. Landholder dominance of the government came under fire by a rising middle class created by the growth of local industry. City workers, their numbers swelled by industrial development, added their voices to the challenge of old style government. The region as a whole began to retreat from its earlier anti-Americanism, forging new areas of cooperation with the United States. Indeed, highly active economic and political forces were creating a Latin America clearly different than before.

We want you to note carefully what has been done here. The student writer has added something to the original list of facts. She has *generalized* ("the period . . . was one of sharp change") and then expressed the same generalization in other terms in the last sentence ("a Latin America clearly different than before"). In her own way she has *interpreted* the facts for us. That always involves an *addition*, which is, essentially, the insight of the historian. (Note also that the student engaged in inference along the way, specifically about "their numbers swelled by industrial development"—a legitimate and proper inference.)

We're now going to give you some exercises that call upon you to interpret an array of facts. This process can be difficult, increasingly so with each exercise. However, this workbook was designed to give you demanding problems that will help you develop historical-mindedness and train your mental faculties to be used beyond history itself in a variety of professions. In many endeavors you will find it necessary to interpret certain facts given you. In each exercise below, you are asked to interpret a set of facts, that is, arrive at some kind of generalization and be able to support it in your paragraph. You need not use all of the statements given in each exercise, but it is important that you use most of them. (It could be argued that the statements used in these exercises are not "facts" in the purest sense but only small-scale generalizations [interpretations] open to debate. To an extent this is true. But rather than venture into an intellectual minefield by trying to define a "fact," for the purposes of this exercise assume that each statement is a solid inference based on the available data. Your task will be to write a larger-scale interpretation that effectively synthesizes the individual statements.)

A. Using the following statements about the impact of the Model-T automobile in America in the 1920s, write an interpretive paragraph in the spaces provided below the statements.

—The Model-T ended the social isolation of the American farmer.
—By enabling children to get away from their parents, the automobile affected American family life.
—The automobile influenced romantic relationships as now lovers could have a privacy not possible before.

—One of the factors contributing to the weakening of neighborhood relationships in America was the car, which enabled people to travel easily outside the neighborhood.

_____

_____

_____

_____

_____

_____

_____

_____

_____

_____

_____

B. Using the following statements about various pieces of British legislation relating to the American colonies in the years preceding the Revolution (1775), write an interpretive paragraph.

—American debtors bitterly opposed the Currency Act of 1764, which outlawed paper money issues thus deflating money values.
—The Quartering Act (1765) permitted public housing facilities in the colonies to be taken over for usage by British troops.
—By the provisions of the Stamp Act of 1765 American merchants found themselves having to purchase a government stamp for each and every business contract into which they entered.
—The Sugar Act of 1764, if enforced (and British officials said it would be enforced strictly), meant major losses to American shippers engaging in trade with the West Indies.
—Western settlers hotly resented the Proclamation Act of 1763, which prohibited colonial settlers from moving to attractive lands beyond the Appalachian mountains.

_____

_____

_____

_____

_____

_____

_____

_____

_____

_____

_____

_____

_____

NOTE: At this point we want to say something more about interpretation. Broadly speaking there are two types of generalization: 1) those that summarize, such as: "It was a very hot day" (based on high temperature readings for several hours) and 2) those that show causal relationships, such as: "High temperatures prevailed today because a lingering low pressure area brought southerly winds." Both of these types of generalization are common in historical discourse. By far the most important of them is the causal, explanatory generalization (type 2). With Item A you could do little more than provide a summarizing generalization; Item B called for a *causal* generalization. The next two units require a generalization of the second type.

C. The following statements relate to the economic interests of the English, Americans, French, and Dutch in the Caribbean during the years 1700–1740. Write an interpretive paragraph in the spaces provided. (Note: You might find it helpful to arrange the statements in chronological order.)

—Sugar planters in the British West Indies suffered major economic losses in the years after 1715.
—American colonial shippers, known throughout the world as sharp traders, had for many years carried on a thriving sugar trade with the British West Indies.
—In 1733, the British Parliament passed the Molasses Act, which placed prohibitive duties on sugar imported into the colonies from non-British possessions.
—After 1715, the French and the Dutch West Indies islands sharply increased their sugar production, and their sugar prices were well below those of the British islands.
—British West Indies planters had many friends in the British parliament.
—The Molasses Act led to smuggling becoming a way of life for American shipping interests.
—Mercantilism (an economic doctrine which dominated British thinking) stressed the importance of keeping colonial trade within the empire.

_____

_____

_____

_____

_____

_____

_____

_____

_____

_____

_____

D. The following statements relate to German plans to repulse the antic-ipated British-American invasion of Western Europe during the waning months of World War II. At that point in the war the German leader, Adolf Hitler, knew that the Allied invasion would determine Germany's fate. If the invasion could be repulsed, he thought, the war might yet be won. Using the following items, write an interpretive paragraph that explains why the Germans failed to repulse the invasion that came in June 1944. You should organize the statements chronologically and topically before you begin.

—Sent from Italy to inspect German defenses against invasion, General Erwin Rommel (the famed Desert Fox of the North African campaign) found them uncoordinated and undermanned.

—German leader Adolf Hitler, though agreeing with Rommel on where the Allies would strike (in Normandy) thought important diversionary activity would occur in the Calais sector, which was well north of Normandy.

—Rommel believed that once ashore the Allies could not be stopped; there-fore, they must be stopped at the water's edge.

—Von Rundstedt thought the main invasion strike would be in the Calais area.

—During the invasion itself Allied air supremacy, destroying German trans-portation and communication facilities, immobilized German forces.

—Hitler compromised between the Von Rundstedt view and the Rommel view; though believing Rommel to be correct, he allowed large army groups to remain committed to the Calais area.

—German western military commander Field Marshal Von Rundstedt saw no hope of preventing an Allied landing; however, he believed a German counterattack could throw them back to the beaches.

—Rommel was convinced that the main Allied invasion effort would be mounted in Normandy, which, as distinct from Calais, had not been mined by the Allies.

_____

_____

_____

_____

_____

_____

_____

_____

_____

Set A, Exercise 2 A famous historian, Fenelon, once said, "The good historian belongs to no time or country: though he loves his own, he never flatters it in any respect. The French historian must remain neutral between France and England. . . ." Difficult counsel indeed. What Fenelon was talking about is *bias,* a crucial issue in any discussion of interpretation.

Earlier in this chapter we discussed the matter of the historian's "intellectual preoccupations"—in other words, biases which might be national (despite the above advice), political, racial, class, religious, or moral. Remember, all interpretations reflect, to some extent, the historian's *frame of reference.* But bias is more than an acceptable intrusion of the historian's point of view; bias is, in the words of Barzun and Graff, "an *uncontrolled* form of interest" (italics ours). The presence of bias does not automatically mean a piece of history is worthless. But it is important that you develop the ability to identify obvious intrusions of bias so that you are better able to weigh the credibility of what you read.

Below are some examples of history writing that reflect authors' biases. Your task with the following excerpts is to identify in each passage any kind of bias you detect. Note each author's choice of words, emphasis, tone, and the like. Under each passage record the type(s) of bias you detect (political, racial, class, national, religious, moral) along with your reasons for thinking so.

1. We love to indulge in thoughts of the future extent and power of this [American] Republic—because with its increase is the increase of human happiness and liberty. . . . What has miserable, inefficient Mexico—with her superstition, her burlesque upon freedom, her actual tyranny by the few over the many—what has she to do with the great mission of . . . the New World. . . .

_____

_____

_____

2. God has not been preparing the English-speaking and Teutonic peoples for a thousand years for nothing but vain and idle self-contemplation and self-admiration. No, He has made us master organizers of the world to establish system where chaos reigns.

_____

_____

_____

3. The Romanism [Catholicism] of the present day is a harmless opinion, no more productive of evil than any other superstition, and without tendency, or shadow of tendency, to impair the allegiance of those who profess it. But we must not confound a phantom with a substance; or gather from modern experience the temper of a time when words implied realities, when Catholics really believed that they owed no allegiance to an heretical sovereign, and that the first duty of their lives was to a foreign potentate. This perilous doctrine was waning, indeed, but it was not dead. By many it was actively professed.

_____

_____

_____

4. An underlying weakness of his [Roosevelt's] leadership lay in his acceptance of the pragmatic approach to the solution of both domestic and foreign problems. In essence, it was a refusal to take the stand for a distinctively American approach to the basic problems of capitalism. No political program that emerged in the Roosevelt administration was distinctly the expression of the American tradition. In the course of twelve years, at home and abroad, the President stood with the radicals, using the political party parlance of the "middle way" in both instances.

_____

_____

_____

5. In fighting the War for Independence in North America, the bourgeoisie led the popular masses of the colonies against the English landed aristocracy and against the colonial yoke of England. This war of the colonies for independence was a bourgeois revolution which overthrew the landed aristocracy and brought to power the American bourgeoisie in union with the slaveholders.

    The American bourgeoisie used the struggle of the popular masses against the English as a means of achieving power; then, having come to power, like the English bourgeoisie of the seventeenth century, they oppressed the popular masses. In North America under the title "sovereignty of the people," (democracy), a so-called bourgeois democracy (in actual fact, the power of the bourgeoisie), was established.

_____

_____

_____

Set A, Exercise 3   *Frame of reference*, obviously, can become extremely dominant when a historian formulates an interpretation. Examples of this tendency were given in the exercise just completed—notably in Item 5, which was taken from a Soviet textbook.

To illustrate this further, we'd like you for a minute or two to think like a Communist. You have been taught to accept the following ideas as *absolutes*:

1. The main theme of all history is class warfare (that is, economic class against economic class).
2. Capitalism, the economic doctrine of the middle classes, is inherently evil.
3. The United States, as the world's strongest capitalist power, is ruthlessly imperialistic and anti-socialist.

Now, we want you to look at the five statements about Latin America on pages 177–178 and write an interpretive paragraph as a committed Communist might write it.

_____

_____

_____

_____

_____

_____

_____

_____

_____

_____

Set B, Exercise 1   Before working on these exercises, you might want to review the discussion that accompanies Set A, Exercise 1.

A. Using the following statements concerning the technological development of the United States in the late nineteenth and early twentieth centuries, write an *interpretive* paragraph in the spaces provided.

—In 1879, Thomas Edison perfected the light bulb and three years later, in 1882, developed the first power transmitting station, thus bringing a major new form of power to U.S. industry.

—In the late nineteenth century the "open hearth" process of steel-making was developed, marking a notable advance in machine tool production.

—By the early years of the twentieth century, American industrial production vastly exceeded that of her nearest rival.

—Development of the internal combustion engine in the late 1800s greatly increased the market for industrial products.

—Continuing developing of petroleum products in the years after 1870 significantly influenced American industrial markets.

_____

_____

_____

_____

_____

_____

_____

_____

_____

_____

_____

B. The following statements relate to the German military campaigns in the early years of World War II. Write an *interpretive* paragraph in the spaces provided.

—In September 1939, led by mechanized divisions and overwhelming air-power, German forces crushed Poland in less than four weeks.

—On May 10, 1940, Germany attacked Holland; and after a savage air bombing of Rotterdam and other cities, Holland surrendered on May 15.

—In the years before 1939, Germans developed the blitzkrieg (lightning war) style of warfare, which involved massive use of tanks and airpower to destroy enemy communications and morale.

—On May 12, 1940, German forces invaded France and, with a lightning thrust to the English Channel, knocked France out of the war within six weeks.

—The German invasion of Russia on June 22, 1941, was a success from the start as German mechanized units, assisted by the German Air Force, conquered dozens of miles a day.

_____

_____

_____

_____

_____

_____

_____

_____

_____

_____

C. These statements relate to events in Eastern Europe in the years following World War II. Write an *interpretive* paragraph in the space provided.

—In January 1944, following the great Russian World War II victory over Germany in Eastern Europe, Yugoslavia adopted a new constitution which closely resembled that of the Soviet Union.

—Influenced by the presence of Russian armies, Bulgaria in 1944 formed a government with Communists in key positions.

—In 1947, Rumania's foreign minister resigned and was succeeded by Communist Ana Pauker.

—In 1948, the refusal of [Catholic] Cardinal Mindszenty in Hungary to make church concessions to the Marxist government led to his trial and conviction, bringing a sentence of life imprisonment.

—Because of the government attempt to destroy the Catholic Church in Czechoslovakia, the Vatican in 1949 excommunicated all active supporters of communism in Czechoslovakia.

_____

_____

_____

_____

_____

_____

_____

_____

_____

_____

D. The following statements relate to the rejection of the Versailles treaty by the U.S. Senate in 1919–1920. President Woodrow Wilson had gone to Versailles and personally negotiated this treaty ending World War I. The treaty he brought home included American acceptance of League of Nations participation. Write an *interpretive* paragraph in the space provided.

—Though temporarily sidetracked in 1917-1918 by anti-German feeling, traditional American isolationism remained strong.

—In 1918, Americans elected a Republican Senate, an ominous sign for the Democrat Administration of President Woodrow Wilson.

—Americans of German and of Irish ethnic background opposed the League of Nations, although for different reasons.

—The wrangling of European diplomats at the Versailles Peace Conference of 1919 confirmed many Americans' view of European countries as narrow and self-serving.

—To get the League of Nations principle accepted in the peace treaty, President Wilson had to compromise several of his ideals.

—The chairman of the Senate Foreign Affairs Committee was Republican Henry Cabot Lodge, a major political enemy of President Wilson.

—Wilson's peace treaty incorporating the League of Nations principle, which had to be approved by the Senate, was eventually decisively rejected.

—Wilson's refusal to take any Republican with him to the Versailles Peace Conference eventually proved costly to his hopes of Congressional acceptance of the treaty.

_____

_____

_____

_____

_____

_____

_____

_____

_____

_____

Set B, Exercise 2   Below are some examples of history writing that reflect authors' biases. Your task with the following excerpts is to identify in each passage any kind of bias you detect. Note each author's choice of words, emphasis, tone, and the like. Under each passage record the type(s) of bias you detect (political, racial, class, national, religious, moral) along with your reasons for thinking so.

1.   The slaveholders controlled the government of the United States during the first half of the nineteenth century. From the War for Independence until the Civil War of 1861–1865, almost all of the Presidents of the United States were slaveholders. The bourgeoisie submissively ceded the direction of governmental affairs to the slaveholders. . . . A democratic system, the sovereignty of the people, existed on paper in the United States. Meanwhile, not only the slaveholders but also the American bourgeoisie used this false mask as a cover. In a capitalist system where factories, mills, and land are the property of the bourgeoisie, there is no real democracy and the masses have to fight to utilize democratic institutions. . . . In a bourgeois democracy, the power of the capitalists is extremely burdensome to the masses.

_____

_____

_____

2.	Cuba, our land, emerged from the condition of being a Spanish colony at the close of the past century, only to become a protectorate and semi-colony of the United States.

	The efforts of the Cuban people to gain full independence and sovereignty—the heroic sacrifices of the Ten Years' War, the Little Way, the War of '95, the aspirations expressed . . . above all by Antonio Maceo and by Jose Marti—were frustrated and flouted by North American intervention in the Cuban-Spanish War at a time when the Cubans had practically defeated Spanish colonialism and were on the verge of gaining full independence.

	In 1902 it was said that Cuba was a free and sovereign republic. It had an anthem and a flag. But above these symbols of sovereignty . . . we had the Platt Amendment, an instrument of oppression and of foreign domination over the country. . . .

	The United States imperialists had militarily occupied the island. They maintained here their army of occupation; by trickery they had disarmed the Army of Liberation and had organized a rural militia and a police force under their command. . . .

3.	Eisenhower and his administration have lived off the accumulated wisdom, the accumulated prestige, and the accumulated military strength of his predecessors who conducted more daring and more creative regimes. If our margin for error is as great as it has traditionally been, these quiet Eisenhower years will have been only a pleasant idyll, an inexpensive interlude in a grim century. If our margin for error is much thinner than formerly, Eisenhower may join the ranks of history's fatal good men, the Stanley Baldwins and the James Buchanans. Their intentions were good and their example is pious, but they bequeathed to their successors a black heritage of time lost and opportunities wasted.

4.	The first element in the negro problem is the presence in America of two alien races, both practically servants. The Indians were savages, and helped to keep alive savage traits in the souls of white settlers; but there was no considerable number of mixed bloods, and the Indians faded away as the white people advanced. The original slaves were also savages, just out of the jungle, who required to be watched and handled like savages, but they steadily increased in numbers, and from the beginning there was a serious race admixture. Their descendants in the second and third generation were milder in character, and were much affected by at least a surface Christianity; but their standards of character were much lower than those of the dominant white community, and tended to pull the superior race down. To the present day the low conditions of great numbers of negroes has a bad effect on the white race.

5.   In pride and vanity, he [Henry VIII] was perhaps without a parallel. He despised the judgment of others; acted as if he deemed himself infallible in matters of policy and religion; and seemed to look upon dissent from his opinion as equivalent to a breach of allegiance. He steeled his breast against remorse for the blood which he shed, and trampled without scruple on the liberties of the nation. When he ascended the throne, there still existed a spirit of freedom, which on more than one occasion defeated the arbitrary measures of the court; but in the lapse of a few years that spirit had fled, and before the death of Henry, the king of England had grown into a despot, the people had shrunk into a nation of slaves.

6.   During the last century the [New England] manufacturer imported the Irish and Fr. Canadians . . . thus the American sold his birthright in a continent to solve a labor problem. Instead of retaining political control and making citizenship an honorable and valued privilege, he intrusted the government of his country and the maintenance of his ideals to races who have never yet succeeded in governing themselves, much less anyone else.

Associated with this advance of democracy and the transfer of power from the higher to the lower races, from the intellectual to the plebian class, we find the spread of socialism and the recrudescence of obsolete religious forms.

Set B, Exercise 3   *Frame of reference* can become extremely dominant in formulating an interpretation. To illustrate this further, we'd like you for a minute or two to think like a total American chauvinist. You have been taught to accept the following ideas as *absolutes*:

1. United States' civilization is vastly superior to that of Latin America.
2. Latin American countries are extremely immature politically, their people having little capacity for democratic self-government.
3. Whatever progress Latin American countries have achieved has been largely due to American aid and intervention.

Now, we want you to look at the five statements about Latin America on pages 177–178 and write an *interpretive* paragraph in the style befitting a chauvinist.

_____

_____

_____

_____

_____

_____

_____

_____

_____

Sources
(Set A, Exercise 2)

1. Walt Whitman, editorial, "Brooklyn Daily Eagle" (July 7, 1846), quoted in *The Mexican War*, Ramon Ruiz, ed. (New York: Holt, Rinehart and Winston, 1963), p. 8.
2. Albert J. Beveridge, *The Meaning of the Times and Other Speeches* (Indianapolis: Bobbs-Merill, 1908), pp. 84–5.
3. James A. Froude, *History of England*, Vol. II (New York: Charles Scribner, 1872), p. 321.
4. Edgar E. Robinson, *The Roosevelt Leadership, 1933–45* (New York: Lippincott, 1955), p. 404.
5. Donald Robinson, ed., *As Others See Us* (Boston: Houghton Mifflin, 1969), p. 321.

Sources
(Set B, Exercise 2)

1. Donald Robinson, ed., *As Others See Us* (Boston: Houghton Mifflin, 1969), pp. 100–101.
2. *Ibid*., pp. 108–109.
3. William V. Shannon, "Eisenhower as President," in *Perspectives on 20th Century America*, Otis L. Graham, Jr., ed. (New York: Dodd, Mead, 1973), p. 323.
4. Albert B. Hart, "Negro Problem," *Cyclopedia on American Government* (Chicago: Appleton, 1914), p. 513.
5. John Lingard, *History of England*, Vol IV (Paris: W. Galignani, 1840), p. 215.
6. Madison Grant, "The Passing of the Great Race," in *Antidemocratic Trends in Twentieth-Century America*, Roland L. DeLorme and Raymond G. McInnes, eds. (Reading, Mass: Addison-Wesley, 1969), p. 45.

CHAPTER 10   THE WRITTEN REPORT

"Research is endlessly seductive; writing is hard work. One has to sit down on that chair and think and transform thought into readable, conservative, interesting sentences that both make sense and make the reader turn the page. It is laborious, slow, often painful, sometimes agony. It means rearrangement, revision, adding, cutting, rewriting. But it brings a sense of excitement, almost a rapture; a moment on Olympus. In short, it is an act of creation."

Barbara Tuchman

Now that we have discussed various skills related to historical reading and research, in the next two chapters we consider the problems anyone faces when trying to commit ideas to paper. In this chapter we give some "nuts and bolts" advice about note-taking, the use of quotations, and the documentation of sources. In the next chapter we will look at the actual process of exposition and narration.

Writing is only a tool not an end in itself. It is a tool for the communication of what we have learned through our research. With respect to the historian, "his subject is the story of man's past. His function is to make it known."[1] In short, the written word is the bridge between the historian's knowledge of the past and the mind of the reader. That is why the historian, or any report writer, must learn to communicate as clearly and effectively as possible. Knowledge is of little use unless it can be transmitted to someone else. Referring to England's Labour Party leader Ramsay MacDonald, Winston Churchill once said, "The Prime Minister has the gift for compressing the largest number of words into the smallest amount of thought." The message of this chapter is: Don't let that happen to you.

We fully admit that advice on the mechanics of writing a decent essay or research paper is not inherently exciting. Nor will the suggestions discussed below magically transform you from the literary equivalent of Archie Bunker into a modern day Lincoln or Churchill, but the recommendations are still important. If you read them, remember them (or some of them), and, most importantly, apply them to your own work, you have a good chance of becoming a better "communicator."

Preparing To Write: The Research Note

Good organization is an essential attribute of most effective historical writing. That dictum applies not only to the actual contents of a paper or report but also to the note-taking stages that lead up to the creative act. To write an organized essay, especially a relatively lengthy research paper or article,

---

[1] Barbara Tuchman, *Practicing History* (New York: Knopf, 1981), p. 32.

you must be able to organize your research notes into a usable format, and that implies effective note-taking.

Note-taking, in the library or the lecture hall, is one of the most important, and underrated, of the scholarly arts. A person who can summarize succinctly a lecture, article, or book has attained a skill that has many uses outside an academic setting. Important mental attributes that students hope to acquire from a university education—the ability to analyze, to synthesize, to organize—are sharpened by conscientious and thoughtful note-taking. In taking notes your aim should be twofold: *to make sure your research notes are both manageable and comprehensible.*

Often novice researchers fear they will not be able to find enough information to write a paper of the assigned length on the chosen topic. Actually, the problem is usually the reverse: you will find far more material on your topic than you can possibly manage in a typical college paper. Furthermore, if you are thorough in the research phase of the project, you may find yourself buried under so many notes that you despair of transforming them into a coherent paper. Thus, it is essential that you create a *system* for ordering your material before you begin writing.

The best way to do so is to use cards or slips of paper of a uniform size for your notes. Avoid transcribing information consecutively in notebooks or tablets. The reason for this suggestion is quite simple. The sequence of information in the final paper is almost never the sequence in which the information was acquired. You have to take notes in such a way that you can rearrange the materials into a logical order before you write the paper. Ideally, you should begin this process of organization (and, usually, reorganization) while you do your research.

We recommend that you take notes on index cards (4″ × 6″ or 5″ × 8″) or on half-sheets of paper. Try to limit yourself to one major idea, point, or piece of information on a single card or sheet. You will then be able to arrange your information in manageable chronological and topical units, and have most of the organizational work done before you write your first word. Also, it will save you time and a good deal of frustration if you write a brief descriptive headline on each card; you won't have to read the entire note to remember what is on it. Finally, as you take notes, make sure that you *record the source and the exact pages* where you found the information. You will use these source references in the footnotes or endnotes that are an indispensable part of any respectable piece of research.

The mechanics are easy to master. The *intellectual skills* associated with note-taking are more difficult to learn. Note-taking is *not* copying; it is an activity requiring thoughtful judgment and selectivity. Remember, the purpose of research is to *learn* something—to gain new knowledge. Writing is the tool for transmitting that knowledge to a reader. The research note is the first step in this process, and as such, should be expressed in your own words. A note should be a *summary* that reflects *your understanding* of what you have read or heard. In short, effective note-taking demands active intellectual work, but the rewards are worth the effort. As Jacques Barzun and Henry Graff point out: "What you have accomplished is threefold: you have made an effort of thought, which has imprinted the information on your mind; you have practiced the art of writing by making a paraphrase;

and you have at the same time taken a step toward your first draft, for here and now these are *your* words, not a piece of plagiarism thinly veiled by a page reference."[2]

Quotations and the Use of Evidence

Once having assembled their research notes, many beginning writers attempt to cram into the final paper all the facts and quotations they have collected. The temptation is completely understandable. After putting in so many hours reading, checking, and cross-checking, it seems wasteful to cast aside any informational tidbit or pertinent quotation. However, the good writer must be ruthlessly selective about what to include in a report. Convincing papers rest not on multiple quotations but on your command of the material.

As noted above, when you complete your research, you will probably have more information than you can possibly use in the paper you are planning to write. (Indeed, if this is not true, the chances are you have done too little research.) Readers are seldom impressed with volume alone, especially since time is a precious commodity. This means you will have to make some difficult decisions as you begin to put your thoughts on paper, or, these days, on a word processor. Just remember, "Distillation is selection, and selection . . . is the essence of writing history."[3]

The question is, *how* to select? Since it is impossible to include all the evidence on any subject, what is included must honestly reflect the total body of evidence with which the historian is familiar. The historian should, according to the nineteenth-century historian T. B. Macaulay, present an account that includes "such parts of the truth as most nearly produce the effect of the whole." That is, the part should be an accurate (or relatively accurate) reflection of the whole. That principle might be called the prime directive for anyone who writes history.

The writer must wield the scalpel with special determination when dealing with lengthy and numerous quotations. There is no better way to drive your reader to the waste basket or the bottle than by presenting an interminable string of quotations tied together with the numbing repetition of "He said," "She responded," and the like. Again, it is hard to abandon the quotations so laboriously transcribed into your notes, but *do it anyway!*

Two rules of thumb might make the task easier:

1. **Quote only primary sources.** There are few reasons to quote secondary sources. The paper you are writing should reflect *your* knowledge and *your* opinions, so write the paper in your own words not those of the historians you have read. This rule, of course, is not an absolute. There are legitimate occasions when you will want to quote another historian. At times you will want to include a passage that is so effective you just can't bear to leave it out. More frequently, to provide the necessary background for your own ideas, you will want to discuss what other historians have said about your topic. If you are going to agree or

---

[2] Barzun and Graff, *The Modern Researcher*, p. 30.

[3] Tuchman, *Practicing History*, p. 62.

disagree with another historian's interpretation, it is certainly proper to use that historian's own words. (One cautionary note here: if you are writing a book review, *the book* is the primary source—i.e., the "document"—you are analyzing. When you quote the author you are conforming with the rule we have been discussing.)

2. **Use quotations as "illustrations" not "proof."** No matter how many quotations you include, you will never be able to prove your point absolutely. There is, remember, always far more evidence available on your topic than you can possibly include in your paper. Thus, what you do include, by itself, proves nothing in any absolute sense. Reflect on how easy it is for narrow-minded or dishonest writers to choose only quotations that support their position, and you will understand why quotations have their limitations as vehicles of truth. The accuracy of a piece of historical writing ultimately rests on the integrity of the historian. The writing must reflect the totality of the available evidence, and the historian must have the honesty to provide a representative selection. It is not the quantity of quotations that is important, but whether they accurately reflect a larger whole. Quotations, in other words, should be used sparingly and only to illustrate salient points the historian has made in the traditional way; quotations should *never* be used to carry the weight of the argument.

Documentation: Footnotes and Bibliography

The quirks and eccentricities of English kings and politicians have long intrigued the history-reading public. In the period during and after World War I there was an especially interesting collection of British public figures who loved to ridicule each other's weaknesses with witty barbs. Lord Kitchener, for instance, said: "My colleagues tell military secrets to their wives, except X who tells them to other peoples wives." X, it has been suggested, was the Prime Minister H. H. Asquith. And Asquith, as historian A. J. P. Taylor notes, "was the first prime minister since the younger Pitt who is said to have been manifestly the worse for drink when on the Treasury Bench. George Robey, says Taylor, was uncomfortably near the truth when he sang: 'Mr. Asquith says in a manner sweet and calm: Another little drink won't do us any harm'." Asquith himself was not above the sarcastic put down. When the ashes of deceased Prime Minister Andrew Bonar Law (d. 1923) were interred in Westminster Abbey, Asquith commented: "It is fitting that we should have buried the Unknown Prime Minister by the side of the Unknown Soldier."

This type of detail makes history come to life. What is curious about the above stories is that they were drawn from footnotes in the first chapter of A. J. P. Taylor's, *English History, 1914–1945*.[4] Taylor is an eminent historian and a master of the informational footnote. Reading some of Taylor's works, which are uniformly provocative and well written, can be slow going since the reader doesn't want to miss the interesting tidbits that Taylor embeds in his footnotes. Where else might we learn that King George V creased his trousers at the sides, not front and back? Or that General Haig

---

[4] A. J. P. Taylor, *English History, 1914–1945* (Oxford: Clarendon Press, 1965), pp. 3, 15.

said of the Earl of Derby: "like the feather pillow he bears the mark of the last person who sat on him"?[5]

In light of this we might be tempted to say: "Footnotes can be fun." We hardly think you would believe it, but such a thought shouldn't be rejected out of hand. What is indisputable is that the use of footnotes is not an affectation or a sign of snobbish pedantry. In history writing, footnoting is essential. (A footnote, by the way, is placed at the "foot" of the page. If the notes are all collected at the end of the paper they are called "endnotes," or, simply, "notes.")

There are two types of footnotes. The first, the *informational footnote*, you are already familiar with from the examples above. Often you have information that could clarify or expand remarks in the text, but would interrupt the flow of the narrative if actually put in the body of the paper. Such footnotes provide a sort of running commentary on the material that forms the central core of your work. Very few students, in our experience, take advantage of the opportunities presented by the informational note. Give them a try, since explanatory footnotes allow you to include a good deal of important information that otherwise might have to be left out.

While the informational footnote is optional, the second type, the *source reference footnote*, is essential. Source references record the origin of, or authority for, material in the text of the paper. We said earlier that the credibility of a piece of historical writing depends on the integrity of the historian. True enough. But we need not rely on blind faith. Through source citations (footnotes) we can hold writers accountable and verify the accuracy and legitimacy of their facts and generalizations. Documentation of this sort helps the reader follow the author's reasoning processes. It allows the reader to test the links between fact and conclusion. From the author's standpoint, footnotes acknowledge the intellectual debt every writer owes to those who have gone before.

A common misconception is that only *direct* quotations need be footnoted. They do, to be sure, but that is not enough. The sources of *indirect* quotations (paraphrases) also need to be documented, if the information or interpretation came from a particular source. If you owe a debt to a specific author, whether you quote directly or not, you should provide a source reference.

Another erroneous belief is that only one source can be cited in a given footnote. This is not true. It is quite common to bunch two or more references together. If, for instance, you have written a paragraph based on multiple sources, you can cite all of them in a single note.

Sample Multiple-Source Footnote:
"For evidence on the growing inequalities in wealth, see James A. Henretta, *The Evolution of American Society, 1700–1815* (Lexington, Mass.: Heath, 1973), 103–06, and Edward Pessen, *Riches, Class and Power Before the Civil War* (Lexington, Mass.: Heath, 1973), 31–45." (From Paul Starr, *The Social Transformation of American Medicine*, [1982], p. 452.)

---

[5] Taylor, *Ibid.,* pp. 2, 53.

How do you know if you have too many or too few citations? Alas, there is no universal standard on this matter. Footnoting, like much else in the world of scholarship, is as much art as science. Gradually, through practice, you will get a "feel" for what is appropriate. You want to avoid cluttering up your writing with an avalanche of references or leaving the reader with the feeling that key references have been left out. Two or three references per typed page is probably adequate. Less or more than that and you come close to doing your reader an injustice. Ultimately, though, the number of citations depends on the type of paper you are writing, the nature of the sources, and the expectations of your reader.

Every paper should include a *bibliography*. A bibliography (list of the sources you consulted) serves a different function than footnotes. The notes help you document specific pieces of information in your essay. A source reference has a one-to-one relationship with a particular segment of the text. A bibliography, on the other hand, gives the reader a complete list of all the sources that were used by the author, whether or not they were cited in the footnotes. In some large works, authors list only the most valuable sources. This is called a "selective bibliography." In either case the lists are alphabetized according to the first letter of the author's last name. Often you will find bibliographies that divide the sources by type: books, articles, manuscripts, government documents, etc., or by primary and secondary sources. In such cases, each section is alphabetized according to the principles mentioned above.

It is not our purpose to teach you proper bibliographic and footnote style. The forms for both are highly standardized and used by scholars all over the world. You will find slight differences in format depending on the style manual you consult, but the differences generally are less obvious than the similarities. The point to remember is that *you should consult a style manual* and then follow that format consistently throughout your paper.

THE LIBERAL ARTS, THE ART OF COMMUNICATION, AND THE "REAL" WORLD

Long ago the Athenian statesman Pericles said, "A man who has the knowledge but lacks the power clearly to express it is no better off than if he never had any ideas." If ever a point sounded purely "academic" that is it. However, Pericles' dictum reflects an eminently practical understanding of the "real" world, and many contemporary business leaders agree. In a series of conferences (1981–1982) on the topic of Liberal Learning and Careers, a group of respected corporate leaders affirmed the importance of being able to do sound research, evaluate data, and clearly communicate the results—i.e., the importance of the skills discussed in this book. Below are a few excerpts from their statements.

"Advanced students of the liberal arts are asked to write research papers. They must learn to collect data and determine what is needed to understand an issue from the plethora of facts available. Then they must evaluate and seek meaning in the data and organize the material into a convincing essay for a discriminating reader. Many young people who work with me must also do this, although they often do not determine well what information to collect, how to evaluate it, or what to emphasize when writing. Liberal arts students gain that training before they join the company." Curtis Tarr, Vice President of Management Development, Deere and Company.

"We seek excellent oral and written communication skills. We also look for a person with strong interpersonal skills and with innate analytical capabilities." Nancy A. Dunston, College Relations Administrator, The Fidelity Bank.

"[C]olleges can make their graduates more employable if they teach them to be problem solvers—to analyze, synthesize issues, and cope with changing situations. As an employer, I would advise colleges first to provide students with a broad background and capacity for rational thought and problem solving. Second, the colleges must help develop students' interpersonal and communication skills—the abilities to get along with others and to write clearly." Sue Dueitt, Vice President, Corporate Communications, Middle South Services.

"The most glaring deficiency we have found in students in general is poor grammatical skills, and it seems to be getting worse. We have to teach college graduates written communication skills. This is an extremely important function that anyone in business or academe must possess." John Connors, Personnel Field Representative, Sears, Roebuck and Co.

"Our government and public affairs department hires people who have the ability to express themselves, to clarify ideas, and to verbalize succinctly. These critical job requirements reflect a need for people who can converse on a broad range of subjects, really on any subject, with their daily contacts." Joyce Bryant, Vice President and Director of the Money Management Institute, Household International.

"Skills that we look for in our candidates include the ability to think clearly and to listen actively and attentively. . . . Often we have to hire consultants to teach business communications skills, such as how to write effectively and succinctly." Carl Braun, Training and Development Coordinator, Lykes Brothers Steamship Company, Inc.

Copyright 1983 by the Association of American Colleges. Reprinted from *Liberal Learning and Careers Conference Report* by Janis L. Moyer.

EXERCISES

Set A, Exercise 1:
Note-Taking

Effective note-taking skills are extremely useful both in the classroom and on the job. This exercise is designed to give you some experience in taking good notes.

As you do the following segments, keep in mind that a good note *summarizes* the important points and it should be written *in your own words*. You should not try to copy the original text or lecture verbatim. Below is an example of the right way and the wrong way to take notes.

Original Passage:

"We cannot leave Versailles without reiterating that it had a purpose beyond being the residence for the king [Louis XIV of France] and his government. This great palace was a keystone in the new cult of royalty. In the preceding eras the great constructions were usually to the glory of God; even Philip II [of Spain], when he built his great palace, made it a monastery with the chapel as the center of interest. At Versailles the bedroom of the king is the center, identifying the king as the highest power on earth, while the chapel is to one side." (John B. Wolf, *Louis XIV*, 1968, p. 362)

I. Sample Note # 1:

```
Wolf
                        Versailles



V. had purpose beyond being king's residence. It was keystone in
new cult of royalty. Previous great constructions usually to glory of
God, like palace of Philip II which was a monastery with chapel as
center of interest. At V. Louis' bedroom was at center, identifying L.
as highest power on earth. p. 362




[Note author's name in corner and page number]
```

COMMENT: This note is sufficient as far as it goes. It records all the essentials, but it is more a literal transcription than a summary. Such a note requires little work on the part of the researcher. Remember, a good note should be a summary written in your own words. Now take a look at another research note based on the same passage.

II. Sample Note # 2:

Wolf

                Versailles

V. not just residence for king & govt.—was center of new "cult of royalty." Previous great buildings were for glory of God. Versailles intended to identify Louis as greatest earthly power. p. 362

COMMENT: This note is much better. It is shorter, and it translates the key ideas into the words of the researcher. In this sort of note some true intellectual work has been done, in that the passage had to be understood fully in order to be summarized effectively in different language. When it comes time to write the paper, there will be no temptation to use John Wolf's words since the note already reflects the style and words of the student.

Notice in both of the sample notes that the researcher has used abbreviations, a legitimate and time-saving practice. Also, the source and page number have been recorded and a one-word heading indicates the general topic of the note.

(Remember: In a real research project another card—a bibliography card—would contain all the pertinent bibliographical information related to Wolf's biography of Louis XIV. Thus the brief notation "Wolf" is sufficient to identify the source on the "information cards" above.)

For each of the passages below write, in your own words, a research note that summarizes the key ideas.

1.   All this emphasis upon grandeur, precedence, rank, and etiquette has led many historians to charge Louis [XIV] with megalomania. . . . But to see the ceremonial life of the court and the demands of his diplomats for recognition of their master's grandeur as megalomania quite misses the point. As Louis' power grew to the point where his officers could really reach into the provinces of his kingdom, and his soldiers could actually assure his government against revolt and rebellions, the *mystique* that has to accompany power had also to grow; this is the most important fact about the elaborate setting for the king. (J. B. Wolf, *Louis XIV*, 1968, p. 366)

_____

_____

_____

_____

_____

_____

_____

_____

2.   Elizabeth [I of England (1558–1603)] had no intention of surrendering her powers, or acquiescing in men's views of women. She had a great longing, she said, 'to do some act that would make her fame spread abroad in her lifetime, and, after, occasion memorial for ever'. 'She seems to me,' wrote Feria, 'incomparably more feared than her sister [Queen Mary], and gives her orders and has her way as absolutely as her father [Henry VIII] did.' She kept matters of state very largely in her own hands, and generally consulted her councillors individually, on the principle of 'divide and rule.' " (J. E. Neale, *Queen Elizabeth I*, 1957, pp. 67–68)

_____

_____

_____

_____

_____

_____

_____

3.   Harriet Tubman was one of the many ex-slaves who served as 'conductors' on the famed Underground Railroad. Along its various routes in the Northeast and Northwest they, together with northern free Negroes and sympathetic whites, sheltered the frightened fugitives and sped them on their way. These runaway slaves did much to disturb the consciences of the northern people and to arouse sympathy for those they left behind.

But southern masters were less disturbed about the ultimate consequences than they were about their immediate losses. Moreover, every successful runaway was bound to encourage other slaves to try their luck in the same enterprise. (Kenneth Stampp, *The Peculiar Institution*, 1956, p. 122)

_____

_____

_____

_____

_____

_____

_____

_____

4.   "In Colonial America, alcohol was vital to the myriad social and cultural expectations which colonists had brought with them from England and the Western world. It was universally honored as a medicine for almost every physiological malfunction, whether temporary or permanent, real or imagined. But even more, it was _aqua vitae_, the water of life, and 'the good creature of God'—in St. Paul's and then Increase Mather's cheerful phrases—a mystical integration of blessing and necessity. And so it had been for as long as men had recorded their fears or their satisfactions. 'Give strong drink unto him that is ready to perish,' reads the _Book of Proverbs_, 'and wine unto those that be of heavy hearts. Let him drink, and forget his poverty, and remember his misery no more.' " (Norman Clark, _Deliver Us from Evil: An Interpretation of American Prohibition_, 1976, p. 1)

_____

_____

_____

_____

_____

_____

_____

_____

5.   "Among professional military men in [President Harry] Truman's inner circle, the influence of General George Catlett Marshall, first as Chief of Staff of the Army, later as Secretary of State, and still later as Secretary of Defense, was supreme. Truman regarded him as the greatest military strategist of our time, the most capable and stalwart director of our foreign policies. He looked uncritically to Marshall for guidance and decision, seldom questioning his opinions, and still more seldom acted contrary to his recommendations. Truman never attributed fault or failure to him. Conjointly, Marshall's prestige in Congress and the country was helpful to the 'upstart' President. Marshall's self assurance gave him confidence." (Herbert Feis, _From Trust to Terror_, 1970, p. 19)

_____

_____

_____

_____

_____

_____

_____

_____

Set A, Exercise 2:
Footnotes

Footnotes (or endnotes) are an integral part of most scholarly writing. Writers use notes to acknowledge the sources of their facts and ideas and to provide additional information or commentary related to material in the text proper. There are a number of places (more than two, less than six) in the following passage that need to be footnoted. At the *end* of the sentences or segments that require a footnote insert the letters "FS" to indicate the need for a source footnote and the letters "FI" to indicate an informational note.

Travel in Nineteenth-Century America

Overland travel in America in the years before 1860 called for the most careful kind of preparation. Especially was this so in the West. The pioneer enroute southwest from St. Louis had to know about wagon maintenance, clothing suitable for prairie travel, use of firearms, and care of mules and oxen. Further, food provisioning was a major problem. The travelers had to take along biscuits, potatoes, sugar, flour, tea, grease, and have the knowledge and skill to make the all-important pemmican along the way. The hard work of travel required substantial amounts of food. One mid-century traveler found that each man in his group consumed 2.35 pounds of food per day.

Once on the road the problems only intensified. There were the difficulties of fording rivers, repairing wagons, or doctoring rattlesnake bites. There were sometimes long distances that had to be traversed without water—"journadas" the Mexicans called them. Such days had to be carefully planned for, as the following advice to travelers illustrates:

> On arriving at the last camping-ground before entering upon the journada, all the animals should be well-rested and refreshed as possible. To insure this, they must be turned out upon the best grass that can be found, and allowed to eat and drink as much as they desire. . . . They should be carefully watered just previous to being hitched up and started out upon the journada, the water-kegs having been previously filled.

If the journada was an occasional problem, the enduring problem was the lack of a good roadway. The traveler had to face dust, ruts, chuck holes, mud, tree stumps in his path, dead carcasses, and deep sand.

Elsewhere in the country, even as late as 1860, America had perhaps the worst roads in the civilized world. The average American preferred to use the railroads when travelling, and so was reluctant to see tax money used for road-building purposes. In fact, at the outbreak of the Civil War in 1861 the national government spent less than 15 million dollars on roadbuilding in all the preceding seventy years. Whatever roads were constructed were most often built by local volunteers as a way of paying their "road taxes." But most citizens regarded their road-building days as "a lark or a picnic," as historian Albert C. Rose puts it. Not much was done.

If you have marked the need for one or more informational footnotes (FI), briefly describe what further information seems to be required.

_____

_____

_____

Set B, Exercise 1: Note-Taking
As you do the following segments, keep in mind that a good note *summarizes* the important points and it should be written *in your own words*. You should not try to copy the original text verbatim.

For this Set B exercise, write research notes for each of the six passages in Chapter 8 ("Evidence") concerning the Kent State incident of May 4, 1970. Assume you are researching a paper on Kent State and these statements are your sources. The passages can be found on pages 155–158.

1. _____

_____

_____

_____

2. _____

_____

_____

_____

3. _____

_____

_____

_____

4. _____

_____

_____

_____

5. _____

_____

_____

_____

6. _____

_____

_____

_____

Set B, Exercise 2: Footnotes

Footnotes (or endnotes) are an integral part of most scholarly writing. Writers use notes to acknowledge the sources of their facts and ideas and to provide additional information or commentary related to material in the text proper. There are a number of places (more than two, less than six) in the following passage that need to be footnoted. At the _end_ of the sentences or segments that require a footnote insert the letters "FS" to indicate the need for a source footnote and the letters "FI" to indicate an informational note.

Renaissance Doctors

So high is the prestige of modern physicians that we forget that, until very recently, doctors knew almost nothing about the causes and cures of disease, and precious little about the structure and function of most human organs. In fact, medicine became a science only in the last half of the nineteenth century, after a long struggle against superstition and ignorance. That struggle began a good deal earlier than the nineteenth century. It was during the Renaissance period, especially in the sixteenth century, that western medicine took its first tentative steps toward modernity.

During the long medieval period (ca. A.D. 500–1500) medical knowledge had advanced at a snail's pace. Medieval medicine was an amalgam of superstition, folklore, and religious dogma. Moreover, doctors believed that everything worth knowing about medicine had already been discovered. The authoritative medical texts were those written before A.D. 200 by Hippocrates and Galen, and by Avicenna, who had died in 1037. If you had a medical question, the answer could be found in their books.

The Renaissance (ca. 1300–1600), however, saw a rebirth of an interest in the study of the world of nature, and by the sixteenth century a number of medical men began to challenge the wisdom of the ancients. For instance, Andreas Vesalius, who taught at the University of Padua, rejected the custom of teaching anatomy by reading extracts from Galen. Instead, he performed dissections himself, and, in the words of Daniel Boorstin, "noted so many instances where Galen described what was not found in the human body that he soon realized that Galen's ostensibly 'human' anatomy was really only a compendium of statements about animals in general." Vesalius then went on to publish his justly famous _De Humanis Corporis Fabrica_ (1543) which became the basis for modern anatomical science.

What distinguished Vesalius, and others like him, was his willingness to believe the evidence of his own senses if what he saw contradicted the ancient texts that most of his contemporaries regarded as only slightly less authoritative than the Bible. This new attitude was best summed up by that remarkable figure, Theophrastus Philippus Aureolus

Bombastus von Hohenheim, better known to history as "Paracelsus." Paracelsus was no respecter of accepted "wisdom." He symbolically burned the books of Galen and Avicenna and said of his contemporaries, who slavishly believed the traditional texts: "Even the flies would disdain to sit on them except to make their dirt." He went on to brag, according to H. W. Haggard, that he alone refused to make up books out of extracts of Hippocrates and Galen but based them on his own experience, "the supreme teacher of all things."

Even by 1600, medicine had a very long way to go. Doctors still understood little about the causes and cures of disease. But the roadblock had been broken. Physicians, and other scientists, were again willing to investigate nature directly rather than meekly accepting the long-revered wisdom of the ancients.

If you have indicated the need for one or more informational footnotes (FI), briefly indicate what further information seems to be required.

_____

_____

_____

_____

_____

CHAPTER 11   WRITING: EXPOSITION AND NARRATION

"Writing is easy. All you do is stare at a blank sheet of paper until drops of blood form on your forehead."

Gene Fowler

It has been said legitimately that writing is the highest of all the arts. It is therefore nonsense to suppose that anyone can be taught "how to write" in the few paragraphs that follow. Better to hear, ponder, and practice the counsel of the great and near-great literary masters, who, in their genius, say so much about writing in a few telling phrases.

As Winston Churchill said, "Short words are best and the old words when short are best of all." Nicolas Boileau, the seventeenth-century French writer, counseled the writer to "twenty times upon the anvil place your work." Mark Twain remarked that "as to the adjective: when in doubt, strike it out." Alexander Pope pointed out that: "whoever thinks a faultless piece to see,/thinks what ne'er was, nor is, nor e'er shall be." Robert Browning urged those who would write to "paint a picture." L. M. Montgomery insisted that "the point of good writing is knowing when to stop." H. L. Mencken approvingly described the man of "verbal delicacy . . . who searches painfully for the right word;" and, finally, an anonymous observer saw the crucial element in writing as "the length of time one could keep the seat of his pants in contact with the seat of his chair."

A major misconception of many students is that history is merely "facts." Not so. *Not so.* The historian, more than simply reciting facts, tries to *explain* them with thoughtful generalizations. As British historian E. H. Carr said: "What distinguishes history from the collection of historical facts is generalization." Facts have no meaning apart from the generalizations (interpretations) the historian supplies. These generalizations, of necessity, become subject to all of the requirements of expositional and narrative form. The sooner this is understood as the fundamental nature of history, the sooner you will be able to write a piece of history that is both coherent and plausible.

Factors That Enhance the Quality of Exposition

Famed essayist E. B. White once remarked that "most readers are in trouble about half the time." What he meant was that reading for understanding is often made unnecessarily difficult by a writer's failure to provide an orderly, systematic *exposition* of the subject. ("Exposition" refers to those techniques writers use to convey information—i.e., set forth essential facts—in a clear and organized manner.)

Writers' faults can be many and varied, but by far the worst of them is lack of orderliness. Orderliness is simply a matter of putting ideas in proper relationship to each other. The correct terms for this process are "superordination'' and ''subordination,'' but such fancy words are unnecessary. What we are talking about is putting smaller details where they belong—under larger generalizations. Readers have a right to expect this basic arrangement and get understandably irritated when they do not find it. Consider this simple illustration:

> We've been having trouble with the family car during the past few weeks. In learning to drive my most difficult task was shifting gears smoothly. My parents didn't allow me to take driving lessons until I was seventeen. As I said, our car seems to vibrate when its speed gets over thirty-five. My driving instructor told our class that we should learn on stick-shift automobiles because it would mean a saving when we get our own cars.

This is an almost ridiculous example, having several themes that don't clearly relate to each other. Truman Capote said it best: ''That's not writing, that's typing!'' Yet such arrangements of ideas are common in history papers and account for much of the red ink that stains work returned to student writers.

Ordering your ideas is a basic task. When you prepare to write, begin by putting down your basic generalization (thesis) in an explicit statement, followed by the two, or three, or four major supporting points that make the generalization plausible. Then add, under each supporting point, the detail necessary for that point to make sense. This is the most fundamental principle of writing. It is not always easy to decide *what* fits *where*, however. To enhance this skill you will be asked to do several exercises at the conclusion of this chapter.

An equally important requirement of effective exposition is to follow certain accepted conventions.

1. **A piece of writing should have a determinable beginning, a developmental middle, and an identifiable end.** The *beginning* (introduction) is usually a paragraph that provides a gradual lead-in, something of a broad stage-setting orientation, to the subject of the paper. Either as a part of such a paragraph or immediately following it, you should unequivocally state the basic interpretive generalization (often called a ''thesis'') whose validity you intend to demonstrate in the pages to follow. The *middle* of the paper sets down the main supporting points along with necessary corroborative detail. The *end* (conclusion) presents a summary of the highlights, along with a restatement or reemphasis of the thesis. This overall structure of beginning, middle, and end may seem simplistic. However, it remains the organizational plan that experienced historians follow, because it is the most comfortable form and the one readers expect.

2. **The basic unit of all effective writing is the paragraph.** A paragraph provides the *thought-unit* which, when well composed, enables the reader to advance forward to the next element in the writer's train of thought. The keynote of the paragraph is the topic sentence (some say ''controlling sentence''), which is essentially a generalization (usually limited) that the rest of the paragraph develops and elaborates. Though it is

not an absolute rule, most effective writers put their topic sentence first. They know that doing so will help readers follow the flow of thought. All the foregoing has probably been covered in your English courses, which only shows that rules don't change simply because you change classrooms.

Paragraphs are the essential building blocks by which a writer develops the central argument of the piece. Consequently, a writer must also give attention to the flow *between* paragraphs. Quite often, as you know, a new paragraph shifts to a different facet of the subject—a turn around a corner, so to speak. It is exactly at such points that readers often get lost unless the writer gracefully steers them into the turn. Experienced writers do this either by making the final sentence of a paragraph "lean" in the direction of the forthcoming shift or by providing a *transitional* paragraph (distinct from the substance paragraph described above). This type of paragraph first summarizes then redirects the reader's attention by announcing that a new aspect of the subject is about to be discussed. Such transitional paragraphs can add greatly to the continuity of a narrative. Writers of history should use them whenever there is a danger that the reader will get lost.

3. **Avoid excessive detail.** When writers follow the foregoing principles, their readers begin to relax a little, knowing that they are being guided by a considerate hand. Yet something more is necessary. An effective writer must not overburden the account with excessive detail, lest readers get to the point where they "can't see the forest because of the trees." Experienced historians make this point over and over: Too much detail can obscure any argument and ultimately confuse the reader. Barbara Tuchman, a superb historian and a fine writer, expresses the same idea in this way:

> The writer of history, I believe, has a number of duties vis-a-vis the reader, if he wants him to keep reading. The first is to distill. He must do the preliminary work for the reader, assemble the information, make sense of it, select the essential, discard the irrelevant—above all, discard the irrelevant . . . . To offer a mass of undigested facts, of names not identified and places not located, is of no use to the reader and is simple laziness on the part of the author, or pedantry to show how much he has read. To discard the unnecessary requires courage and also extra work. . . .[1]

Thus, we can say too much information is the enemy of form. In the next breath, however, we must also say that too little in the way of supporting detail robs a generalization of its substance, as well as its validity. In short, the key principle must be that of *selectivity*, which, as a famous ballerina once said, is "the soul of art."

In summary, effective communication requires the writer to observe certain standard forms: proper ordering of ideas; use of the paragraph as the

---

[1] Barbara Tuchman, *Practicing History* (New York: Knopf, 1981), pp. 17–18

basic unit of exposition; and selectivity in regard to the amount and kind of specific information incorporated in the writing.

Factors That Enhance the Quality of Narration

If you follow the steps of historical inquiry discussed in earlier chapters, and observe the requirements of exposition described above, you will be well on your way toward doing good history. However, there is something more to writing effective history, simply because history is *narrative* as well as expository. Remember that *exposition* involves ordering your ideas and presenting them clearly. *Narration*, on the other hand, means, essentially, telling a story—relating a sequence of events.

Before examining the art of historical narration, we need to look briefly at the distinction between "narrative" history and "analytical" history. In its pure form narrative history tells a story in more or less chronological order, along the lines of Julius Caesar's "I came, I saw, I conquered." Analytical history, on the other hand, frequently puts the chronological movement of events into the background in favor of emphasis upon the characteristics of a given time and place such as *political, social, economic,* or *ideological* elements. Such writing, though having roots in the day-to-day and month-to-month rush of events, tends to separate itself from them, concentrating on a deeper explanation of vital forces operative during a time.

Analytical history can explain how the past lingers in a certain institution of the time; it may explore the origins and structure of a key idea that influenced the main historical figures or perhaps examine the technological setting that generally shaped the historical situation. An example of such analytical history is Peter Laslett's *The World We Have Lost* (1965). In this study Laslett examines the social and economic structure of preindustrial England without concerning himself with the day-to-day movement of events. He draws examples from many places and years in order to show, in general terms, what English life was like during the century or so before the industrial revolution.

It must be emphasized that both narrative and analytical approaches qualify as history. While the distinction is essential, it is still true that in practice narration and analysis tend to blur, as it is impossible to *narrate* events of a period without *analyzing* certain of its aspects. Likewise, analysis must be firmly based on the concrete events that constitute the backbone of history. The typical way in which narrative and analysis are combined in a piece of written history is illustrated in the passage below, which discusses the end of World War II in 1945. Note our bracketed remarks:

> On August 6, after an ultimatum to surrender, the first atomic bomb destroyed rather more than four square miles of Hiroshima and killed upward of seventy thousand persons. [*A narrative sentence—note the action verbs.*] Since the Japanese high command still ignored the ultimatum, a second and more powerful bomb was dropped three days later on Nagasaki, destroying six square miles and killing an unknown number. [*Again, part of the basic narrative flow.*] These two holocausts were on about the same scale as an Anglo-American triple air raid on Dresden, which had been undertaken in support of the Russian winter offensive in February, 1945. [*This is a bit of comparative analysis enabling the reader*

to appreciate the destructive force of just two bombs.] The new bomb was, however, decisive because it appeared capable of limitless, pitiless, irresistible repetition. [*Again analysis of the threat the bomb posed.*] The Japanese government resolved to submit before a third bomb fell, leaving the conquerors to wrestle with the problem of atomic weapons which still darkens the thoughts of mankind. [*Basically narrative, though the latter part of the sentence does briefly describe the long-term menace of the bomb.*][2]

We ask you to keep this basic distinction in mind as we proceed to examine the techniques of narrative history. Perhaps the best way to obtain a deeper insight into narrative history is to discuss it in the context of fiction at one end of a spectrum and empirical studies (economics, sociology, etc.) at the other end. History lies between them. It is not an empirical study (that is, one in which the researcher can directly observe, or measure, or experiment upon the "thing" being investigated) for it is predominantly concerned with past events, each of which is in some sense unique and thus unrepeatable. Nor is history fiction, since its characters and actions are taken from reality rather than from imagination.

Still, while distinct, written history does have a good deal in common with fiction. Both historical narratives and novels deal with the gradual unfolding of a causally connected series of incidents (i.e., they both have a "plot"). Both must make human acts meaningful within the context of a society's central values; both must blend description and background with action to make their accounts understandable. Many historians do not understand or fully appreciate these parallels, and all too often write accounts that dull the intellect as well as the imagination. Not surprisingly, students find such writing boring and put it aside with relief when the required reading is finished.

In your own writing try to use the narrative techniques historians share with fiction writers. Among them are the following:

1. **Character development:** Any account of the past has human beings moving in and out of it to one degree or another, and many historical situations are crucially influenced by the strengths, weaknesses, and peculiarities of single individuals. In fact, for the most part, characters are the primary vehicles through which a narrative becomes meaningful. Consequently, the novelist's habit of putting individuals at the center of the story is one well worth imitating. There's nothing forced about this, either, for given our ambitions, hates, and loves, all of us are continually being carried decisively across the paths of others, often with fateful consequences. This means that in a narrative the writer must present us with more than a character's actions. The person must also be seen remembering, reflecting, fearing, worrying, predicting, yearning. In other words, a historical figure is both a doer *and* a thinker, and an examination of the contemplative side will help clarify the basis on which action is taken.

It is true, of course, that a historian cannot invent motivations as can a novelist. But, provided there is a basis in evidence, the historian can legit-

[2] Ernest J. Knapton and Thomas J. Derry, *Europe and the World Since 1914* (New York: Scribner, 1966), p. 289.

imately *infer* motivation, states of mind, and character qualities. Here are a couple of examples of historical passages that do this well:

> For Churchill it [the Japanese attack on Pearl Harbor and U.S. entry into World War II] was a moment of pure joy. So he had won, after all, he exulted. Yes, after Dunkirk, the fall of France, the threat of invasion, the U-boat struggle—after seventeen months of lonely fighting and nineteen months of his own hard responsibility—the war was won. England would live; the Commonwealth and the Empire would live. The war would be long, but all the rest would be merely the proper application of overwhelming force. People had said that Americans were soft, divided, talkative, affluent, distant, averse to bloodshed. But he knew better; he had studied the Civil War, fought out to the last desperate inch; American blood flowed in his veins. . . . Churchill set his office to work calling Speaker and whips to summon Parliament to meet next day. Then saturated with emotion, he turned in and slept the sleep of the saved and thankful.[3]

> Henry VIII, fat-cheeked, sensual, greedy, and unscrupulous, became King of England in 1509. He had hot, sultry eyes, a small tightly closed mouth, and a beefy coarseness of feature. Like a wrestler he stood habitually with his legs far apart, his hands on his hips. His mentality was simply an aggregation of desires. He loved meat and drink—and finery. He loved money and power, and he loved women. He loved women almost as much as he loved power. When he got tired of his wives he treated them very badly; he sent two of them to the Tower and had their heads cut off.[4]

Such commentaries add a note of "inwardness" (getting inside an individual's mind) to a historical account. It is an important technique of narrative form frequently employed by many historians and is simply a frank recognition that human beings contemplate before they act. Because of the limitations of evidence, historians cannot use it to the same extent as can a novelist. Rightly used, however, this technique can add much to the vitality and reality of the story the historian tells.

2. **The role of plot:** As we mentioned earlier, plot refers to the gradual unfolding of a causally connected series of motivated actions. A typical example of a summarized plot would be the following: "Lisa, angry that Chris was having an affair with Miriam, told his boss that Chris had been padding his expense account. An investigation followed, and Chris was discharged. Suspecting that Lisa had been the informant, Chris confronted her, and after an angry exchange, struck her just as Miriam walked into the room." Yes, a soap opera plot, so familiar to most of us. Soap opera is interesting because it intensifies life, with crisis following crisis like box-

---

[3] James M. Burns, *Roosevelt: Soldier of Freedom* (New York: Harcourt Brace Jovanovich, 1970), p. 163.

[4] W. E. Woodward, *A New American History* (New York: The Literary Guild, Inc., 1937), p. 7.

cars racing past a railroad crossing. Our own lives move at a slower pace and so, too, did the lives of the people of the past. History "plots" don't move like soap opera. Still, historians can learn something from those media products. All of the action is *motivated*. In the example above Lisa has good reason to be furious with Chris, and no one can blame him for his resentment at her underhanded revenge against him. However frivolous the whole scenario seems to be, historians can draw from it a significant insight: for an action to be believable, it must be motivated, whether on the high plane of ideals, the middle plane of ambition or party loyalty, or the lower plane of avarice, meanness of spirit, or other inclinations too numerous to mention. In other words, enough of abstract forces. In history we are talking about human beings.

What the writer needs to do in many cases is develop the inherent drama of the historical situation: highlight the basic conflict between differently motivated individuals and describe the action and reaction that led to a resolution of the issue. Never mind about naming the heros and villains of the piece—they are useful but not essential in dramatic situations. The following passage is a good illustration of the way in which a writer can bring out motivations and develop conflict. In it, author James M. Burns describes the split between President Franklin D. Roosevelt and labor leader John L. Lewis, earlier an ardent FDR supporter:

> Conflict between the two men was inevitable even if they both had not been prima donnas. To speak and act for his followers, Lewis had to move toward leftist politics and direct action. Roosevelt, with a different constituency and needing support in Congress, had to continue his delicate balancing act among power blocs. Lewis derided Roosevelt's public role as a great humanitarian and forthright fighter for the underdog; Roosevelt, he said, was weak, tricky, and lacking in conviction. Distrusting the mine leader, and fearing that he would disrupt the coalition, Roosevelt struck out at him at critical moments. And Lewis, fighting for his organization's life during the crucial organizing drives, recoiled from what he called Roosevelt's "catlike scratches."[5]

Perhaps the best way to finish this little essay on plot is to say that we are bored by an account that simply tells us that "The king died and then the queen died." Change this to "the king died, and then the queen died of grief" and you have a story of inherent promise. We learn not only what happened but *why*. In other words we have the element of plot. What is necessary, then, is that the writer of history clearly recognize that some historical situations can best be made coherent through the use of dramatic form.

3. **Description of setting:** Because as readers we employ mental pictures to facilitate our understanding, novelists take care to describe the physical setting in which their action takes place. Historians can afford to do much less with physical setting (though occasionally that too can be important). Instead, they concentrate on setting in another sense—the social, ideolog-

---

[5] Burns, *Roosevelt*, p. 351.

ical, and cultural environment in which historical action takes place. We've already discussed this matter at some length, so we will simply note that cultural conditions really are the "scenery" necessary to appreciate the action. Of course, if a historian shifts the focus of the action to a totally new setting, he or she must reorient the reader by describing the different cultural and ideological conditions.

4. Other narrative techniques:

Word Choice: Seeing that history is a way of reexperiencing reality as structured by the historian, it follows that the writer should use language that reflects reality—its pulse, its density, its vitality. The language of the senses does this. Concrete rather than abstract terms provide something of the flavor of day-to-day life; common, even idiomatic, language is preferable to jargon or highly technical words; action verbs give an impression of human beings in motion; and dialogue between historical figures (if available) does the same.

Management of (Historical) Time: A historian is something like a wilderness guide who takes a tenderfoot through the woods to view a backwoods stream—the stream of time. The reader is invited to step into the stream to meet some of the people there, to look, at times, upstream to an embankment that redirects the water's flow or downstream to a quickening of the current. At other times the reader is asked to step back out of the flow so that a larger view might be taken.

What we are speaking of here is the importance of a narrator's management of time. The reader is willing to stay in the stream for awhile and follow the struggle going on there, or to get back on the bank, or to look upstream, or downstream—all provided the narrator gives the proper signals. Suspension of the story for political analysis, or sociological commentary, or psychological insights, or geographical fact are all tolerable provided the writer gives signals of the shift in attention. It is perfectly acceptable for a writer to break the flow of action, provided it is done with careful concern about the reader's switch in mental orientation.

Shift in Perspective: Given the fact that one person's path often crosses another's, a story of the past is the story of conflicting individuals and groups. But the dramatic values evident in conflict will remain dormant unless clearly developed by the narrator. The primary means for doing so is technically called "perspectivism." That is, the narrator is obliged to shift at critical points in the story from a description of the viewpoint or perspective of one historical figure to that of another with whom there is conflict. Thus, after a discussion of, say, Adolf Hitler's grand strategy for conquering Russia (including timetables, tactics, and political factors) to give shape to the dimensions of the conflict, one is then bound to evaluate the views and projections of the Soviet high command.

Certainly there are other valuable narrative techniques, but those mentioned above are the most important for the writing of history. The principles of narration, along with those of exposition, are not easily mastered; but if you learn to use them in your own writing the rewards will be great.

EXERCISES

Set A, Exercise 1   A hallmark of an effective writer is the ability to subordinate less important facts and generalizations to those that are more important. This first exercise requires you to list a number of items in descending order from general to specific. In the spaces provided, number the items in sequence, using "1" for the most general item and so on. In some cases you may have to assign the same number to two or more items.

a.   _____   city government
     _____   national government
     _____   organized neighborhood
     _____   state government
     _____   county government

b.   _____   a history of North America
     _____   a history of the world
     _____   a history of the United States
     _____   western hemisphere history
     _____   history of General Washington as a military leader
     _____   a history of the American Revolution
     _____   a military history of the Revolution

c.   _____   One of Vallee's favorite songs was the "Stein Song."
     _____   Though some parts of the country could get no radio signal, urban areas were quite well served by 1925.
     _____   Radio broadcasting began in 1920 and quickly spread across the land.
     _____   In the 1920s the electronic media changed American entertainment habits.
     _____   Radio listeners soon warmed to the baritone voice of Rudy Vallee.

Set A, Exercise 2   This exercise extends further the principle of organizing from the general to the specific. Here the task is to find the most general point (the most comprehensive topic sentence) and label it "1." Then find the most logical sequence in which the other sentences should follow, using "2," "3," "4," etc.

     _____   Nebraska farmers stopped trains and took off carloads of cattle.
     _____   Wisconsin farmers dumped milk on the roadsides and fought with deputy sheriffs.
     _____   Especially in the Midwest were extreme actions taken by farmers.
     _____   In the depression summer of 1932, American farmers organized and prevented products from reaching the market, the movement moving gradually westward as the summer wore on.

_____ In eastern Iowa many farmers drowned pig litters because it was unprofitable to raise them.

_____ Near Spragueville in eastern Iowa, some farmers reverted to subsistence farming, refusing to send anything to market.

_____ In the states further west, such as Colorado and Wyoming, the movement lacked force because of the low productivity of these areas.

Set A, Exercise 3 This exercise is a somewhat more complex version of the one just completed. You must do two things: 1) work out the relations between the general and the specific and 2) organize the pieces so they are logically related. What follows is a scrambled paragraph; unscramble it, using number "1" for the first sentence, "2" for the second, etc., to indicate the proper sentence order. It's a good idea to keep a couple of points in mind, namely that identification of the topic sentence is half the battle and that in some cases chronology is a good clue to proper order.

_____ Surface raiders, such as the pocket battleships *Graf Spee* and *Deutschland* caused much concern.

_____ But the enduring enemy was the U-boat [submarine].

_____ But later in the war U-boats found it very difficult to operate, as the British used a version of sonar, and American hunter-killer groups sent many submarines to the bottom.

_____ The Germans successfully planted magnetic mines which did much damage to British shipping in coastal waters.

_____ If, in 1940 the defeat of France had been offset by the British success in the Battle of Britain, in 1941 the defeat of Great Britain became once more a possibility to be reckoned with.

_____ In 1940, however, the U-boat fleet, reinforced by a production drive, began to score abundantly.

_____ One British convoy lost thirty-two ships in a U-boat attack which continued through four consecutive nights.

_____ In the first year of the war, 1939, the German U-boat fleet had been small and was not particularly successful.

_____ Because Britain was an island nation she was especially vulnerable to German sea warfare, which included mines, surface raiders, and U-boats.

Set A, Exercise 4 The following exercise presents ten pieces that, when put together correctly, represent a simplified sentence outline for a short essay. Though much is missing, we specifically include a main thematic statement (topic sentence), three main points, five subpoints belonging somewhere under the main points, and a summary statement. Put all the pieces in their proper places (by number) in the form provided below.

1. A powerful new military bureaucracy developed during the war, with increasingly strong links to major industrial firms.
2. During the war more than a million Blacks moved out of the South to northern cities seeking a better life than they had known on southern farms.

3. The deficit mentality lingered on after the war, and contributed to the acceptance of new governmental programs in later years.
4. Indeed these three changes brought by the war affected American society permanently.
5. The war also deepened public willingness to accept enormous government deficits as the national debt doubled and redoubled from 1941 to 1945.
6. Huge numbers of civilians migrated to ship and aircraft production facilities, seeking the high wages paid there.
7. World War II brought deeper changes in American life than any other development since the Civil War.
8. In fact much later, President Dwight Eisenhower, himself a military man, was to warn the nation of the dangers of this combination of interests, often called the "military-industrial complex."
9. First and foremost it caused a vast uprooting of Americans from their traditional homes.
10. Millions of men and women became temporary citizens of military camps all across America.

_____   Main thematic statement

_____   A. Main point

_____   1. Subpoint (if any)

_____   2. Subpoint (if any)

_____   3. Subpoint (if any)

_____   B. Main point

_____   1. Subpoint (if any)

_____   2. Subpoint (if any)

_____   C. Main point

_____   1. Subpoint (if any)

_____   2. Subpoint (if any)

_____   D. Summary statement

Set A, Exercise 5   No topic sentences appear in the following paragraphs. Compose a topic sentence for each of them, expressing the main idea of the paragraph. Use the space provided.

a. _____

_____

The chain-store method of marketing was furthered by F.W. Woolworth as he opened a number of "Five and Ten Cent Stores" during the 1880s. In 1881, James B. Duke had brought a change in American smoking habits when he first marketed "ready-made" (machine made) cigarettes. Meat marketing was revolutionized by Gustavus Swift's use of the refrigerated railroad car in the early 1880s. And by the late 1880s A. Montgomery Ward had perfected the mail-order method of marketing goods.

b. _____

_____

This war (World War I) brought the first widespread use of poison gas, which killed or permanently disabled hundreds of thousands of soldiers, both Allied and German. The submarine became a successful arm of the German navy as their U-boats threatened Britain's life lines. World War I also saw the first usage of the airplane as an offensive weapon. The tank was introduced in the middle of the war and gave a hint of what future wars would be like.

c. _____

_____

[During the period of the Great Depression the] loss of a job—and the status that went with it—caused suffering and brought much personal unhappiness into the lives of millions of Americans. Families were disrupted. Some took to the road in a vain search for better employment opportunities elsewhere. Often the women in families sought to earn an income for the first time. Sometimes families moved in with friends or relatives. Other families disintegrated as individual members tried to make it on their own. Many young men and women—perhaps as many as 2 million—became "tramps" riding the rails to nowhere in particular, hoping to get a job or a meal at every stop. Numerous others were homeless—sleeping in parks, subways, or abandoned buildings . . .[6]

Set A, Exercise 6 In this chapter we briefly considered a basic distinction between narrative and analytical history. Narrative history provides a chronology of events; in analytical history the writer pauses for a sentence, or a paragraph or more, to show the significance of an event, or some such other matters as description of the surroundings, comment upon motivation, discussion of participants' reaction, etc. Narrative and analytical history are mixed together in many historical passages. Such is the case with the following short excerpt. Your task here is to indicate after each sentence in the space provided whether it is narrative (using an N) or analytical (using an A). The passage concerns the major drive of the Union army against the Confederates in 1864.[7]

The final drive toward Richmond began on May 3, 1864, when Grant crossed the Rapidan and encountered Lee. _____ The fierce fighting of the next two days left both armies almost exhausted. _____ The bat-

---

[6] Gerald D. Nash, *The Great Depression and World War II* (New York: St. Martin's Press, 1970), p. 7.

[7] W. E. Woodward, *A New American History*, p. 564.

tle of the Wilderness, as this engagement is called, was a revelation to Grant of the energy and martial spirit of the Confederates. _____ He had seen nothing like it in his Western campaigns. _____ At the end of the second day's struggle most of the Union officers thought the army would retreat across the Rapidan during the night. _____ General James H. Wilson says that at the end of the first day's battle Grant threw himself down on his cot and sobbed. _____ I can well believe it; Grant did weep at times when his affairs were not going well. _____ After the sobbing spell he ordered a forward movement. _____ Before daybreak the sorely tried army was on its feet and moving toward Richmond. _____

At Spottsylvania Court House Lee faced them again, standing squarely across their road. _____ As at the Wilderness, the Union losses ran into terrifying figures, but Lee had to give way, and Grant went on a few miles farther. _____ It was then that he sent his famous dispatch in which he said: "I propose to fight it out on this line if it takes all summer." _____

The fighting went on steadily, day after day. _____ The opposing armies rolled over each other in the mud and dirt, like two determined and blood-smeared football teams. _____ At the end of each bout the Confederates had been pushed back a few yards, or a few miles. _____

Set B, Exercise 1   A hallmark of an effective writer is the ability to subordinate less important facts and generalizations to those that are more important. This first exercise requires you to list a number of items in descending order from general to specific. In the spaces provided, number the items in sequence, using "1" for the most general item and so on. In some cases you may have to assign the same number to two or more items.

a. _____ National [baseball] League
   _____ major league teams
   _____ baseball
   _____ St. Louis Cardinals
   _____ American sports

b. _____ a history of England
   _____ non-fiction books
   _____ a history of the political affairs of King Henry VIII of England
   _____ history books
   _____ a European history survey textbook
   _____ a history of the reign of Henry VIII

c. _____ Indeed, South Carolina produced little else.
   _____ In that section Georgia and South Carolina were among the leaders in cotton-growing acreage.
   _____ The city of Charleston in South Carolina was almost totally dominated by the cotton trade.
   _____ Invention of the cotton gin made cotton growing profitable all through the South.
   _____ Especially well suited to cotton culture were the states of the lower South.

Set B, Exercise 2   This exercise extends further the principle of organizing from the general to the specific. Here the task is to find the most general point (the most comprehensive topic sentence) and label it "1." Then find the most logical sequence in which the other sentences should follow, using "2," "3," "4," etc.

_____   Perhaps the most important of them was what we would call an "image" problem.

_____   To Truman's dismay, both houses of Congress went Republican in the election of 1946.

_____   He found it necessary to fire a number of the carryovers because they were less than cooperative with him.

_____   Roosevelt had been urbane and eloquent, but Truman was stodgy and a boring speaker.

_____   Finally, he had a major political problem.

_____   After assuming the presidency in 1945 Harry Truman had several problems.

_____   The public compared him unfavorably with his predecessor, Franklin D. Roosevelt.

_____   Secretary of Commerce Wallace was dismissed from the Cabinet.

_____   Even with his "inner circle," the Cabinet, he had a problem.

Set B, Exercise 3   This exercise is a somewhat more complex version of the one just completed. You must do two things: 1) work out the relations between the general and the specific, and 2) organize the pieces so they are logically related. What follows is a scrambled paragraph; unscramble it, using number "1" for the first sentence, "2" for the second, etc., to indicate the proper sentence order. It's a good idea to keep a couple of points in mind, namely that identification of the topic sentence is half the battle, and that in some cases chronology is a good clue to proper order.[8]

_____   His [John F. Kennedy's] backing of the Cuban invasion in April 1961 further fanned the Cold War.

_____   (It may be that "needlessly" is too strong a word; perhaps Kennedy thought he needed to arouse the country to obtain a more balanced military program. . . .)

_____   At a Vienna conference with Khrushchev in June he over-reacted to Khrushchev's ultimatum, for in recent years Khrushchev's repeated deadlines and backdowns over West Berlin had become a kind of pattern.

_____   His [Kennedy's] inaugural address was alarmist, already historically off key, more suited to the Stalinist era than to 1961.

_____   His statement to newspaper publishers and editors gathered at the White House in May—that the United States was in the most critical period of its history—increased the popular anxieties.

_____   His late January State of the Union message was even more alarmist, as Kennedy told the nation that we were drawing near the maximum danger.

---

[8] Based loosely on a paragraph in William G. Carleton, "J.F.K.: History's Romantic Hero," in Stephen B. Oates, ed., _Portrait of America_, Volume II (Boston: Houghton Mifflin, 1973), p. 468.

_____ On his return from Vienna he appealed to Americans to build do-it-yourself bomb shelters, an appeal that produced a war psychology in the country and all manner of frenetic behavior.

_____ During his first two years in office, beginning in January, 1961, President John F. Kennedy seemed needlessly to have fanned the tensions of the dying Cold War.

Set B, Exercise 4 The following exercise contains ten pieces that, when put together correctly, represent a simplified sentence outline for a short essay. Though much is missing, we specifically include a main thematic statement (topic sentence), three main points, five subpoints belonging somewhere under the main points, and a summary statement. Put all the pieces in their proper sequence (by number) in the form provided below.

1. The strong, jungle-like beat of early '60s music brought another phenomenon: the twist.
2. This four-person group powerfully affected American youth in clothing, in hair fashion, and in drug usage.
3. He dressed shabbily and had wild long hair.
4. Taken together these developments formed the foundation of an alternative American life style.
5. Beatlemania began in England in 1963 and crossed the ocean to America in 1964.
6. He exploited the generation gap and soon developed a large cult following.
7. Three major developments in the world of music were influential in shaping the counter-culture of the 1960s.
8. No group was as influential as the Beatles, who were perhaps artistically superior to most other musical quartets.
9. The twist was a highly individualistic dance form completely divorced from the romantic foxtrot of earlier years.
10. Of foremost importance was Bob Dylan, whose hard-driving version of folk music brought sympathy to "down and outers."

_____ Main thematic statement

_____ A. Main point

_____   1. Subpoint (if any)

_____   2. Subpoint (if any)

_____ B. Main point

_____   1. Subpoint (if any)

_____   2. Subpoint (if any)

_____ C. Main point

_____ 1. Subpoint (if any)

_____ 2. Subpoint (if any)

_____ 3. Subpoint (if any)

_____ D. Summary statement

Set B, Exercise 5 No topic sentences appear in the following paragraphs. Compose a topic sentence for each of them, expressing the main idea of the paragraph. Use the space provided.

a._____

_____

By the terms of the Webster-Ashburton Treaty of 1842 the Maine boundary dispute was settled on a basis favorable to American claims. In 1845, the independent nation of Texas was annexed to the United States. The Oregon Treaty of 1846 settled the territorial dispute between Britain and the United States and these new lands stretched American sovereignty to the Pacific. The Treaty of Guadalupe Hidalgo completed America's westward expansion as the southwest corner of what is now the United States became American property in 1848.

b. _____

_____

Senator Huey Long, with his "share-our-wealth" proposal, emerged in 1934 as a major threat to President Roosevelt's political combination. Further, Dr. Francis Townsend's seemingly bizarre organization of older Americans was daily winning converts from the mainstream Democratic party. Father Charles Coughlin's radio fans, enthused by his radical proposals, were fast becoming anti-Roosevelt, thus further weakening the coalition that had won in 1932. And conservative Republicans, stung by the leftist tendencies of Roosevelt's New Deal, loomed as dangerous political adversaries in the forthcoming election of 1936.

c. _____

_____

With men away in the armed forces—or engaged in demanding occupations—millions of women became the effective heads of families. In a sense many families became matriarchal. No less striking was the increase in the number of working women. The number of females who took jobs rose from 12.0 million in 1941 to 16.5 million in 1945. Many were in occupations once considered exclusively the domain of males such as locomotive oilers or welders. During the war many women worked on assembly lines, and others could be found in steel plants around blast furnaces or rolling mills. For the first time in an American war, women were permitted to join the armed forces as other than nurses. In the Women's Army Corps (WACs), Women's Auxiliary Naval Service (WAVES), and in the Marines, women performed varied duties as officers or enlisted personnel which freed men for combat service.[9]

Set B, Exercise 6   In this chapter's section on narration, we briefly considered a basic distinction between narrative and analytical history. Narrative history provides a chronology of events; in analytic history the writer pauses for a sentence, or a paragraph or more, to show the significance of an event, or some such other matters as description of the surroundings, comment upon motivation, discussion of participants' reactions, etc. Narrative and analytical history are mixed together in many historical passages. Such is the case with the following short excerpt. Your task here is to indicate after each sentence in the space provided whether it is narrative (using an N) or analytical (using an A). The passage concerns the actions of the British army after an attack upon Washington, D.C., during the War of 1812.[10]

After the British left Washington they went back to the Chesapeake and made an unsuccessful attack on Baltimore. _____ It was no use to take the town without taking Fort McHenry, which commanded the harbor. _____ The fort was strong and well manned, and the water roundabout was too shallow for the ships to come into close range. _____ After an all-night bombardment the Stars and Stripes still waved over the fort, and Francis Scott Key, by the dawn's early light, was patriotically moved to write "The Star-Spangled Banner". _____

The British loitered in the Chesapeake for two months and then sailed for New Orleans, where they arrived in December, 1814, after having stopped at Jamaica to take on board several thousand additional men. _____ It is rather surprising that they had not made a major attack on Louisiana much earlier in the war, as New Orleans was the strategic key to the whole Mississippi valley. _____ With the mouth of the river in their hands the British commissioners would have had a trump card to play at the peace conference. _____

Their delay was due chiefly to the fact that they could hardly spare the troops, as almost all their available forces were fighting in Europe, or in Canada, or were scattered throughout the colonies. _____ Early in 1814 the war in Europe came to an end, and Napoleon was exiled to Elba. _____

All the troops in the New Orleans expedition were veterans, with a few exceptions. _____ They had been in many battles, and were cool, steady, and well-disciplined. _____ Their commander was General Sir Edward Pakenham; he had been a soldier all his life. _____

---

[9] Gerald D. Nash, *The Great Depression and World War II*, p. 146.

[10] W. E. Woodward, *A New American History*, pp. 334–35.

CHAPTER 12

HISTORIOGRAPHY

"History does not repeat itself. The historians repeat one another."

Max Beerbohm

"History has to be rewritten because history is the selection of those threads of causes or antecedents that we are interested in."

Oliver Wendell Holmes, Jr.

A university professor once berated a young graduate student for what he termed "stale historiography." A fellow student later said this sounded something akin to bad breath. What the professor meant, of course, was that the student was not familiar with the most recent scholarly interpretations in a particular subfield of history.

"Historiography" is not a word one normally finds in casual reading; nevertheless, the concept behind the word should be familiar to every student of history. In fact, you probably already know the concept even if the word itself is unfamiliar. Literally the word means "the writing of history." In modern usage, however, the word refers to the *study of the way history has been and is written—the history of historical writing, if you will.* When you study "historiography" you do not study the events of the past directly, but the changing *interpretations* of those events in the works of individual historians. To acquaint yourself, for example, with the variety of ways historians have tried to explain the coming of the American Civil War is to become familiar with the historiography of that subject.[1] Graduate students in history spend years mastering the major interpretations in their particular specialties, including the most recent scholarship.

In this chapter it is not our intention to recruit fledgling graduate students, but, by examining a few important interpretive "schools" and trends, to help you read history more critically. Before beginning, though, a few cautions are necessary.

Trying to summarize even a few historiographical trends in capsule form is a sin only slightly less serious than omitting the subject altogether. Not only is the topic immense, but any secondhand account of another historian's work should be viewed with suspicion. If you want to know what a historian says about a subject, you should read that historian's work.

Furthermore, every historian's work is to some extent unique, reflecting individual values, assumptions, interests, and abilities. Yet below we discuss

---

[1] Some historians see that war as a conflict between an agrarian economy (the South) and an industrializing economy (the North); others emphasize slavery as the primary cause; still others see states' rights versus federal sovereignty as the issue at stake.

historiography in terms of exceedingly broad trends and generalized characteristics. We suggest a number of patterns that seem to be reflected in a significant number of historical works. As you read what follows keep in mind 1) that other historians writing such a book as this could legitimately emphasize wholly different patterns and 2) that no single work of history will fit a pattern exactly. Again, the only way to study the subject properly is to read a lot of history.

**History:
The Beginnings**

The Western tradition of historical writing began with the ancient Hebrews and Greeks. The Jews, in their long struggle for freedom and autonomy, developed the belief that their people were special in the eyes of God (Yahweh) and that their historical experiences reflected God's will. Conscious of their special role as God's "chosen people," the Jews wrote history as a chronicle of their continuing and evolving relationship with the Creator. Essentially the books of the Old Testament comprise a written history of the Jewish people and Hebrew nation. In summary, Jewish historical writing was very "God-centered" and would have an immense influence on the Western historical tradition, especially during the Christian Middle Ages.

If Jewish historical writing was "God-centered," it was the ancient Greeks who first wrote history in self-consciously *human* terms. At first the Greeks saw both their own past and the workings of the physical universe as the products of supernatural forces and the intervention of the gods. Later, in the sixth century B.C., a number of Greek philosophers began to reject supernatural explanations in favor of natural ones. They saw nature as functioning according to concrete "natural" laws that could be comprehended through human reason. The past, long explained through myths and legends, came to be explained as the product of human actions and decisions.

Herodotus (fifth century B.C.), the so-called Father of History, wrote the first systematic historical work based on personal observations and the examination of witnesses and surviving records. In his account of the Greek wars against the Persians he also included many fanciful myths and unsubstantiated legends, but essentially his was a history of human actions told in human terms. Thucydides, who, a generation later, wrote a justly famous account of the Peloponnesian Wars (431–404 B.C.), was even more careful in his use and analysis of evidence. He insisted that his history include only relevant, verifiable facts, and that it explain events only in ways that could be substantiated by the evidence. (The English word "history" comes from the Greek word for "research.") In Thucydides we first see what moderns would call a true historical spirit.

There was little change in the nature of written history when the glory that was Greece succumbed to the power that was Rome. However, during the European Middle Ages (ca. A.D. 500–1500), a change of some magnitude took place. With the triumph of Christianity, history writing again became more concerned with the relationship of the human experience to what was perceived as God's eternal plan. Christian historiography mirrored that of the Hebrews not that of the Greeks and Romans, although Greek and Roman influences were strong. To Christian writers in the Middle Ages, human experiences on earth were but a minor part of a larger design. It was the job of written history, therefore, to find and reveal the transcendent design of God hidden in the chaos of day-to-day events. That is why many histories written in the Middle Ages began with the biblical story of creation and incorporated that part of the Jewish Old Testament tradition that fit the redemptive message of Christianity. The proper concern of written history, in the eyes of the Christian monks who wrote it, was not the earthly fate of a particular state or people, but the universal drama of humanity's quest for salvation.

Only in the Renaissance (1400s and 1500s) did historians again return to the more secular, humanistic style of the Greeks. Especially important were a number of fifteenth-century Italian historians, Niccolo Machiavelli (1469–1540) and Francesco Guicciardini (1483–1527) being the best known. Although the Renaissance historians were Christians, they believed that the function of history was to narrate the experiences of particular states and individuals not, as in the Middle Ages, to reveal God's designs in the earthly affairs of humanity. The Renaissance also saw the gradual emergence of new critical standards for collecting, reading, and interpreting evidence. History was not yet a recognized independent field of study (like theology or law), but the path was clearly marked.

Progress was slow. In spite of the long tradition of history writing in the West, the discipline of history as we know it is relatively young. Indeed, history emerged as a formal academic study only in the early nineteenth century. To be sure, many pre-nineteenth-century historians produced works of great power and sophistication, as any reader of Gibbon (*The Decline and Fall of the Roman Empire*) or Thucydides can attest. On the whole, though, such works were few and far between, for history still lacked a coherent and workable critical methodology. Much history was written, but seldom did the historians consider the question: "What are the criteria for writing good history?" Many pre-nineteenth-century historians handled evidence with a cavalier disregard for critical standards. Often they cited no sources whatever; on other occasions they accepted myth, legend, and gossip as established fact; on yet others, they read or interpreted records with too much credulity and too little skepticism.

In another way, the pre-nineteenth-century historians had a blind spot. They did not fully understand that in some respects past ages differed from their own; they had difficulty realizing that styles, habits, and values changed over time. There exist many Renaissance paintings, for example, in which biblical scenes are portrayed with figures dressed in "modern"—that is, fifteenth-century—garb and surrounded by the latest architectural styles. The equivalent today would be a painting of George Washington dressed in a three-piece pin-striped suit and driving a motor launch across the Delaware River.

Conversely, when many of the early historians did perceive differences between their age and another, their response was not to try to understand that which was different but to denounce it. Thus did Voltaire, in the eighteenth century, dismiss the Middle Ages as unworthy of study because medieval men and women were not "enlightened," as he felt himself to be. Such an attitude, as we have seen, is unhistorical. (See Chapter 6, Context.)

Leopold von Ranke and the Rise of Modern History

Historical studies came into their own following the immense political and social upheavals that accompanied and followed the French Revolution (1789–1815). The Revolution represented a massive break with the past and, accordingly, made people much more "history-conscious" than ever before. Thus, it was in the nineteenth century that history became the "Queen of the Sciences" and earned a permanent place in the academy.

The man most responsible for elevating the study of history to a new plateau was the German historian Leopold von Ranke (1795–1886). Ranke was the George Washington of academic history—the founding father of the modern discipline as we know it. Ranke's contributions were threefold: 1) he played a leading role in establishing history as a respected discipline in the universities, 2) he firmly established the notion that all sound history must be based on primary sources and rigorous "scientific" method, and 3) he reflected the broader nineteenth-century attempt to define the concept of "historical-mindedness." Of these, the latter two points require further elaboration.

Ranke and Historical Method: Previously, as we mentioned above, much history was written, but "there was no systematic use of sources and no accepted methodological principles."[2] Many pre-Rankean historians relied heavily on the work of other authors (secondary sources) rather than going to the original documents (primary sources). Ranke, on the other hand, stressed the importance of basing any historical narrative firmly on the reading of primary sources. Furthermore, he insisted that the historian constantly inform the reader of the specific sources upon which a given point was based. Hence the central importance, after Ranke, of thorough footnotes and bibliographies. (Now you know whom to blame.) In a word, Ranke popularized the idea that history could be "scientific" not in the sense that history could discover general laws of behavior but that historical writing should be based on rigorous critical standards.

Ranke and Historical-Mindedness: Ranke also contributed to the rise of the conviction that one should not study a past age in terms of one's own values and culture but in terms of the values and realities of the age itself. According to Ranke, one should not make moral judgments on past individuals and past cultures but try to understand them on their own terms. To Ranke, every age and individual was "immediate to God" (did not need to be justified) and worthy of our sympathy and understanding. Ranke appreciated the fact that things do change over time, and this basic insight is central to the whole process of thinking historically.

Ranke, then, and many other eminent scholars, established the study of history on a firm methodological foundation. What did these pioneers write about? Space forbids a detailed treatment of history and historians in the nineteenth century, but two general points can be made:

1. Most nineteenth-century history was political, legal, or diplomatic in emphasis, as historians began to get access to government archives that

---

[2] Arthur Marwick, *What History Is and Why It Is Important* (Bletchley, England: Open University Press, 1970), p. 42.

had been closed to researchers. Their work, which reflected the character of the documents, naturally focused on the actions of kings, parliaments, law courts, armies, navies, and diplomats—"drum and trumpet" history as it came to be called.

2. Nineteenth-century history, especially in Europe, tended to have a *national* focus—more in the sense of "nationality" than "nation." During that era a number of "new" nations, or ethnic groups, perceiving their cultural and historical uniqueness, began vigorously to explore their own historical roots. Even history coming out of the more established nations, such as England and France, reflected this compulsion to probe the depths of their national experience. Much the same could be said of the histories produced in nineteenth-century America. Across the board, historiography during this period tended to be ethnocentric and nationalistic.

Karl Marx and History

If Ranke and his contemporaries saw only politics and diplomacy as worthy of the historian's attention, it was the German economist and revolutionary philosopher Karl Marx who opened historians' eyes to the importance of social and economic forces in human affairs. Marx (1818–1883) is widely recognized as one of the most influential thinkers of the last one hundred and fifty years. Much modern scholarship in history, economics, political theory, sociology, and philosophy cannot be fully appreciated without some understanding of Karl Marx's ideas. This is not the place to discuss Marx's system in detail, but a few words concerning his impact on the discipline of history are in order. It should be noted from the start, however, that a consideration of Marx the historian can be effectively divorced from consideration of Marx the prophet of socialism. In the latter guise Marx, and his collaborator, Friedrich Engels, postulated a broadly "progressive" theory of history, which held that human societies would evolve through a number of stages. These stages would culminate in the establishment (through revolution) of a "dictatorship of the proletariat" and, eventually, a classless society. This was a secular version of the story of the human race moving toward a "preordained goal." The validity of this vision is best left to the philosophers, since historical evidence can never confirm or deny such all-encompassing metaphysical theories.

More important for our purposes is the fact that Marx opened new intellectual vistas by breaking out of the political-diplomatic straitjacket that had bound most historical investigations before his time. Marx, says one American historian, "became the first to formulate, in explicit fashion, the economic interpretation of history."[3] Marx (and Engels) argued that, at any given point in time, the mode of economic production determined, to a great extent, the character of the entire society—its ideas, values, political structure, and social relations. To some of Marx's more dogmatic followers, this insight was converted into a thoroughgoing economic determinism. That is, economic forces were seen *totally to determine* the nature of society, and changes in the economic structure were considered the *sole* engine of

---

[3] Allan Nevins, *The Gateway to History* (Chicago: Quadrangle Books, 1963), p. 268.

historical change. Marx himself never went so far; late in life he even commented: "I am not a Marxist." Marx and Engels did not deny that non-economic factors could be contributing causes of events. They simply asserted that economic factors were of primary importance.

Within this general framework, the history of economic and social classes was more relevant than the history of great men or ruling elites. "The history of all hitherto existing society," wrote Marx and Engels in one of their more famous lines, "is the history of class struggle." This, of course, is a debatable conclusion. Of significance, though, is the fact that Marx and Engels saw class interests as a vital element in any historical equation.

Marx's impact on politics and political thought has been immense and requires no further comment. But what of Marx's impact on the writing of history?

In communist countries, of course, where Marxism in some form or another is an official ideology, historical writing is "Marxist" in the extreme. Quite frankly, much of it is not good history. Evidence is chosen, organized, analyzed, and interpreted more with an eye to validating the ideology than establishing the best true account of the past. Much official communist history written in Russia, the eastern European countries, and other communist nations suffers from this defect. In fairness, we should also note that noncommunist history is not immune from this failing. Any time scholarship is subordinated to the dictates of an ideology—Marxist or non-Marxist—the truth suffers.

In the noncommunist West, the influence of Marx, while great, has been less direct. In the broadest sense Marx is significant because, by emphasizing the importance of economic factors in history, he opened the door to a new approach to the past. Few historians today, whatever their political orientation, would deny the validity of exploring the role of classes, economic interests, and modes of production in the historical process. Economic interpretations have, in fact, become a staple of American historiography. A famous (if not unanimously respected) example would be Charles A. Beard's *An Economic Interpretation of the Constitution of the United States* published in 1913. In that work Beard examined the economic interests of the framers of the Constitution and concluded that the Constitution was designed more to protect property rights than political rights. Whatever the accuracy of this interpretation (and it has been vigorously challenged), the important thing to note is the explicitly economic focus of the work. Beard was no Marxist, but he acknowledged a debt to Marx just the same. Few historians have gone as far as Beard in emphasizing economic factors so single mindedly, but even fewer would deny that the economic question is one that must be asked in order to understand any given segment of the past.[4]

---

[4] For some Western scholars the Marxian impact has been more direct. There are many scholars, historians among them, who consciously call themselves "Marxists," and they have adopted an explicitly Marxian (class-oriented) approach to the study of history and society. Within the ranks of historians, such scholars are a distinct minority. Yet certain Marxist historians have produced solid, scholarly works, which have greatly enriched our understanding of many historical events. Remember that the test of good history is not the author's ideology but the thoroughness and accuracy of the work produced.

The Twentieth Century

The twentieth century, especially the decades since 1945, has witnessed a "knowledge explosion" of sorts. Books, articles, reports, and the like have been pouring off the presses at an ever-increasing rate. The explosion has been most dramatic in the sciences, but the generalization is applicable to history as well. It is safe to say that more history has been written and published in the twentieth century than in all the previous centuries combined. Moreover, recent historical writing has displayed such kaleidoscopic diversity that history is a more exciting field than ever before. Unfortunately, the mass and diversity of recent historical scholarship also makes it impossible to summarize neatly even the most prominent trends in twentieth-century historiography. What follows, therefore, is a very selective and idiosyncratic sampling of what we see to be some of the defining characteristics of recent historiography—especially American historiography.

The New Social History

There is nothing especially new about social history. Social history, simply put, is the history of life in the broadest sense; the history of the everyday experiences of average men and women. It is the history of occupations, life styles, leisure activities, family structures, eating habits, sexual practices, reading preferences, beliefs, and values; it is "grass roots" history; it is, in the memorable words of G. M. Trevelyan, "history with the politics left out"—or, to the irreverent, "rum and strumpet history." Historians have been writing social history for some time. Even today, one of the most frequently cited examples of brilliant social history is the famous portrait of English society during the 1680s in Macaulay's *History of England*, written in the nineteenth century.

Although social history has long been with us, only in recent decades has it become an important area of specialization within the historical profession. In the nineteenth century social history was strictly subordinated to the more important priority of telling the story of political, constitutional, and military affairs. Social history was used to set the scene or provide a pleasant interlude in the narrative. Today, however, social history is taught and studied as a field of inherent interest and importance. Only to this extent is social history "new."

Social history is new in another sense—it is much more scientific and less anecdotal than had previously been the case. Social history is one area where the application of statistical methods and computer analysis has been especially productive. Much social history today is, in effect, *historical demography* (demography is the statistical study of population). In such work, historians systematically analyze large-scale population trends and calculate such factors as average family sizes, death and birth rates, marriage ages, and average incomes. The more literary tradition of social history has by no means been abandoned, but statistical methods have given the social historian another potent analytical weapon.

The most fruitful contribution of the social historians has been to cast the spotlight on groups that typically have been ignored in traditional history—workers, farmers, peasants, women, children, ethnic minorities, and the aged. In fact, the popularity and vitality of social history is in part a reflection of the increasing sense of identity among various ethnic subcultures. Witness the proliferation of books on black history, Chicano history, native American (Indian) history, and the like. The feminist movement has likewise inspired a great many valuable studies, which highlight the role of women in history, not to mention histories of family life, child-rearing practices, and sexuality. In sum, the "new" social history has brought to life the experiences of countless groups previously overlooked by the mainstream historical surveys.

Psychohistory

Psychohistory is another growing and popular subfield of historical scholarship but still somewhat a black sheep in the eyes of traditionalists. In the late nineteenth century a number of researchers, of whom Sigmund Freud (1856–1939) was the most influential, began to draw attention to the importance of the unconscious mind and irrational impulses in human behavior. Just as Marx had emphasized the importance of economics in human affairs, Freud's many trailblazing studies underscored the role played by hidden psychological drives. Freud's message was reinforced by the senseless slaughter of World War I (1914–1918), which dramatized for a complacent Europe how easily irrationality and animal brutality could triumph over intellect and reason. In the years after the war, psychiatry and psychoanalysis came into their own; following World War II (1939–1945), the insights of psychiatry were applied to figures of historical significance, both alive and dead. Psychohistory was born.

Perhaps the best known of the psychohistories is Erik Erikson's masterful study, *Young Man Luther* (1958). Since the publication of Erikson's book, many other historians and psychologists have attempted to apply psychological or psychoanalytical theories to the study of past individuals and events—sometimes successfully and sometimes not. Nevertheless, psychohistory seems here to stay. Even the more traditional historians are paying closer attention to the psychological dimensions of the events and individuals they study.

Computers and Quantification

Another distinctly twentieth-century phenomenon is the growing use of computers and statistical methods in history. These techniques have been especially productive (as noted above) in the realms of economic and social history. Historical studies of voting behavior have also benefitted from the application of well-designed computer programs to historical evidence. There is, however, a problem with this type of history. Most historical questions cannot be answered with computers, however sophisticated the machines or their programs. Too often scholars become so hypnotized by the attractions of new statistical methodologies that they end up letting the methodology dictate the type of research done. This, in the words of one political scientist, is akin to buying a leash and then looking for a dog to attach to it. Quantification has a place in historical studies, but the limitations of mere numeration must be kept firmly in mind.

Popular History

Our century, especially since the advent of cheap paperback books and television, has been the age of popularized history par excellence. There has been tremendous growth in the amount of history written for the viewing or reading enjoyment of a mass audience. Ultimately this is a good trend, for unless historians communicate their findings to a larger audience, they are serving no useful function in the society. On the other hand, popular history (whether presented in books or on television) can also be dangerous. Frequently, good entertainment is bad history, for to emphasize the dramatic and sensational is often to distort the truth. More than ever the reading and viewing public must be able to discriminate between good history and bad history.

Moreover, so insatiable is the public appetite for the inside story of recent dramatic events that "instant" histories have become commonplace. Almost before events have run their course, popular histories are on the drugstore reading racks. Whether the subject is the Kennedy assassination, the Falklands War, a sensational murder case, the death of a rock star, or the latest terrorist outrage, paperback "histories" are available days or a few weeks after the event. The dangers inherent in such books should be apparent. They are put together in haste on the basis of incomplete evidence, and public passions may still be fully aroused. The authors, in many cases, are not trained historians or even trained journalists. Obviously, such books should be read with a highly critical eye.

This advice applies even more to television shows that purport to document "real" events through dramatic re-creations. Many such shows in recent years (a number of BBC historical dramatizations come to mind) have been excellent as history as well as entertainment. Others, however, have obscured the line between truth and fiction so badly that their value as history is limited. In our modern world, it is more important than ever to have a historically literate population if for no other reason than to judge critically the mass of popularized and instant histories that bombard us.

If one can perceive a trend over time, it is this: historical writing in the West has become broader in geographic scope, casting its attention on civilizations and cultures hitherto ignored; it has become more eclectic, with few aspects of life escaping critical attention; and it has become ever more rigorous and imaginative in its use of evidence, our comments on "instant history" notwithstanding. History as a discipline is alive and growing, telling its story of change but telling also of how tenaciously the past survives in the present.

EXERCISE

The answers to the crossword puzzle below are based on the information in this chapter. Enjoy.

ACROSS CLUES

2. Psychohistorian
4. English word "History" derived from Greek word for this
5. 19th-century history was very _____ in focus
7. Wrote history as story of the relationship with Yahweh
9. Wrote economic interpretation of the Constitution
13. Renaissance historian
14. Father of critical history
16. Wrote history of the Peloponnesian War
17. Believed economic forces were key to historical change
18. History with the politics left out
21. Period saw the return to secular history of Greeks
22. Considers role of subconscious drives

DOWN CLUES

1. First to write history in human terms
3. Wrote early example of social history
6. Erickson's "Young Man _____ "
8. Increased attention payed to this group in new social history
10. Period of God-centered history
11. The history of history
12. The "Father of History"
15. Macaulay's "History of _____ "
19. Created psychoanalysis
20. Partner of Marx

HISTORY AND THE DISCIPLINES

In Chapter 1 we made some brief and tentative comparisons between the discipline (or study) of history and other academic disciplines in the sciences, social sciences, and humanities. History, clearly, is something of an intellectual chameleon. In its attempt to establish solid "truths" (or at least viable hypotheses) about humans and their world, history shares a good deal with the sciences; as a discipline concerned primarily with women and men as social beings, it shares much with the social sciences; and as a discipline that so often emphasizes telling a story about the past in a literate and engaging fashion, it aspires to the status of an art. Yet the differences between history and her sister disciplines are equally striking.

History and Science

In the nineteenth century some of the pioneers of modern historical studies were convinced that history could attain the status of a pure science like chemistry or physics. N. D. Fustel de Coulanges, a nineteenth-century French historian, was typical when he claimed: "History is and should be a science." A moment's reflection will show that such optimism was misplaced.

The aim of science is to discover regularities ("laws") in nature—that can be used to generalize (i.e., predict) about future occurrences. Precise measurement, careful observation, and laboratory experiments are the basic methods used for establishing such scientific "laws." For instance, repeated experiments at sea level will show that water boils at 100 degrees Celsius (212 degrees Farenheit). On the basis of such experiments the scientist (and the rest of us) can be reasonably sure that under similar circumstances water will always boil at that temperature.

Historians, obviously, can never discuss the past with such precision, since past events are unique and unrepeatable. The historians cannot experiment on the past. They can't, for instance, run the French Revolution over and over again to discover which variables were the critical ones nor can they interview the participants. Historians can never establish the boiling point of a human community with anything like the precision with which the scientist can establish the boiling point of a liquid. The historian, then, does not aim (at least does not primarily aim) to establish universally convincing generalizations on the scientific model. Given the nature of the subject matter (unique, concrete, unrepeatable events) the historian is more interested in reconstructing *specific episodes* in all their diversity and particularity. The historian aims at truth, but not universal, timeless truth.

In spite of these differences, history shares more with science than first meets the eye. First, originally "science" simply meant "knowledge." If we think of a science as any search for knowledge based on a rigorous and objective examination of the evidence (whether the evidence is a beaker of boiling water or a diplomatic dispatch), then clearly history has some claim to being a science. Second, not even all the so-called sciences are totally experimental in approach. Such fields as astronomy, geology, medicine, and even biology are much akin to history in their methodology. All, like history, rely heavily on systematic *observation* and *classification of data*. Moreover, sciences like astronomy and geology are (like history) concerned with studying the "records" of past events—the light and radio waves that originated eons in the past and the rock formations that betoken upheavals thousands of years ago.

To sum up, even though history can never hope to achieve the level of certainty that is possible in the pure experimental sciences, it can still, through the application of rigorous canons of research, strive to attain closer and closer approximations of the "real" past it seeks to recover. Remember, as difficult as it is to reconstruct the events of the past, those events *did* happen. Historical study can be used to understand and illuminate those events.

History and the Social Sciences

History is related even more closely to the social and behavioral sciences (e.g., anthropology, sociology, political science, economics, psychology). Indeed, many would include history among the social sciences. Whether history is a bedfellow or simply a close relative of the social sciences need not, for the moment, concern us. What is clear is that historians and social scientists share much in common. On the simplest level it is fair to claim that history provides much raw material for the social sciences. It would even be arguable (rightly we think) that history is in many ways the mother of the social sciences. Historians Jacques Barzun and Henry Graff have noted that the social sciences "are in fact *daughter* disciplines [to history], for they arose, each of them, out of historical investigation, having long formed part of avowed historical writing."[1]

Both history and the social sciences are bodies of knowledge that deal with women and men in society. Indeed it is often difficult to tell where one discipline leaves off and another begins. It is best to think of history and the social sciences not as distinct categories, but as colors in an intellectual spectrum where one hue shades imperceptibly into another. But as much overlap as there is, each discipline approaches the study of the individual and society in a slightly different way.

Anthropology literally means the "study of humanity." Physical anthropologists study the centuries-long physical evolution of human beings, whereas cultural anthropologists attempt to describe similarities and differences among peoples and cultures around the world (often concentrating on primitive cultures) and to explain the evolution of human social patterns. Anthropologists are historians of a sort, and history has been defined as "retrospective cultural anthropology." In general, though, the anthropol-

---

[1] Barzun and Graff, *Modern Researcher*, p. 218.

ogists have traditionally concentrated on preliterate peoples, whereas the historians have emphasized the study of civilizations for which there are written records.

Sociology, a close relative of anthropology, studies the characteristics and behavior of social aggregates and groups, especially their institutions and modes of social organization. Whereas anthropologists have focused attention on primitive societies, sociologists have concentrated on more advanced, technologically sophisticated societies. To the extent that anthropology and sociology might study the same cultural groups and institutions, they are almost indistinguishable as disciplines. Again, the overlaps with history are many. Much sociology is based on historical evidence, and many historians have adopted a sociological approach in their historical studies of social classes, occupational groups, institutions, and the like.

Political Science, like sociology, attempts to unlock the secrets of institutional and group behavior. However, as the name implies, political science concentrates especially on political behavior and governmental and legal institutions. The evolution and nature of political and legal ideas (political theory) also has been a longtime interest of the political scientist. The shared interests of the political scientist and historian are many, since law, politics, war, and diplomacy are among the most traditional objects of historical study. Many scholarly works on government, international relations, and politics are impossible to categorize as history or political science with any degree of certainty.

Economics is the discipline that attempts to lay bare the mechanisms through which a society produces, trades, and distributes material goods. That the historian too is vitally interested in the economic side of human affairs goes without saying (recall our comments on the influence of Marx).

Finally, **psychology** is the study of "mental, emotional, and behavioral processes." The psychologist is interested in the unseen forces within the individual and within the social environment that make people behave the way they do. More than the other social and behavioral sciences, *psychology emphasizes the mental processes and behavior patterns of the individual*, although some branches of psychology (e.g., social psychology) do deal with group behavior. Recently, as we have seen, historians have shown a growing interest in the psychological dimension of human behavior. A growing number of studies have attempted to apply the insights of psychology to historical individuals and groups.

Clearly, there are many parallels between history and the various social sciences. But how do they differ? First, and this verges on massive oversimplification, a major preoccupation of the social sciences is to explain how societies, economies, groups, governments, etc. behave *today*. History, on the other hand, is more interested in explaining how societies functioned and developed *in the past*—that is, how they changed through time. Of course, the political scientist or economist does not ignore history (i.e., the past); nor does the historian ignore the lessons of the present. But generally the social sciences are much more "present oriented" than is history. The social scientist (often using historical evidence) tries to account for present behavior; the historian (often using current insights) tries to account for past behavior.

History and the social sciences diverge in yet another way. The social sciences, like the physical sciences, emphasize the precise quantification (measurement) of data, experiments (when appropriate), and the development of "laws" that permit prediction (and even control) of future behavior. *While the historian attempts to reconstruct individual events in all their uniqueness, social scientists attempt to discover general principles of behavior that can be used to understand many events.* To oversimplify, the historian examines the uniqueness of past events; the social scientist searches for their commonalities. For instance, a historian may desire to know all there is to know about the 1968 presidential election to write a thorough history of that event. A political scientist, however, might want to compare voter behavior in 1968 with that in 1972, 1976, 1980, and 1984 to discover voting patterns that might help predict the outcomes of future elections.

Of course, the historian will be more than happy to utilize whatever information the political scientist discovers (intellectual parasitism has a long and noble history), but it is not the historian's primary purpose to establish such regularities. Nor is the historian especially interested in prediction, as it is difficult enough to find out what has already happened. "It is the historian's aim," claims one writer, "to portray the bewildering, unsystematic variety of historical forms—people, nations, cultures, customs, institutions, songs, myths, and thoughts—in their unique, living expressions and in the process of continuous growth and transformation."[2]

Whether history is a bona fide social science or just a close relative is a matter best left unresolved at this time. Whatever your view of the matter, it is clear that the line separating history from the social scientific disciplines discussed in this section can never be drawn with absolute clarity.

History and Art   If, at times, history seems to "belong" to the social sciences, at other times it seems more reasonable to count it among the literary arts. After all, in its most basic form, written history is, as the name suggests, a "story." To tell a story well, as we have seen, the good historian must use the literary skills and conventions of the novelist or poet. Arnold Toynbee, the famous British historian, said that "no historian can be 'great' if he is not also a great artist." It is true that some of the "greatest" (at least most widely read) historians have been superb literary stylists. The war histories of Winston Churchill, Lord Macaulay's *History of England*, Edward Gibbon's *Decline and Fall of the Roman Empire*, and, more recently, the works of Barbara Tuchman are worth reading as much for their literary qualities as for what they say about the past. And what they say about the past, we might add, is very much worth our attention.

---

[2] Hans Meyerhoff, ed., *The Philosophy of History in Our Time* (New York: Doubleday, 1959), p. 10.

The historian must be an "artist" in another sense. To make the past come alive for current readers, a historian must be able to re-create on paper the passions, beliefs, and feelings of people long dead. This requires more than literary grace. The historian, as we have noted more than once in this book, must be able to empathize and sympathize with individuals, institutions, customs, and ideas that may seem foreign or strange. Like poets or novelists, historians must be able to "feel" themselves into the periods and cultures they are studying. Dispassionate objectivity is, of course, essential to good history; but so, too, is the imaginative insight and vision of the creative artist. The basic difference between a great historian and a great novelist is that the historian's story must conform to known facts. The plausibility of the historian's narrative is determined by its adherence to the evidence. Good fiction, on the other hand, must be internally consistent and correspond to common-sense notions of human behavior, but it need not conform to any external body of source materials.

SUGGESTIONS FOR FURTHER READING

The Nature of History—Philosophy of History

Becker, Carl. *Everyman His Own Historian*. New York: Appleton-Century-Crofts, 1935.

Bloch, Marc. *The Historian's Craft*. New York: Knopf, 1961.

Braudel, Fernand. *On History*. Chicago: University of Chicago Press, 1980.

Butterfield, Herbert. *The Historical Novel*. Cambridge: Cambridge University Press, 1924.

———. *History and Human Relations*. London: Collins, 1951.

———. *Man on His Past*. Cambridge: Cambridge University Press, 1955.

———. *The Whig Interpretation of History*. London: G. Bell, 1931.

Carr, E. H. *What Is History?* New York: Knopf, 1962.

Collingwood, R. G. *The Idea of History*. Oxford: Clarendon Press, 1946.

Commager, Henry Steele. *The Nature and Study of History*. Columbus, Ohio: Charles E. Merrill Books, 1965.

Dray, William H. *Philosophy of History*. Englewood Cliffs, N.J.: Prentice-Hall, 1964.

Fischer, David Hackett. *Historians' Fallacies: Toward a Logic of Historical Thought*. New York: Harper & Row, 1970.

Gardiner, Patrick L. *The Nature of Historical Explanation*. New York: Oxford University Press, 1952.

———, ed. *Theories of History*. New York: Free Press, 1959.

Gottschalk, Louis. *Understanding History*. New York: Knopf, 1950.

Gustavson, Carl G. *The Mansion of History*. New York: McGraw-Hill, 1976.

———. *A Preface to History*. New York: McGraw-Hill, 1955.

Hexter, J. H. *The History Primer*. New York: Basic Books, 1971.

Hughes, H. Stuart. *History as Art and as Science*. New York: Harper & Row, 1964.

Kitson Clark, George. *The Critical Historian*. London: Heinemann, 1967.

Marwick, Arthur. *The Nature of History*. London: Macmillan, 1970.

Meyerhoff, Hans, ed. *The Philosophy of History in Our Time*. New York: Doubleday, 1959.

Nash, Ronald H., ed. *Ideas of History*. 2 vols. New York: E. P. Dutton, 1969.

Nevins, Allan. *The Gateway to History*. Chicago: Quadrangle Books, 1963.

Norling, Bernard. *Timeless Problems in History*. Notre Dame, Ind.: University of Notre Dame Press, 1970.

———. *Toward a Better Understanding of History*. Notre Dame, Ind.: University of Notre Dame Press, 1960.

Rowse, A. L. *The Use of History*. Rev. ed. London: English Universities Press, 1963.

Smith, Page. *The Historian and History*. New York: Knopf, 1964.

Tholfsen, Trygve R. *Historical Thinking*. New York: Harper & Row, 1967.

Trevelyan, G. M. *An Autobiography and Other Essays*. London: Longmans, Green, 1949.

———. *Clio, A Muse and Other Essays*. New ed. London: Longmans, Green, 1930.

Walsh, W. H. *An Introduction to Philosophy of History*. 3rd ed. rev. London: Hutchinson University Library, 1967.

Historical Methodology

Altick, Richard D. *The Scholar Adventurers*. New York: Macmillan, 1950.

Aydelotte, William O. *Quantification in History*. Reading, Mass.: Addison-Wesley, 1971.

Barzun, Jacques. *Clio and the Doctors: Psycho-history, Quanto-history and History*. Chicago: Chicago University Press, 1974.

———, and Henry F. Graff. *The Modern Researcher*. Rev. ed. New York: Harcourt, Brace, 1970.

Cantor, Norman F., and Richard I. Schneider. *How to Study History*. New York: Thomas Y. Crowell, 1967.

Daniels, Robert V. *Studying History: How and Why*. 2nd ed. Englewood Cliffs, N.J.: Prentice-Hall, 1972.

Davidson, James W., and Mark H. Lytle. *After The Fact: The Art of Historical Detection*. New York: Alfred A. Knopf, 1982.

Elton, G. R. *The Practice of History*. London: Sydney University Press, 1967.

Gawronski, Donald V. *History Meaning and Method*. 3rd ed. Glenview, Ill.: Scott, Foresman, 1975.

Gray, Wood, et al. *Historian's Handbook: A Key to the Study and Writing of History*. 2nd ed. Boston: Houghton Mifflin, 1964.

Handlin, Oscar. *Truth in History*. Cambridge: Harvard University Press, 1979.

The History Teacher. Long Beach, Calif.: The Society for History Education. Published Quarterly.

Marwick, Arthur. *What History Is and Why It Is Important; Primary Sources; Basic Problems of Writing History; Common Pitfalls in Historical Writing*. Bletchley, England: The Open University Press, 1970.

Neugent, Walter T. K. *Creative History*. Philadelphia: Lippincott, 1967.

Nye, Russel B., "History and Literature: Branches of the Same Tree," Robert H. Bremner, ed. *Essays on History and Literature*. Columbus: Ohio State University Press, 1966.

Renier, G. J. *History: Its Purpose and Method*. New York: Harper & Row, 1965 (1950).

Scholes, Robert, and Robert Kellogg. *The Nature of Narrative*. New York: Oxford University Press, 1966.

Shafer, Robert Jones, ed. *A Guide to Historical Method*. Rev. ed. Homewood, Ill.: Dorsey, 1974.

Shorter, Edward. *The Historian and the Computer*. Englewood Cliffs, N.J.: Prentice-Hall, 1971.

Stephens, Lester D. *Probing the Past: A Guide to the Study and Teaching of History*. Boston: Allyn and Bacon, 1974.

Tollivar, Harold. *Animate Illusions. Explorations of Narrative Structure*. Lincoln: University of Nebraska Press, 1974.

Tuchman, Barbara W. *Practicing History*. New York: Alfred A. Knopf, 1981.

Winks, Robin W., ed. *The Historian as Detective: Essays on Evidence*. New York: Harper & Row, 1968.

Historiography

Barker, John. *The Superhistorians*. New York: Charles Scribner's Sons, 1982.

Barnes, Harry E. *A History of Historical Writing*. 2nd rev. ed. New York: Dover, 1963.

Gay, Peter, and Gerald J. Cavanaugh, eds. *Historians at Work*. 2 vols. New York: Harper & Row, 1972.

Geyl, Pieter. *Debates with Historians*. New York: Meridian Books, 1958.

Gilbert, Felix, and Stephen R. Graubard, eds. *Historical Studies Today*. New York: Norton, 1972.

Gooch, George Peabody. *History and Historians in the Nineteenth Century*. Rev. ed. London: Longmans, Green, 1952.

Halperin, S. William, ed. *Some Twentieth-Century Historians*. Chicago: University of Chicago Press, 1961.

Higham, John, Leonard Krieger, and Felix Gilbert. *History: The Development of Historical Studies in the United States*. Englewood Cliffs, N.J.: Prentice-Hall, 1964.

Kraus, Michael. *The Writing of American History*. Norman, Okla.: University of Oklahoma Press, 1953.

Kren, George M., and Leon H. Rappoport, eds. *Varieties of Psychohistory*. New York: Springer, 1976.

Neff, Emery. *The Poetry of History*. New York: Octagon Books, 1979.

Stannard, David E. *Shrinking History*. New York: Oxford University Press, 1980.

Stephens, Lester D. *Historiography: A Bibliography*. Metuchen, N.J.: Scarecrow Press, 1975.

Stern, Fritz, ed. *The Varieties of History from Voltaire to the Present*. Cleveland: World, 1956.

Thompson, James Westfall. *A History of Historical Writing*. 2 vols. New York: Macmillan, 1942.

Wolman, Benjamin B., ed. *The Psychoanalytic Interpretation of History*. New York: Harper & Row, 1971.

INDEX

1992

University of St. Francis
O 371.9046 M281
Mann, Philip H.
A guide for educating mainstre

3 0301 00071942 3

Philip H. Mann
Florida International University, Miami, Florida

Patricia A. Suiter
House of Learning, Miami, Florida

Rose Marie McClung
Florida International University, Miami, Florida

A Guide for Educating Mainstreamed Students

Allyn and Bacon
Boston   London   Toronto   Sydney   Tokyo   Singapore

LIBRARY
College of St. Francis
JOLIET, ILLINOIS

Copyright © 1992 by Allyn and Bacon
A Division of Simon & Schuster, Inc.
160 Gould Street
Needham Heights, Massachusetts 02194

All rights reserved. No part of the material protected by this copyright notice may be reproduced or utilized in any form or by any means, electronic or mechanical, including photocopying, recording, or by any information storage and retrieval system, without written permission from the copyright owner.

The second and third editions of this book were published under the title *Handbook in Diagnostic-Prescriptive Teaching,* copyright © 1987, 1979 by Allyn and Bacon, Inc. The first edition of the book was published under the title *Handbook in Diagnostic Teaching: A Learning Disabilities Approach,* copyright © 1974 by Allyn and Bacon, Inc.

Library of Congress Cataloging-in-Publication Data

Mann, Philip H.
  A guide for educating mainstreamed students / Philip H. Mann, Patricia A. Suiter, Rose Marie McClung.
      p.   cm.
  Includes bibliographical references (p.) and index.
  ISBN 0-205-13225-1
    1. Learning disabled children—Education—United States. 2. Mainstreaming in education—United States.
I. Suiter, Patricia. II. McClung, Rose Marie.   III. Title.
LC4705.M37   1992   91-4162
371.9'046—dc20   CIP

Printed in the United States of America
10   9   8   7   6   5   4   3   2   1   95   94   93   92   91

371.9046
M281

Contents

143, 106

Contents

Preface

Research during the past five years has added to our knowledge about learning and learners. New insights into how the brain works and how individuals process information, new uses for technology, and the identification of new instructional alternatives have opened vistas for both research and practical application in the classroom.

Greater control by teachers over instructional decisions and more involvement in program development requires a higher degree of accountability. Educators at all levels will be required to accelerate their own learning and enhance their own knowledge base. It is said that the chains of habit are too weak to be felt until they are too strong to be broken.

Cooperation and collaboration will be the mode for the 1990s. The diversity and complexity of the demands made on teachers will require a greater in-depth understanding of the possible roles they will be called on to play. It appears that some type of consultation system will occur in most schools.

The book is divided into twelve chapters. Chapter 1 addresses general concepts related to learning and covers currently defined clusters of behavior and their related causation. Constructs such as mildly handicapped, learning disabilities, attention deficit disorder, dyslexia, and developmental language disorders are discussed. Chapter 2 follows with an analysis of currently accepted learning theories. Theories are important because they provide a means of explaining the underlying structures and functions that affect student performance.

Chapter 3 introduces the neurobiology of learning and the physiology of memory. A discussion of the structures and functions of the brain is also included.

Chapter 4 on behavior management defines the behavioral and cognitive areas of study. It also presents suggestions for dealing with problem behavior at home and in school. This chapter contains important information on classifications of behavior, dropouts, substance abuse, child abuse, suicide, and depression.

Chapter 5 presents a rationale for the organization and management of assessment. Descriptions of consultation approaches, along with ideas for school-based management of assessment, will provide the educator with suggestions for how to structure a school for effective and efficient evaluation.

Chapter 6 continues the discussion on assessment, providing examples of various assessment instruments. These include those suggested by the authors, as well as tests gleaned from the field that are currently in use. Practical assessment tips are provided, along with appropriate worksheets needed for documentation. All of the testing in the book (except for vocational assessment) is located in this chapter.

Chapter 7 deals with organization and management for instruction. This chapter contains useful ideas for setting up and managing instructional programs for individuals and groups with the appropriate activities. Cooperative learning is highlighted, encompassing how a classroom should be designed and how to work with other professionals, peer tutors, and parents.

Chapter 8 contains a thorough examination of language and its components. It contains a discussion about language and how students are affected by language problems. Many suggestions for the classroom and the home will be found that address what can be done about specific problems. All language testing is located in Chapter 6.

Chapter 9 contains reading, spelling, and written language expression instructional activities. These teaching approaches are comprehensive and can be used with the young child as well as the older secondary student. All of the testing for reading and spelling is contained in Chapter 6, along with the special forms to be used for documentation.

Chapter 10 deals with the gross and fine motor areas and handwriting. The discussion and instructional activities appropriate to this area of study are presented in this chapter, whereas the testing for this area and special forms are found in Chapter 6.

Chapter 11 is comprised of a discussion of mathematics and a variety of teaching ideas and activities. The testing for arithmetic is located in Chapter 6.

Chapter 12 contains discussions about and suggestions for teaching science, social studies, study skills, and vocational education. It also has a comprehensive list of science and social studies items that are free or inexpensive that can be acquired. These materials deal with a variety of content areas and issues in ecology.

As a totality, the text offers a practical guide to mainstreaming students with learning needs.

Introduction

Within the past few decades the education of students with learning problems has gone through a number of changes. In the 1970s, concerns by parents and other advocates for handicapped students led to the passage of landmark legislation in 1975—the Education for All Handicapped Children Act, also known as Public Law 94–142. Important aspects of this law addressed such concerns as the misclassification of students, the abridgment of due process procedures of parents and students, and the exclusion of many handicapped students from contact with their age-mates.

P.L. 94–142 introduced the concept of least restrictive environment and encouraged a shift of many students from isolated "tributaries" back into the "mainstream" of the educational community. The movement resulted in an inclusion within the general education system of students with physical disabilities in wheelchairs, with vision and hearing impairments, and those with emotional and learning handicaps.

The delivery system for the mild and some moderate special education students moved along a continuum in the last 10 years, from special schools and self-contained classrooms to a joint sharing between general educators and special educators for specified hours or periods during the day. Some students have even returned to the regular class full time. Classes for the severely involved, for the most part, still remain in self-contained areas, but seem to be more integrated within school buildings.

A parallel movement to the categorically labeled handicapped students being returned to general education is the emergence of many students being diagnosed as having learning disabilities. With more federal, state, and local funds designated for services, a plethora of assessment devices, and a fresher look at students with learning problems in the regular classroom, the learning disabled prevalence figures have rapidly increased. More and more students are being reclassified as learning disabled and referred for learning disability classes. The resource model for addressing the needs of these students in most districts is based on pulling students out of the regular classes for anticipated benefits.

In the late 1980s, high costs resulted in a reexamination of the services for the mildly handicapped, including the service delivery system and the categorical classifications. The efficacy of the "pull-out" resource program model began to be questioned. There is a move today to reduce the overidentification of learning disabled students, to simplify the referral and placement process, and to reduce the stigma felt by labeled students. There is also a desire to provide a higher level of education for all learners, especially the growing numbers of underserved students not considered handicapped.

Advocates of this new approach are recommending that most students should stay in regular classes. This concept is one that is also promoted by a recent movement called the Regular Education Initiative (REI). As a result, it is anticipated that new configurations of collaboration among professional school personnel will appear nationwide and will promote a healthier, more productive school climate.

Mainstreaming in the 90s is to some extent different from the 70s. The concern for access and civil rights is still a primary consideration and has been extended through the amendments of P.L. 94–142 in 1986. The recent legislation, P.L. 99–457, extends special education services to children ages 3 through 5. Preschool intervention is a proactive movement designed to look at at-risk students before labels are required.

A teacher in today's classroom has to be prepared to respond to the variability among all of the students. The competencies required to be effective and to enjoy teaching as a career are changing. Knowledge of content is only one criteria for effective teaching. Others include consultative interactions with other professionals, communication with pupils and their parents or guardians, classroom management and personal coping skills, as well as a wide variety of new teaching and assessment procedures.

This book is designed to give administrators, general and special education teachers, and professionals from other disciplines current information that will make mainstreaming work.